SE: A PRIMER

C. J. Date

DATABASE: A PRIMER

Addison-Wesley Publishing Company
Reading, Massachusetts • Menlo Park, California
London • Amsterdam • Don Mills, Ontario • Sydney

This book is in the
Addison-Wesley Microcomputer Books
Popular Series
Marshall Henrichs, *Cover Design*
Ellen Klempner, *Design*

SQL is a trademark of International Business Machines, Inc.; dBase II is a trademark of Ashton-Tate; NOMAD is a registered trademark and proprietary product of National CSS, Inc.

Library of Congress Cataloging in Publication Data

Date, C. J.
    Database: a primer.

    Bibliography: p.
    Includes index.
    1. Data base management. I. Title.
QA76.9.D3D366 1983   001.64′2   83-3786
ISBN 0-201-11358-9

ISBN 0-201-11358-9
ABCDEFGHIJ-HA-89876543

For Sarah and Jennie

FOREWORD

This book is a user's introduction to database technology—with the emphasis on the *user*. It is concerned with how database systems are used, rather than with how they work. Database technology is, of course, built on an underlying foundation of computer technology; indeed, as you are probably aware, database systems represent one of the most important application areas for the modern computer. But the book is not really about computers as such at all—it is (to repeat) about how those computers can be used. It treats computers as a means, not an end.

The assumption is, then, that you need to use or understand a database system but have little or no knowledge of how computers work. If that description fits your case, then this book is for you. The fact is, you should not *need* to know much about the computer itself in order to use a database system. (What little you do need will be explained at appropriate points in the text.) It is the great achievement of modern computer technology that computers—in particular, microcomputers—are at last beginning to become tools in the service of people who do not have, and do not need to have, any knowledge of how the machine actually works internally. Fundamentally, there is no more need to know how a computer functions internally in order to use it than there is to know how the internal combustion engine works in order to drive a car. However, it is a fact that, until comparatively recently, only those with very specialized training were capable of exploiting computer systems to the full. But this situation is changing rapidly, for a variety of reasons, one of which is (laudably enough) simple user demand.

So who exactly is this book intended for? The answer is, "All of the following:"

- **Home computer owners**

  In this category I include anyone who owns, or is considering owning, a personal computer as a tool to help with some kind of home filing system (as opposed to someone who is interested in a home computer more as an electronic hobby). The scope for ordinary households in applying such a tool will grow by leaps and bounds over the next ten or fifteen years.

- **Small business owners**

  It is becoming increasingly common to find small corporations acquiring their own (micro- or mini-) computer to help in running their business. Frequently, the fact that there is a database system available on that computer is the overriding reason for using the computer at all. As with the home computer owner above, the person who actually interacts with that system (who may even be the corporation president) will not be a computer specialist, nor will he or she have any desire to be.

- **End-users in a larger corporation**

  In a medium-to-large corporation there will typically be some large central computer and some large number of "end-users," who are certainly not computer specialists themselves but who need to use that computer and are therefore allowed to access it from some remote terminal. Once again, those users will probably have no particular interest in exactly how the machine works, but they *will* be interested in what the database system can do for them and what they have to do to make use of it.

  If you fit into any of these three categories, then this book should give you a good idea of what to expect. It describes the kinds of things you will have to do and the kinds of behavior you can expect on the part of the system. But there are others who should also gain from reading this book:

- **User management**

  If you are not a direct user yourself but instead are in the position of being able to request other people (the end-users mentioned above) to obtain information from the system on your behalf, then you should have some idea of what those other people have to do, so that you can communicate with them properly and can understand what is and is not reasonable to expect of them. This book will provide you with that necessary background knowledge (but, of course, you may be able to skip some of the detail).

- **College students**

  The field of database management is (as indicated above) becoming increasingly important, not only in computer science per se but also in many related disciplines such as business administration. A student in a community college or in an undergraduate course in one of those related disciplines should find that the book provides a good grounding in this new field.

- **Home students**

  Finally, the book should prove suitable for the "intelligent amateur"—by which I mean anyone who may be interested (for whatever reason) in studying database technology at home, without any kind of formal instruction (especially if that person has a home system at his or her disposal on which to try out some of the examples and exercises).

The book is *not* intended for data processing professionals such as application programmers or database software specialists—though such readers may perhaps learn something too, inasmuch as they may gain an appreciation of how end-users wish or need to use the systems that they build.

Some of you will be aware that I have already published two other books on the subject of database technology—*An Introduction to Database Systems*, Volume I (Addison-Wesley, 3rd edition, 1981) and Volume II (Addison-Wesley, 1st edition, 1983)—and may be wondering how the present book differs from those existing books. In fact, there is not really very much overlap at all. The present book does necessarily cover some of the same ground, but:

- As already stressed, it is aimed at the user, not the data processing specialist. There is far less technical detail in this book. (What detail there is is detail the user needs in order to use the system properly.) The overall slant is different.

- It assumes less. Specifically, the two existing books assume that the reader is familiar with at least one programming language and understands what is involved in "file processing" in that language. By contrast, the present book assumes simply that the reader is interested in getting the system to do something useful.

- It includes a good deal of different (more user-oriented) material. For example, it covers NOMAD (a very "user friendly" system) and dBASE (one of the most powerful microcomputer systems) in some depth; neither of those systems is touched on at all in the other books. It also devotes an entire chapter to the question of displaying results and formatting reports, and it provides some guidelines for database design (another topic that is not really addressed in the existing books).

One technical point: All of the systems described in this book are *relational* systems. Those of you who follow the trade or technical press will be aware that a debate has been going on for some time in the database world regarding the relative merits of the newer, so-called relational systems versus the older *hierarchical* and *network* systems. There is no need to air the issues in that debate here. Suffice it to say that (a) most database professionals now believe that relational technology is the way of the future—so much so that new users have no need even to be aware of the older technologies—and (b) just about every product announcement in the database field these days is either for an entirely new relational system or for relational enhancements to one of the older systems. In particular, systems for smaller machines (micros or minis) are almost invariably relational. (But if you do wish to understand exactly what it means for a system to be relational, I have included in Appendix A a more technical discussion of the subject, under the heading "The Relational Model." More information on this topic, and specifically on the differences between relational and nonrelational systems, can be found in the two books mentioned above.)

Acknowledgments: It is a great pleasure to acknowledge the following people, who assisted me in the preparation of this book in a variety of ways: Roger Reinsch of IBM and Tom Dwyer of the University of Pittsburgh, both of whom read the manuscript in its entirety and made many helpful suggestions; Roger Harvey of IBM, who answered numerous technical questions concerning Query By Example; Brad Whitlock of NCSS, who very kindly furnished me with a copy of the NOMAD *Reference Manual*; and George Tate of Ashton-Tate, who equally kindly supplied me with a copy of the dBASE system for my own use in trying out some of the examples. To all these people, my grateful thanks. I would also like to thank Tom Bell of Addison-Wesley for his cheerful support throughout the entire production process.

Finally, I am pleased to acknowledge the support I have received from IBM in preparing this book. Needless to say, however, the content of the book is entirely my own responsibility; the views expressed are my own and in no way represent an official statement on the part of IBM.

Saratoga, California
June 1983

C. J. D.

CONTENTS

FOREWORD   *vii*

PART I: DATABASE ACCESS AND MAINTENANCE   *1*

1   INTRODUCTION TO PART I   *3*

Objectives   3
Structure of this book   4

2   AN OVERVIEW OF DATABASE MANAGEMENT   *9*

What is a database system?   9
Benefits   1 1
A multitable example   13
Query languages and data manipulation   16
Other operations   18
Further examples   20
Summary   23

3   WHAT THE MACHINE IS DOING   *25*

Introduction   25
Computer system structure   25
Programs   29
The Database Management System   30
Language level   32
Natural languages   38
Data independence   40
Other database management functions   41
Summary   43

4 A CASE STUDY: DATABASE CREATION AND SAMPLE QUERIES 45

Introduction 45
Creating the database 46
Loading the database 51
Sample queries 53
Summary 66
Exercises 67
Answers 67

5 A CASE STUDY (CONTINUED): SAMPLE MAINTENANCE OPERATIONS 69

Introduction 69
Exceptions 70
Multistatement updates 72
Canned procedures 77
Application generators 80
Summary 81

6 DATA DISPLAY AND REPORT WRITING 83

Introduction 83
Data display 83
Report writing 85

7 THE DATABASE CATALOG 91

Introduction 91
An example 91
Querying the catalog 94
Updating the catalog 95
Catalog versus dictionary 97
Conclusion 98
Answers 98

8   QUERY BY EXAMPLE   101

Introduction   101
Queries   104
Updates   107
Data definition   109
Querying the catalog   110
Summary   111
Answers   112

9   NOMAD   115

Introduction   115
Data definition   117
Query and formatting operations   120
Update operations   127
Querying the catalog   131
Summary   131
Answers   132

10   dBASE II   135

Introduction   135
Data definition and loading   136
Queries   137
Update operations   140
Canned procedures   143
Report writing   149
Querying the catalog   154
Summary   155
Answers   155

PART II: DATABASE DESIGN AND CONTROL   159

11   INTRODUCTION TO PART II   161

Preview   161
Structure   163

12 INDEXES 165

Introduction 165
Direct access versus sequential access 167
Further considerations 170
System examples 174
Summary 175

13 VIEWS 177

Introduction 177
Further examples 180
NOMAD facilities 182
Advantages of views 184

14 SECURITY 187

Introduction 187
Granting authority 188
Views and authorization 190
Revoking authority 191
QBE facilities 191
Other aspects of security 192

15 INTEGRITY 197

Introduction 197
Integrity constraints 197
Primary keys 198
Foreign keys 200
Format constraints 202
Range constraints 203
Conclusion 204

16 LOCKING 207

Introduction 207
Locks 209
Releasing locks 212
Deadlock 213
Summary 214

17 DATABASE DESIGN   217

Introduction   217
Departments and employees: a good design   219
Departments and employees: a bad design   220
Departments and employees: another bad design   224
Discussion   226

18 DATABASE DESIGN (CONTINUED)   231

Introduction   231
Suppliers and parts: a good design   231
Discussion   233
Further remarks   235
Individual user views   236
Summary   238
Exercises   239
Answers   241

AFTERWORD   245

APPENDIX A: THE RELATIONAL MODEL   249

APPENDIX B: A GUIDE TO FURTHER READING   257

INDEX   263

DATABASE: A PRIMER

PART I

Database Access and Maintenance

1   *Introduction to Part I*

OBJECTIVES

Database management is one of the most important functions provided by modern computer systems. So important is it, in fact, that very often it is the principal justification for acquiring the computer in the first place. The primary objective of this book is to explain what database management means to you, the user. Thus the aim is to describe what database systems look like *externally*, rather than how they work internally—though we will delve (not very deeply) into some internal aspects from time to time. But first let me make clear what I mean by the term "user."

Broadly speaking, a user is anyone who is interested in using some automated (i.e., computerized) system for maintaining and interrogating data files, on any subject whatsoever, at any level of sophistication. More specifically, the term "user" will be taken throughout this book to mean any one of the following:

1.   A person with his or her own private home computer, presumably some kind of microcomputer such as an Apple II or a TRS 80 or an IBM Personal Computer or any of the many others now available;

2.   A person in a small business, such as a small accounting corporation or a local retail store, with a micro- or minicomputer to help in running that business;

3.   An end-user in a larger organization, such as a bank, industrial company, hospital, or university, who has access via a computer terminal to some large, possibly remote, central computer operated by some specialist data processing department.

These different classes of people, though clearly having different overall requirements, nevertheless have a lot in common when it comes to the question of what they want the database system to do for them. In all cases the requirements are to be able to store data records in the system, to be able to retrieve them on demand, and to be able to update them as and when necessary. Externally, therefore, systems should look pretty much the same in all three cases, even though internally their structure will probably vary considerably. Since (as already indicated) this book is concerned with externals, there is little need for us to make much distinction among the three cases.

A secondary objective of this book—or, perhaps, a different way of expressing the primary objective—is to *remove the mystery* from database systems. For some reason a considerable mystique has grown up around the topic of database management, and it is not uncommon to find people (even computer professionals) who seem to be almost scared of the subject: "Oh, that's much too complex for me, I'd never understand it, don't you need a math degree before you can use a database?" and so on. We might add that the terminology of the subject tends to foster this attitude: In a field that is generally notorious for its bewildering array of jargon—namely, computer science—database management stands out specifically as one of the worst offenders. Now it is true that database *internals* is a complex subject. It is also true that the job of designing and administering a large, sophisticated database is a complex one. As a result, the tasks of *database system implementation* and *database administration* (in a large organization) are both very specialized, and both require highly skilled people to do them. But those tasks are not performed by *users*, in our sense of the term. The whole point of all that complexity is to make life *easy* for the user. From the user's perspective, database systems are simple. (Perhaps in honesty we should add "or should be"—some of the older systems are not as easy to use as they might be! But the claim is generally becoming truer and truer as time goes on, and it is certainly true of the newer systems.) It is, however, unfortunately still the case that the terminology is sometimes obscure. We will try to lighten some of that obscurity in this book.

STRUCTURE OF THIS BOOK

As you can see, the book is divided into two parts. Part I consists of ten chapters and Part II consists of eight. The questions addressed in Part I are the ones you should be most immediately interested in—namely, how to get data into the database in the first place and how to get it back out subsequently (and how to change it, when necessary). These aspects are referred to generically as *database access and maintenance.* The topics of Part II, by contrast, are ones you do not need to understand just to start using the system initially, but should know something about as part of your general appreciation of what the system is doing. Part II has its own introduction (Chapter 11).

The structure of Part I is as follows. Following this introductory chapter, Chapter 2 provides an overview of the entire database management function. It does so by plunging instantly into a complete example, showing what a simple database might look like and showing how you can access (interrogate and/or update) that database whenever you want to. If you and I could sit down together at the computer right now, this is the first thing I would show you on the system. Since that is not possible, the next best thing is to try and do the equivalent thing on paper—hence the introductory example. That example is, of course, very simple, but it *is* complete. I believe it is most important for you to get the overall picture right at the outset, so that you have a framework into which you can fit the material of later chapters as you read them. Thus by the end of Chapter 2 you should have gained some overall appreciation of the kinds of things you can do with a database system, even though you will not have seen very much of the detail (and perhaps not have followed all the detail you have seen).

The idea of sitting down at the computer raises another point. This book contains numerous worked examples and some exercises for you to do (sometimes answers are provided, too, but not always). *If you have access to a machine, it is a good idea to try these examples and exercises on that machine whenever possible.* You will learn more, and more quickly, if you can use the book and the machine in conjunction.

Back to the structure of the book. Chapter 3 takes a brief look at what the machine has to do in order to provide the capabilities sketched in Chapter 2. This material is more in the nature of background information: You do not have to understand it in order to use the system, but it is certainly possible that you will use the system better if you have some appreciation of how it works—and in any case I hope you will find the material interesting. Of course, if you are already familiar with the basic idea of how a computer works, you can skip this chapter.

Chapters 4 and 5 are concerned with a case study (a real application). Chapter 4 discusses retrieval and Chapter 5 update. Since the application is a real one, it contains some unavoidable complexities (real life is never as simple as invented textbook examples); in many ways, in fact, these two chapters—especially Chapter 4—are the most difficult in the entire book. Please do not let that fact deter you! Both chapters start off simply enough but get progressively more complicated; if you find you are getting bogged down in detail, simply skip ahead to the next chapter. It is not necessary to follow all the detail of these chapters in order to be able to proceed with later material in the book. But you may like to come back to study that detail if and when you start using a database of your own.

Chapter 6 discusses the question of "report writing," that is, the question of obtaining printed reports from your system. Chapter 7 describes a useful feature of database systems known as the *catalog*.

It is not the purpose of this book to deal in depth with specific systems. For one thing there are far too many of them (and more are appearing almost daily, it seems). For another (and more importantly), we are concerned with *concepts*, *principles*, and *ideas* rather than with system-specific details (which in any case change all the time as systems are enhanced). Nevertheless, Chapters 2–7 are primarily expressed in terms of one specific system (called SQL), simply for reasons of consistency and ease of learning. Therefore, to show that there are other ways of doing things (ways that are different from the SQL way, that is), Chapters 8–10 sketch the details of three other systems: QBE, NOMAD, and dBASE II. Please note that I chose to include those particular systems simply because they illustrate very nicely the points I want to make in the text. I do not necessarily mean to imply any personal endorsement of those systems. Equally, the fact that some system is not described should not be interpreted as a lack of such endorsement or as disparagement.

Let me stress again that the overall objective of the book is not to teach the fine detail of any specific system, but rather to give some idea of what you can expect in general. In fact, let me make a couple of points quite clear right at the outset:

1. In the interests of clarity and consistency I have not hesitated to simplify certain minor points, nor to ignore certain minor restrictions, in the description of any given system.

2. I have deliberately not even attempted to describe every aspect of each system. Several quite important features are not even mentioned.

These two points apply to all the systems discussed and will not be repeated in every chapter.

Despite these disclaimers, however, you may still find that there is more system-specific detail than you feel you need. I cannot deny that there is quite a lot of detail in places. But this detail is quite deliberate. From my experience in both learning and teaching this material, I firmly believe that you need to see a few concrete examples, *with no major details omitted*, before you can truly appreciate what database systems can and cannot do. Now I do not mean by this remark that you must absorb all of the detail—merely that you should have given it at least a "once over lightly" reading and that you should generally be aware of the fact of it. But let me stress the "lightly." Again, it is important not to get bogged down; if you find this is starting to happen, then simply move on to the next topic or next chapter. The material is not really difficult, but sometimes it can be a little overwhelming.

By the end of Chapter 10 you should have gained a fairly good overall understanding of what database systems can do and should be ready to tackle Part II. As indicated earlier, the chapters of Part II provide an introduction to a variety of additional topics—topics, however, that are for the most part system considerations rather than direct user considerations. An outline of the structure of Part II is given in Chapter 11, the introduction to that part of the book.

You should now be ready to embark on Chapter 2, the overview. Let me conclude this introduction by saying that I welcome any and all comments, criticisms, questions, and suggestions regarding the content of this book. Please address any correspondence to C. J. Date, c/o Addison-Wesley Publishing Company, Reading, Massachusetts 01867. Thank you; and good reading!

2 *An Overview of Database Management*

A database system is essentially nothing more than a *computerized record-keeping system*. Many of the data files traditionally kept on paper could more conveniently be kept in a database. For example, I have a (rather small) database on my computer that helps me keep track of the contents of my wine cellar. To see exactly what I have in stock at any time, I can type in the command:

```
SELECT * FROM CELLAR
```

(We will examine the details of this command in a moment.) The computer responds by displaying the information I am looking for on its screen:

BIN	WINE	PRODUCER	YEAR	BOTTLES	READY	COMMENTS
2	Chardonnay	Buena Vista	79	1	82	
3	Chardonnay	Louis Martini	79	5	82	
6	Chardonnay	Chappellet	79	4	82	Thanksgiving
11	Jo.Riesling	Jekel Vineyard	80	6	82	
12	Jo.Riesling	Buena Vista	77	1	80	Late Harvest
16	Jo.Riesling	Sattui	79	1	81	very dry
21	Fume Blanc	Ch.St.Jean	79	4	81	Napa Valley
22	Fume Blanc	Robt.Mondavi	77	2	80	
25	Wh.Burgundy	Mirassou	80	6	82	
30	Gewurztraminer	Buena Vista	80	3	82	
43	Cab.Sauvignon	Robt.Mondavi	77	12	83	
50	Pinot Noir	Mirassou	77	3	82	Harvest Sel.
51	Pinot Noir	Ch.St.Jean	78	2	84	
64	Zinfandel	Mirassou	77	2	84	Anniversary
72	Gamay	Robt.Mondavi	78	2	82	

This table (the CELLAR table) represents a complete listing of all the wine I have in stock.

Now suppose I have decided to put aside a bottle of Chardonnay for dinner, but I am not sure exactly which one I want and wish to contemplate just my stock of that particular wine. I type in the following:

```
SELECT * FROM CELLAR WHERE WINE = 'Chardonnay'
```

The computer responds as follows:

BIN	WINE	PRODUCER	YEAR	BOTTLES	READY	COMMENTS
2	Chardonnay	Buena Vista	79	1	82	
3	Chardonnay	Louis Martini	79	5	82	
6	Chardonnay	Chappellet	79	4	82	Thanksgiving

Compare this table with the previous display. By specifying a *WHERE clause* in the SELECT command, I have caused the computer to restrict its output to just those records—that is, rows —that satisfy the *condition* in that WHERE clause. It is also possible to restrict the display to just certain columns, or indeed to a combination of certain rows and certain columns, as in the following example:

```
SELECT BIN, PRODUCER, READY, BOTTLES
FROM   CELLAR
WHERE  WINE = 'Chardonnay'
```

(It doesn't matter whether the command is typed entirely on one line or is spread out over several lines, as here.) Note, incidentally, that I have also changed the left-to-right order of columns in this example, just to show that it can be done. Display:

BIN	PRODUCER	READY	BOTTLES
2	Buena Vista	82	1
3	Louis Martini	82	5
6	Chappellet	82	4

"SELECT *" in the earlier examples is simply a shorthand for "SELECT every column in the table."

Suppose I decide on a bottle of the Louis Martini (bin 3). To reflect the fact that I am going to remove that bottle from stock, I should now *update* the database:

```
UPDATE CELLAR
SET    BOTTLES = 4     (previously 5)
WHERE  BIN = 3
```

If I now entered

```
SELECT *
FROM   CELLAR
WHERE  BIN = 3
```

I would see the effect of my UPDATE on the database:

BIN	WINE	PRODUCER	YEAR	BOTTLES	READY	COMMENTS
3	Chardonnay	Louis Martini	79	4	82	

Suppose I had chosen the (only) bottle of Buena Vista instead. Then there would no longer be any need to keep that record in the database at all:

```
DELETE
FROM  CELLAR
WHERE BIN = 2
```

The other operation I will need to perform from time to time on my wine cellar database is to INSERT a new record (or UPDATE an existing record to increase the number of BOTTLES) to reflect new acquisitions. For example:

```
INSERT
INTO   CELLAR
VALUES (53, 'Pinot Noir','Franciscan',76,1,83,'present from Joan')
```

We have now seen all four of the basic operations on data: *retrieval* (SELECT), *modification* (UPDATE), *deletion* (DELETE), and *insertion* (INSERT). These four operations are often referred to generically as *data manipulation* operations. These are the operations (most especially retrieval) that you will find yourself using constantly if you use a database system.

BENEFITS

Why use a database system? What are the advantages? The wine cellar example is so small and so simple that the benefits in this case are not particularly striking. But imagine a similar database for a large restaurant, with a stock of perhaps thousands of bottles and with very frequent changes to that stock; or think of a liquor store, with again a very large stock and with high turnover on that stock.

In these situations the advantages of a computerized system over traditional, paper-based methods of record keeping are perhaps more obvious. Here are some of them:

- Compactness: No need for possibly voluminous paper files.

- Speed: The computer can retrieve and change data far faster than a human can (in particular, spur-of-the-moment queries—e.g., "Do we have more Zinfandel than Pinot Noir?"—can be answered quickly without any need for time-consuming manual or visual searches).

- Less drudgery: Much of the sheer tedium of maintaining files by hand is eliminated (mechanical tasks are always better done by machines).

- Currency: Accurate, up-to-date information is available on demand at any time.

A hidden benefit—one that the wine cellar example is really too simple to illustrate—is that the exercise of designing the database can be valuable, in and of itself. The fact is, it can sometimes be quite difficult to come properly to grips with the problem at hand—difficult, that is, to acquire a proper understanding of the data you have to work with. You need a discipline, a set of guidelines, that can help you think about that data in a systematic manner; and designing the database provides just such a discipline. Having to produce a database design forces you to approach the problem systematically and generally helps you to organize your thinking appropriately. However, these remarks are really more applicable when the database is "large." (Generally speaking, the greater the data volume, and/or the more complicated the data structure—see the next section—the more necessary such a discipline becomes. Equally, of course, the use of a database system becomes particularly attractive, if not essential, in such an environment.) For "small" databases the structure is usually intuitively obvious. Most of the databases discussed in this book will be "small" in this sense. The database design discipline and "large" databases will be discussed in Part II.

Still further advantages apply when the data is shared by multiple users. However, we do not discuss shared data in any depth until Part II of this book.

A MULTITABLE
EXAMPLE

The wine cellar example is particularly simple in that it involves only a single table. Most databases consist of multiple, interrelated tables. Here is an example (still very simple):

FLIGHTS table:

FLIGHT	FROM_CODE	TO_CODE	DEP_TIME	ARR_TIME
TW750	SJC	STL	0745	1321
DL834	STL	ORD	1725	1822
AA160	SFO	ORD	1203	1750
UA095	BOS	SFO	1005	1310
UA122	SFO	ORD	0730	1330
PA072	LAX	JFK	0830	1700
AA214	SFO	ORD	1215	1820
TW066	LAX	BOS	0845	1658
EA224	LAX	JFK	0900	1649

CITIES table:

CODE	CITY
SJC	San Jose
STL	St. Louis
ORD	Chicago
SFO	San Francisco
BOS	Boston
LAX	Los Angeles
JFK	New York

The interrelationship between the tables here is that every city code (SJC, STL, etc.) appearing as a FROM_CODE or TO_CODE value in the FLIGHTS table must also appear as a CODE value in the CITIES table (thus identifying some CITY in that table). Suppose I want to find all flights from San Francisco to Chicago. First, I can look up the codes for these two cities in the CITIES table:

```
SELECT CODE
FROM   CITIES
WHERE  CITY = 'San Francisco'
```

Result (on the screen):

```
CODE

SFO
```

Now Chicago:

```
SELECT CODE
FROM   CITIES
WHERE  CITY = 'Chicago'
```

Result:

```
CODE

ORD
```

Now I can ask the real question:

```
SELECT *
FROM    FLIGHTS
WHERE   FROM_CODE = 'SFO'
AND     TO_CODE   = 'ORD'
```

Notice the use of AND in the WHERE clause here to connect two conditions together, incidentally. The SELECT will retrieve just those records that satisfy *both* those two conditions. Result:

FLIGHT	FROM_CODE	TO_CODE	DEP_TIME	ARR_TIME
AA160	SFO	ORD	1203	1750
UA122	SFO	ORD	0730	1330
AA214	SFO	ORD	1215	1820

The foregoing procedure (involving three separate queries) obviously works. However, *it is also possible to express the entire problem by means of a single SELECT that refers to both tables.* Instead of issuing the two preliminary queries and then writing 'SFO' and 'ORD' explicitly in the "real" query, as above, I could ask the *system itself* to go and look in the CITIES table for the necessary city codes:

```
SELECT *
FROM    FLIGHTS
WHERE   FROM_CODE =
        (SELECT CODE
         FROM   CITIES
         WHERE  CITY = 'San Francisco')
AND     TO_CODE =
        (SELECT CODE
         FROM   CITIES
         WHERE  CITY = 'Chicago')
```

} This inner SELECT looks up the code for San Francisco.

} And this one looks up the code for Chicago.

Now the entire problem has been reduced to a single query—a single query that involves, however, two inner or "nested" queries (each enclosed in parentheses). Under the covers the system will first perform the two inner SELECTs, obtaining the results 'SFO' and 'ORD'. However, it will not display those results on the screen but will simply plug them into the outer SELECT and then go on to obtain the desired final result. The overall query process has thus been mechanized still further: The machine is doing more work and the user is doing less (obviously a good thing). In general, the more complex the SELECT is, the more the problem has been mechanized, and the more this last statement is true. We will see more examples of such complex SELECTs in Chapter 4.

Aside: At this point you may be feeling that the whole process is far more trouble than it is worth. In the case at hand it is obviously easier—and quicker—to find the required information (flights from San Francisco to Chicago) by simply scanning the two tables by eye. Why go to the length of constructing an undeniably complex SELECT statement just so the system can do the scanning instead? The answer, of course, is that it is *not* usually easier and quicker to scan the tables yourself. Real tables will frequently contain many hundreds or thousands of rows, not just a few as in our simple example. What is more, the system is not liable to the kinds of error (such as overlooking entries) that human beings make all too easily when faced with a boring and highly repetitive task like this one. Third, once we have constructed the SELECT for flights from San Francisco to Chicago (say), it is a comparatively simple matter to get the system to find flights between *any* specified pair of cities, using a facility known as "canned procedures" (to be discussed in Chapter 5). Finally, the query does not look quite so complicated anyway in some query languages; a more "user friendly" example can be found in the answers section in Chapter 8.

To return to the example: One further useful feature of most query languages is the ability to get the system to display the result in some specific order. For example, I could have asked to see the requested flight information in departure time order by specifying an appropriate *ORDER BY* clause in the SELECT:

```
SELECT  *
FROM    FLIGHTS
WHERE   FROM_CODE =
        (SELECT CODE
         FROM   CITIES
         WHERE  CITY = 'San Francisco')
AND     TO_CODE =
        (SELECT CODE
         FROM   CITIES
         WHERE  CITY = 'Chicago')
ORDER   BY DEP_TIME
```

The ORDER BY clause causes the system to arrange the result rows in the specified order before displaying them on the screen:

FLIGHT	FROM_CODE	TO_CODE	DEP_TIME	ARR_TIME
UA122	SFO	ORD	0730	1330
AA160	SFO	ORD	1203	1750
AA214	SFO	ORD	1215	1820

Unless the result table is very small, it is usually a good idea to ask the system to put it into some specific sequence before displaying it, for obvious reasons.

QUERY LANGUAGES AND DATA MANIPULATION

As mentioned earlier, the four operations retrieval, modification, deletion, and insertion are usually grouped together under the general heading of *data manipulation*. Thus one of the primary functions of a database system is to permit such data manipulation —or, more precisely, to support a *database language* (or *query language*) in which the user can formulate commands that will cause such data manipulation to occur. The examples in this chapter are all expressed in a specific database language called SQL (Structured Query Language; the acronym SQL is usually pronounced "sequel"). The data manipulation operations are expressed in SQL by means of commands (also called *statements*), as follows:

Retrieval	SELECT
Modification	UPDATE
Deletion	DELETE
Insertion	INSERT

Each database system typically supports its own unique query language; that is, retrieval, for example, is written SELECT in some systems, READ in others, RETRIEVE in still others, and so on. For reference, the terms used in the systems discussed in this book (SQL, QBE, NOMAD, and dBASE) are summarized in Fig. 2.1. That table will be repeated at appropriate points in later chapters.

The differences among different languages are not very important for our purposes, and for consistency we will use SQL for all examples in the first few chapters of this book (as explained in Chapter 1). Please remember, however, that it is *not* the purpose of this book to teach the details of the SQL language per se. All features of SQL used in examples will be explained when they first appear.

Figure 2.1

	SQL	QBE	NOMAD	dBASE
Retrieval	SELECT	P.	LIST	DISPLAY
Modification	UPDATE	U.	CHANGE	REPLACE
Deletion	DELETE	D.	DELETE	DELETE
Insertion	INSERT	I.	INSERT	APPEND

Note: SQL was originally designed by D. D. Chamberlin and others at the IBM Research Laboratory in San Jose, California. Numerous experimental implementations of the language (for a variety of different machines) have been built, at IBM and elsewhere. A commercial implementation of SQL for medium to large IBM machines (SQL/Data System, abbreviated SQL/DS) is now available from IBM; another, called ORACLE, is available for both IBM and DEC machines from ORACLE Corporation (3000 Sand Hill Road, Menlo Park, California 94025). More recently, a number of other vendors have also announced systems that support SQL, or at least something very close to it, and further implementations are rumored to be in the pipeline also.

One question that may have occurred to you is: Why do we need a query language at all? Or, rather, why can't we formulate queries in plain English, instead of having to learn SQL or some other special language? We will not try to answer this question now but defer discussion of it to Chapter 3.

One further point: The term "query language," common though it is, is really a misnomer, inasmuch as the English verb "query" suggests *retrieval* (only), whereas query languages typically provide UPDATE, DELETE, and INSERT operations as well. And while we are on the subject of terminology, I may as well mention two more points:

1. The term "update" is, confusingly, often used to mean not just UPDATE operations per se, but rather all three of the operations UPDATE, DELETE, and INSERT.

2. You have probably noticed that the terms *row* and *record* can be used interchangeably. The same applies to *column* and *field*; that is, "field" is often used as an alternative to "column." Thus we might describe the CELLAR table as having seven fields. As a matter of fact, computer professionals normally talk in terms of records and fields; on the other hand, "row" and "column" have the advantage of being more immediately understandable and so are in some ways preferable. But both sets of terms are in common use, and we will use both in this book.

You can see that (as indicated in Chapter 1) database terminology is sometimes rather confusing, not to say confused. We will do our best to avoid as much of that confusion as possible.

OTHER OPERATIONS

Data manipulation is obviously important, but it is not the end of the story. A variety of additional functions are also needed. For example, it should be possible to *print* the result of a SELECT, instead of merely displaying it on the screen. For example:

```
SELECT *
FROM    CELLAR

PRINT
```

(There are two commands here, one to retrieve the required data and one to print it.)

It may also be desirable to "format" the result before printing it—for example, to introduce suitable page headings or to get the system to append certain summary information to the output, such as totals and subtotals. Another feature that is clearly needed is the ability to deal with results that are too large to fit on a single screen. In this latter situation you might think of the screen as a kind of window, through which only a limited portion of the total result can be seen at any one time, and special display, or *scrolling*, commands (typically UP, DOWN, LEFT, RIGHT) will let you move the window around (conceptually, of course, not physically) to bring different portions of the result into view. Formatting, scrolling, and similar operations will be discussed in Chapter 6.

Finally, certain *data definition* functions (as opposed to data manipulation functions) are also needed. In particular, it must be possible to create new, empty tables (you cannot INSERT any data into the database until there is a table in the database to hold that data; all the examples so far have tacitly assumed that appropriate tables were created ahead of time). For example, the CELLAR table might have been created by means of the following SQL statement:

```
CREATE TABLE CELLAR
      ( BIN        DECIMAL(3),
        WINE       CHAR(25),
        PRODUCER   CHAR(20),
        YEAR       DECIMAL(2),
        BOTTLES    DECIMAL(3),
        READY      DECIMAL(2),
        COMMENTS   CHAR(25)  )
```

The effect of this statement is to build a table called CELLAR, with columns as indicated but with as yet no rows (other than the row of column headings):

CELLAR table:

BIN	WINE	PRODUCER	YEAR	BOTTLES	READY	COMMENTS

DECIMAL(n) means that the column concerned will contain decimal numbers (positive or negative) up to n digits long. CHAR(n) means that the column concerned will contain "character strings" (i.e., data values that are strings of characters, such as the string 'Chardonnay') up to n characters long, where a character is anything you can type by means of a single key (or key combination) at the keyboard. By "key combination" we mean, for example, the combination of the shift key and the "c" key that you use to obtain an uppercase "C".

You will probably have noticed in the examples earlier that when actual data values such as 6 or 'Chardonnay' are used in a SQL statement, those values must be enclosed in single quotes if they are character strings but not if they are decimal numbers. One reason for this rule is that a character string without quotes might be confused with a table name or a column name. Incidentally, of course, a character string value can include numeric digits as well as letters. For example, '23 Main Street' is a perfectly valid character string, and so is '123456789'. However, data that needs to be operated on arithmetically—for example, a dollar balance—should be specified as DECIMAL, not CHAR. (That is what DECIMAL is for.)

We have now briefly described all of the major functions provided by a typical database system (from the user's point of view, that is). To summarize, those functions include the following:

- Data definition functions (such as CREATE TABLE);

- Data manipulation functions (such as SELECT, UPDATE, etc.);

- Scrolling and formatting functions (such as UP, DOWN, totaling, subtotaling, etc.).

These functions, together with others not yet discussed, are collectively referred to as *database management.* Thus the overall purpose of a database system may be described (rather tautologically) as *the provision of database management functions.* In Chapter 3 we will expand on this description somewhat.

FURTHER EXAMPLES

In this section we briefly sketch a few more possible applications for a database system. Most of the examples are deliberately small and simple in nature, in order to give you some idea of the range of applications that might be useful even on a microcomputer in the home. However, from the list you should also begin to see some of the possibilities in a larger commercial, industrial, or scientific environment. A somewhat more complex (and complete) example is examined in detail in Chapters 4 and 5.

- **People file**

Use the system to maintain your personal list of names, addresses, and phone numbers, perhaps divided into sublists of friends and relatives, professional contacts, emergency contacts, and so on. For friends and relatives you might also include birthdays, names of children, a Christmas card list, a Christmas gift list, and so forth. Some typical queries:

"What's the plumber's phone number?"

"When is Uncle George's birthday?"

"What did Betty give the children last Christmas?"

- **Recordings library**

  Use the database to keep track of your personal collection of phonograph records, tape cassettes, and so on. Typical queries:

  "What recordings do we have of music by Sibelius?"

  "How many Haydn quartets do we have?"

  "Which Creedence Clearwater record has *Born on the Bayou*?"

- **Professional library**

  I have a collection of several hundred technical papers, books, and journals on database technology and related fields, dating back to the mid 1960s. For many of these I also have a paragraph or two of annotation, representing my own summary of, criticism of, or reaction to the item in question. What I need, badly, is an automated system that would enable me to locate specific items quickly:

  "List title, source, and shelf location for all papers by Stonebraker."

  "Display my comments on the paper by Codd in *Communications of the ACM*, Vol. 13, No. 6."

- **Other libraries**

  Whatever your interests (chess? photography? science fiction?), it is likely that you have some kind of personal library that could benefit from a similar treatment.

- **Bank accounts**

  Keep your checkbook entries in a database table.

  "Display date, payee, and amount for check number 1253."

  "How much interest have I received so far this year?"

  "List all school fees paid since August 1981."

Here are some other examples of accounts that you might wish to keep in a database: monthly household expenses, professional expenses, legal expenses, investment accounts, entertainment expenses, utility expenses.

- **Tax records**

  Keep current and detailed records of income received, deductible items, withholding, estimated tax payments.

- **Insurance inventory**

  For insured items, maintain a table giving item descriptions, item serial numbers if applicable, date of purchase, cost.

- **Personal calendar**

  This item is self-explanatory. Typical queries:

  "Are we doing anything on 20th June?"

  "When does school resume?"

  "What are the dates of our trip to Mexico City?"

- **Scientific tables**

  Scientific tables present an ideal application for students, as well as for professional (or amateur) scientists. For example, a table of the elements could be used to answer these queries:

  "What is the atomic weight of iodine?"

  "Which elements are in Group VIII?"

  "What is the symbol for ruthenium?"

Another database table might contain information on the planets and satellites to answer queries like these:

"List the moons of Saturn."

"What is the diameter of Neptune?"

And so on.

Exercise: Try taking one of the examples above (or one of your own devising) and designing a suitable table structure for it. Your design might involve one table or several. Write some appropriate CREATE TABLE statements. Try also writing some sample data manipulation statements (SELECT, UPDATE, DELETE, INSERT). Better still, if you have access to a computer of your own, try these exercises on your own system. (In this case, how-

Figure 2.2

PEOPLE:

LASTNAME	OTHERNAMES	ADDRESS	PHONE

BIRTHDAYS:

PERSON	DATE

XMAS81:

LASTNAME	OTHERNAMES	CARDTO	GIFTTO	CARDFROM	GIFTFROM

XMAS82:

LASTNAME	OTHERNAMES	CARDTO	GIFTTO	CARDFROM	GIFTFROM

XMAS83:

LASTNAME	OTHERNAMES	CARDTO	GIFTTO	CARDFROM	GIFTFROM

ever, you will first have to find out how your system requires you to spell CREATE TABLE, SELECT, etc.; unfortunately, it is almost certain to be different from the way shown in this chapter. You will also need to INSERT some sample data into your tables before your queries etc. will make much sense.) To help you get started, we give an outline design in Fig. 2.2 for a possible "people" database. The fields CARDTO and CARDFROM in this design are intended to take the values 'YES' and 'NO' only; the fields GIFTTO and GIFTFROM are intended to identify the actual gift (e.g., 'SWEATER', 'FOUNTAIN PEN', 'MOBY DICK', etc.).

SUMMARY

We conclude this introductory chapter by briefly reviewing the main points covered. We have defined a database system as a computerized record-keeping system, and we have shown how data records can be stored in such a system in the form of rows in tables.

A database is a collection of one or more such tables, typically interrelated (as in the example of the flight information database). We have discussed data manipulation operations (represented in SQL by the statements SELECT, UPDATE, DELETE, and INSERT); in particular, we have shown how SELECT can be used to retrieve any combination of rows and columns from a table, how it can be made to look over at other tables for needed data values (via nested queries), and how the result can be ordered into some desired sequence before it is displayed. We have mentioned formatting, scrolling, and data definition operations (specifically, CREATE TABLE). Finally, we have sketched the advantages of database systems and have indicated a range of possible applications for such systems. In the next chapter we will take a look at what the computer has to do to support all of these functions.

3   *What the Machine Is Doing*

INTRODUCTION

From the previous chapter you should have gained a broad appreciation of what is meant by the term "database management." To review briefly, a database system is a computer system that allows you to do the following:

- *Create* tables (also called files) for the storage of data records;

- *Maintain* those tables via operations such as UPDATE, DELETE, and INSERT;

- *Retrieve* data from those tables, selectively, on demand, and fast, via operations such as SELECT;

- *Display* that retrieved information (via scrolling operations, if necessary) and/or *format* that information for printing.

What exactly does the computer have to do to provide these functions? Although you do not really need to know the answer to this question in order to use the system, there is no doubt that a general understanding of what the machine is doing can help you to use it better. In this chapter, therefore, we take a brief look at what is going on under the covers in a database system.

Note: Although you may already have some experience, extensive or otherwise, of interacting with a computer system, it is simplest to assume at this point that you have no prior computer knowledge. Thus the explanations in this chapter will all start from scratch. Of course, if you do not need this preliminary material, you can just go on to the next chapter. Another general point: We will do our best to minimize the amount of jargon, though in this field that is sometimes difficult. Certainly all new terms will be defined as they are introduced.

COMPUTER SYSTEM STRUCTURE

Figure 3.1 represents the logical structure of a typical small computer system. As the figure shows, such a system consists of six principal components, the functions of which are highly interrelated. Figure 3.2 is a photograph of a real system (an IBM Personal

Figure 3.1

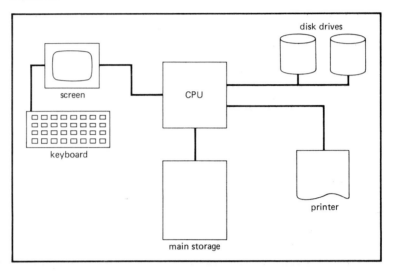

Computer) in which most of the six components can clearly be distinguished. The components and their functions are as follows:

1. The central processing unit (abbreviated CPU)

The CPU is "the computer proper"; it is the unit that actually performs all computations. It does so by *executing instructions.* Those instructions are typically at a very fine level of detail; for example, there will be an instruction to add two numbers together, another to subtract one number from another, another to test two numbers for equality, and so on. Thus, for example, to compute the value of the expression

$$((a - b) \times c)/d,$$

where a, b, c, and d are numeric values, the CPU would have to execute the following sequence of instructions:

Subtract b from a (giving result x, say);

Multiply x by c (giving result y, say);

Divide y by d (giving final result z).

Two particularly important instructions from a database standpoint are "read" and "write" (see paragraph 2 below).

Figure 3.2

2. Main storage (also called main memory)

Main storage is essentially a device in which information can be recorded (*stored*) electronically. It typically has sufficient capacity to allow many thousands of separate data values (such as the numbers a, b, c, x, y, z in the example above) to be stored simultaneously. However, placing a particular value at a particular position in main storage will erase whatever was stored there previously. Before any data can be operated on by the CPU, it must first be placed in main storage. Data can be *read into* main storage from a disk or from the keyboard. Likewise, data can be *written out of* main storage to a disk or to the printer or to the screen.

Note: Reading data from a disk actually reads a *copy* into main storage; the original data still remains on the disk. Similarly, writing data out of main storage really writes a copy and leaves the original data unchanged in storage.

One point that it is important to understand is that main storage is *volatile:* If the computer is turned off, or if a power failure occurs, then everything in main storage will be lost (i.e., automatically erased).

3. Disk storage (also called secondary storage)

Disks are also storage devices. They differ from main storage in two principal ways:

*   They provide a *permanent* (nonvolatile) storage medium. Turning the machine off has no effect on the content of the disks.

*   Individual disks can be *removed* and *replaced*; that is, one disk can be taken off its disk drive and another one mounted in its place, thus making an entirely different set of data available for reading into main storage and processing. Hence the total database (which will be kept on disk) can exceed the capacity of a single disk, if necessary. Remember, however, that no piece of data can be processed by the CPU without first being copied from disk into main storage (via a read operation), and this fact in turn implies that the appropriate disk must first be mounted on one of the disk drives.

Data is recorded on disks magnetically, much as sound signals are recorded magnetically on conventional audiotapes. Disk capacity is typically greater than that of main storage, but disk *access time* is typically greater too (it takes longer to find a piece of data on a disk than it does in main storage). Disks are also much cheaper than main storage: A disk for a home computer will cost in the region of $5, whereas the main storage on that same computer may cost $1000 or even more.

As with main storage, recording data at a given position on a disk will erase whatever was there before.

4. Keyboard

The keyboard is the *primary input device.* It is the unit that allows you to enter data and commands into the system. Everything you enter will be displayed on the screen as you type it; the "carriage return" or "enter" key causes the text you have just typed to be sent to the CPU. Usually, you will have the ability to correct typing errors before sending the text to the CPU (i.e., before hitting "enter").

5. Screen (also called visual display)

Just as the keyboard is the primary input device, so the screen is the primary *output* device. The screen is the unit the system uses to display information (messages and results) back to you. As indicated under paragraph 4, the screen is also used to display your input to the system as you enter it.

6. Printer

The printer is the device that allows you to obtain a printed-paper copy ("hard copy") of various information from the system. In particular, it allows you to obtain *formatted reports* (reports are discussed in detail in Chapter 6).

Not all systems will have exactly the structure indicated here. Some, for example, may have no printer; some may have a printer but no screen; others will have cassette tape storage instead of, or as well as, disk storage; and so on. *Large* systems will typically have many additional components, and also many instances of each type of component; in particular, they will normally have many *terminals*, perhaps as many as a thousand or more, each with a keyboard and a screen, so that many users can be accessing the system at the same time. But all systems will have a CPU, main storage, secondary storage, and some means of getting information into and out of the system. "Getting information into and out of the system" is usually referred to as *input/output* (I/O); thus terminals and printers are "I/O devices." Other kinds of I/O devices exist, but will not be discussed in this book. The operations *read* and *write* mentioned above are "I/O operations."

PROGRAMS

So far we have not mentioned *programs*, at least not explicitly. The central processing unit (CPU) is just a machine that is capable of executing a limited set of very simple instructions (such as "Add A to B") very fast. It cannot directly execute complicated operations such as a SQL SELECT statement at all. Instead, it provides the *effect* of such complicated operations by executing a large number (probably millions) of the simple instructions, in some suitable sequence. But it cannot do this unaided; it needs to be told exactly *which* instructions to execute *when*. This is where programs come in. A program is basically a list of instructions for the CPU to execute. [The sequence of instructions shown in the previous section (p. 26) for computing the value of an arithmetic expression is in fact an example of a very simple program.] Now, in all but the very simplest programs there will be some instructions of the form "Go back and execute the last N instructions again." Thus even though there may be millions of instructions *executed*, the list of instructions constituting the program as written down may be only a few hundred or few thousand instructions in length. Nevertheless, the job of constructing such a program is a highly skilled and complex one, as you can imagine.

THE DATABASE MANAGEMENT SYSTEM

The CPU *always* operates under the direction of a program (different programs at different times, of course). The program that is currently in control is kept in main storage; other programs will be stored on a disk somewhere, ready to be read into main storage when they are needed. One particular program—the one we are primarily interested in—is the *database management system* (DBMS). The DBMS is the program that enables the system to perform all those functions that we classified as "database management" at the beginning of this chapter. Thus, when you are issuing commands such as SELECT or UPDATE or CREATE TABLE at the keyboard, the DBMS is the program that is sitting in main storage and is running the system for you. How did it get there? The answer is that it was read in from disk when you started your session at the keyboard. Quite likely you had to type in START SQL, or something of the kind, before you could issue any SQL commands; that START is what caused the system to read the DBMS program into main storage in the first place.

Now you should be in a position to understand what happens when you enter a SQL statement, say a SELECT. Let us go through the process step by step; see Fig. 3.3.

1. You type in the statement. It appears on the screen as you do so.

2. The DBMS reads the statement from the keyboard into main storage. (More precisely, the CPU reads the statement, under the direction of the DBMS. It is usual not to be this precise in informal discussion.)

Figure 3.3

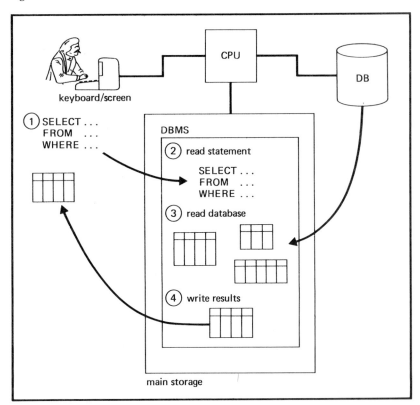

3. The DBMS analyzes the statement to work out what it means, decides what data is needed from the database, and issues instructions to read that data into main storage.

4. The DBMS writes the required result out to the screen. (*Note:* The term "data" is generally used to include results—i.e., output data—as well as input data. Thus we might express this step as "The DBMS writes the required *data* out to the screen.")

Similarly, for an UPDATE statement:

1. You type in the statement.

2. The DBMS reads it into main storage.

3. The DBMS analyzes it and reads the required data into main storage.

4. The DBMS changes the data in main storage.

5. The DBMS writes the changed data back out to the database.

6. The DBMS writes a message to the screen, telling you what it has done.

LANGUAGE LEVEL

In the previous section we saw the steps the DBMS has to go through to deal with a SELECT or UPDATE statement. One particular step of the process, step 3, bears closer examination. That step involves analyzing the SQL statement and issuing the appropriate CPU-level instructions ("machine instructions") to get the CPU to do whatever is necessary. In effect, the DBMS is *constructing a program*, that is, a sequence of machine instructions, the effect of whose execution is to achieve exactly the result requested via the original SQL statement. In other words, the original SQL statement is *already* a program (consisting of just one instruction) *at a very high level*, and what the DBMS is doing is *translating* that program into an equivalent program at a much lower level (and then executing that lower-level program). Because that equivalent program is at a lower level (namely, the level of machine instructions), it is much more detailed and much less concise (it involves many thousands of instructions instead of just one).

Aside: In Chapter 5 we will see that it is also possible to construct SQL-level programs consisting of multiple SQL statements instead of just one.

We have already said that SQL is a language—a query language, to be more specific. Machine instructions constitute another language, *machine language* or (more usually) *machine code*. We have also indicated that SQL is a very high level language and machine code is a very low level language. Are there any levels in between? The answer is, Yes, there are. In fact, we can identify a whole spectrum of languages, with machine code at the lowest level and many other languages at various higher levels. Some of them are illustrated in the following diagram:

INTELLECT, RENDEZVOUS	High level
SQL, QBE, QUEL, NOMAD, dBASE	
COBOL, FORTRAN, PL/I, PASCAL, BASIC	
ASSEMBLER LANGUAGE	
MACHINE CODE	Low level

All of these languages can be regarded as *programming* languages, in the sense that "programs" can be formulated in any of them. Traditionally, however, the name "programming language" is reserved for languages at the level of COBOL, FORTRAN (etc.), and below. As we have already indicated, languages higher up in the spectrum are more usually referred to as *query* languages. We will follow tradition and reserve the term "programming language" for languages at the lower levels.

Generally speaking, the higher up in the spectrum a given language is, the further away the user of that language is from tedious machine details, and the more productive that user is therefore likely to be. On the other hand, there are some advantages to be obtained from using a lower-level language (see below). Thus some systems do allow appropriately skilled users to construct programs directly at some lower level. In fact, in older systems one had to work at such a level—languages like SQL did not even exist a few years ago. By way of illustration, we show on the next few pages a possible COBOL program for the query "List all flights from San Francisco to Chicago, in departure time order." For purposes of comparison, we first repeat the SQL version from Chapter 2.

```
SELECT *
FROM    FLIGHTS
WHERE   FROM_CODE =
        (SELECT CODE
         FROM    CITIES
         WHERE   CITY = 'San Francisco')
AND     TO_CODE =
        (SELECT CODE
         FROM    CITIES
         WHERE   CITY = 'Chicago')
ORDER   BY DEP_TIME
```

In COBOL (with a few details omitted):

```
DATA DIVISION.

SUBSCHEMA SECTION.

DB FLIGHTS-AND-CITIES WITHIN OAG.

WORKING-STORAGE-SECTION.

01 FCITY-FOUND        PIC XXX.
01 TCITY-FOUND        PIC XXX.
01 FCITY-CODE         PIC XXX.
01 TCITY-CODE         PIC XXX.

01 EOT                PIC XXX.
01 NOT-FOUND          PIC XXX.
01 CITY-NOT-FOUND     PIC XXX.

01 RESULT-TABLE.
   02 TEMP-REC OCCURS 25 TIMES.
      03 FLIGHT       PIC X(6).
      03 F-CODE       PIC XXX.
      03 T-CODE       PIC XXX.
      03 DEP-TIME     PIC XXXX.
      03 ARR-TIME     PIC XXXX.

01 TEMP.
   02 FLIGHT          PIC X(6).
   02 F-CODE          PIC XXX.
   02 T-CODE          PIC XXX.
   02 DEP-TIME        PIC XXXX.
   02 ARR-TIME        PIC XXXX.

01 I                  PIC S999  COMP.
01 J                  PIC S999  COMP.
01 N                  PIC S999  COMP.

PROCEDURE DIVISION.

DECLARATIVES.
```

```
       USE FOR DB-EXCEPTION ON '0502100'.
EOT-PROC.
    MOVE 'YES' TO EOT.


       USE FOR DB-EXCEPTION ON '0502400'.
NF-PROC.
    MOVE 'YES' TO NOT-FOUND.


       USE FOR DB-EXCEPTION ON OTHER.
OTHER-PROC.

          . . . (Code omitted here.) . . .

       END DECLARATIVES.


MOVE 'NO ' TO EOT
MOVE 'NO ' TO NOT-FOUND
MOVE 'NO ' TO FCITY-FOUND
MOVE 'NO ' TO TCITY-FOUND
MOVE '   ' TO FCITY-CODE
MOVE '   ' TO TCITY-CODE


READY F-C-REALM USAGE-MODE IS RETRIEVAL


FIND FIRST CC-REC WITHIN CITIES
PERFORM UNTIL (FCITY-FOUND = 'YES' AND TCITY-FOUND = 'YES')
             OR EOT = 'YES' OR NOT-FOUND = 'YES'
    GET CC-REC
    IF CITY IN CC-REC = 'San Francisco'
       MOVE CODE IN CC-REC TO FCITY-CODE
       MOVE 'YES' TO FCITY-FOUND
    ELSE
       IF CITY IN CC-REC = 'Chicago'
          MOVE CODE IN CC-REC TO TCITY-CODE
          MOVE 'YES' TO TCITY-FOUND
       END-IF
    END-IF
    FIND NEXT CC-REC WITHIN CITIES
END-PERFORM
```

```
      MOVE 'NO ' TO CITY-NOT-FOUND
      IF FCITY-CODE = '    '
         DISPLAY 'FROM CITY NOT LOCATED'
         MOVE 'YES' TO CITY-NOT-FOUND
      END-IF
      IF TCITY-CODE = '    '
         DISPLAY 'TO CITY NOT LOCATED'
         MOVE 'YES' TO CITY-NOT-FOUND
      END-IF
      IF CITY-NOT-FOUND
         GO TO EXIT-PGM
      END-IF

      MOVE FCITY-CODE TO FROM-CODE IN FLIGHT-REC
      MOVE TCITY-CODE TO TO-CODE   IN FLIGHT-REC
      FIND FLIGHT-REC WITHIN FLIGHTS USING FROM-CODE IN FLIGHT-REC,
                                    TO-CODE IN FLIGHT-REC
      PERFORM VARYING I FROM 1 BY 1 UNTIL EOT = 'YES'
                                    OR NOT-FOUND = 'YES'
         GET FLIGHT-REC
         MOVE FLIGHT-REC TO TEMP-REC (I)
         FIND DUPLICATE WITHIN FLIGHTS USING FROM-CODE, TO-CODE
      END-PERFORM

      FINISH F-C-REALM

      SUBTRACT 1 FROM I GIVING N
      PERFORM VARYING I FROM 1 BY 1 UNTIL I > N - 1
         PERFORM VARYING J FROM 1 BY 1 UNTIL J > N - I
            IF DEP-TIME OF TEMP-REC (J) > DEP-TIME OF TEMP-REC (J + 1)
               MOVE TEMP-REC (J) TO TEMP
               MOVE TEMP-REC (J + 1) TO TEMP-REC (J)
               MOVE TEMP TO TEMP-REC (J + 1)
            END-IF
         END-PERFORM
      END-PERFORM

      DISPLAY 'FLIGHT' 'FROM_CODE' 'TO_CODE' 'DEP_TIME' 'ARR_TIME'
      PERFORM VARYING I FROM 1 BY 1 UNTIL I > N
         DISPLAY TEMP-REC (I)
      END-PERFORM

  EXIT-PGM.
     GOBACK.
```

The *advantages* of operating directly at the COBOL level are as follows:

- It may be more efficient—efficient, that is, in terms of machine performance, not human performance. In some applications today this consideration outweighs all others. However, most experts believe that the time will come when the machine performance obtainable from higher-level languages such as SQL will be as good as, or even better than, that of COBOL, in all but a handful of applications. Thus we are likely to see a gradual (or perhaps not so gradual?) movement away from COBOL and toward those higher languages.

- There may be things you can do at the COBOL level that you cannot do at the higher level. For example, SQL does not currently provide the full range of computational facilities that are available in COBOL. It is likely to be only a matter of time before such facilities are provided in the higher languages; but for the present it is still necessary to operate at the COBOL level in some situations. (At least, this statement is true assuming that you want to get the machine to do as much of the work as possible; in a small system it may well be easier simply to do a little more manual work yourself. Certainly it would be unreasonable to require you to be proficient in COBOL before you could use the system at all. We will touch on this point again in Chapter 5 in our discussion of canned procedures.)

In passing, we note that these claimed advantages of COBOL over SQL are precisely the advantages that were cited for machine code over COBOL when COBOL first appeared. Today nobody writes in machine code, except for those who design or build CPUs and others performing similar specialist tasks.

The *disadvantages* of operating at the COBOL level should be clear:

- COBOL-level programs are large and complex. The COBOL program above is over ten times as long as the SQL equivalent shown earlier and much more than ten times as complicated. The job of producing and maintaining such programs obviously requires highly specialized skills. Writing, testing, and "debugging" (i.e., fixing the errors in) such a program to the point where it is fully operational can take months or even years. Changing that program later to deal with changes in requirements can be a nightmare.

- As a corollary of the first point, it may be impossible to obtain information from the database *at the time it is needed.* The language acts as a *barrier* between the data and the user; the user cannot get to the data directly but has to go through an intermediary, the COBOL programming specialist, who may not even be available at the time (see the next point below).

- The COBOL programming department can become a bottleneck. If all access to the database requires a COBOL program to be written, it may be months or years before the necessary skills are available to write that program. One large computer installation estimates its "application backlog" at approximately *thirty years.* Backlogs of seven to ten years are by no means uncommon.

One of the advantages of a language like SQL is precisely that it enables users to get at data *directly,* at the time that data is needed, bypassing the COBOL programming department entirely. Usability, responsiveness, and productivity are all thus greatly enhanced.

NATURAL LANGUAGES

Let us return for a moment to the questions raised in Chapter 2: Why do we need query languages at all? Why can't we use ordinary English (or some other natural language)? Perhaps the best answer to these questions is, "We're getting there." For example, the following might be legal queries on the wine cellar database in the language INTELLECT:

```
WHAT WINES WILL BE READY IN 1986?
WHICH OF THEM ARE FROM MIRASSOU?
```

These queries certainly look like ordinary English; notice in particular how the second query here "remembers" the result of the first. Considerable success has been achieved with languages such as INTELLECT in certain applications. However:

- Look back at the language spectrum shown on page 33. A general rule is that the higher up in the spectrum a given language appears, the more computer resources are needed to analyze queries in that language and to translate them into machine code equivalents. Notice the position of INTELLECT on the spectrum! It follows that, at the time of writing at least, natural language systems are generally available only on large machines—though once again, given the pace at which the database field is moving, this restriction is unlikely to apply for very much longer.

• The process of installing a natural language system is more complex than that of installing a (comparatively) lower-level system such as SQL and requires certain special skills. This is because a natural language system has to be tailored to the particular database it is going to deal with, so that it can (for example) understand what is meant by expressions such as READY IN 1986 or MIRASSOU WINES. (These expressions would have no meaning in the context of, for example, the flight information database. Equally, the flight information database would have specialized expressions of its own that would have no meaning in the wine cellar example.)

• A problem with natural language systems in general is that they are liable to encourage users to ask questions that the system cannot answer (even though those queries may be superficially similar to ones that it can). For example, the query

```
WHAT WINES DID I BUY IN 1980?
```

cannot be answered, because the information is not in the database—but is that fact obvious to the user? Another example:

```
WHICH WINE GOES BEST WITH ALMOND CHICKEN?
```

The system is unlikely to deal with this query in a very intelligent fashion. The danger is that the user will become frustrated with the system and will therefore cease to use it.

• Finally, there are many application areas in which a more stylized language may actually be preferable to natural language. Such applications are ones in which the user is entering rather stereotyped queries over and over again as part of a regular job. Consider a travel agent, for example, who wishes to query the flights database for flights from San Francisco to Chicago. For that user, the somewhat cryptic expression

```
JUL20SFOORD1P
```

may actually be easier to use, and certainly will take less time to type, than an English language equivalent (or a SQL equivalent, come to that).

**DATA
INDEPENDENCE**

One term that you will often hear in a database context is "data independence." Like so many other terms in this field, it is not particularly apt; indeed, it does not really have a single, specific meaning, but serves rather as a blanket term for a variety of somewhat distinct notions. Broadly speaking, however, what the term means is that *users are not dependent on the precise details of how data is physically stored in the database* (i.e., on the disk). In particular, when we say that a database "consists of tables," we do not really mean that data is physically stored in that tabular form, exactly as the user sees it. The physical arrangement is certain to be something quite different. Apart from anything else, each individual data value, such as 8 or 'ZINFANDEL', must be represented as a sequence of *bits*, or binary digits, because, fundamentally, bits are all that the machine can understand. The character string 'ZINFANDEL', for example, would be represented by the bit sequence

0101101001001001010011100100011001000010100111001000100010001010101001100

(using a certain "character code" known as ASCII). But this fact is of no concern to the user. Likewise, the precise physical location of such bit sequences on the disk is equally immaterial. All these considerations are the concern of the DBMS, not the user (see Fig. 3.4); the user is thus free to act as if the database really did consist of tables. (However, Chapter 12 in Part II of this book contains a brief discussion of how data may actually be represented on the disk.)

The advantage of data independence is that it enables the user to concentrate on the *logical* structure of the data and to ignore irrelevant physical details—much as a language like SQL enables the user to concentrate on the logical structure of the query and to ignore details of the machine code instructions needed to execute that query. Thus data independence, like a high-level language, is a significant factor in increasing user productivity (indeed, data independence and high-level languages are really just two sides of the same coin). In fact, direct user access to the database would not even be feasible without some reasonable measure of data independence.

We will discuss further aspects of data independence in Part II. It is of even more significance in a large, shared database environment.

Figure 3.4

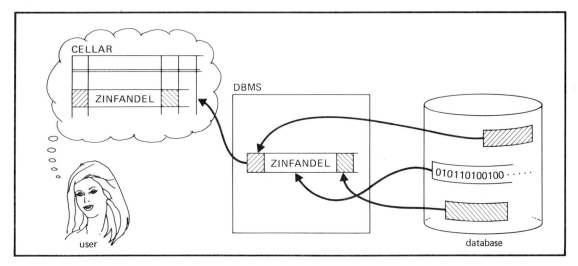

OTHER DATABASE MANAGEMENT FUNCTIONS

We have now outlined what database management means to the user. However, a database expert, or anyone knowledgeable in the database field, will probably object strongly at this point that we have not even mentioned some of the most important aspects at all! Or, equivalently, that our example databases (Chapter 2) are scarcely worthy of the name, since they make little or no use of the functions that distinguish database systems per se from other kinds of systems (such as file systems, text-editing systems, etc.). And these objections do have some validity. Let us consider them carefully.

The basic point is that we have almost totally ignored the possibility of *sharing* the data. Historically, sharing was one of the prime motivations, if not *the* prime motivation, for going to a database system in the first place. Indeed, a database is frequently *defined* as a collection of data that is intended to be shared by multiple users. Incidentally, "sharing" here is usually taken to mean, not only that the database can be accessed by multiple users, but that it can be accessed by multiple users *at the same time.* See Fig. 3.5. We will discuss this aspect of sharing in Part II.

Of course, sharing does have numerous advantages. For example, it means that data does not have to be stored redundantly to be used for multiple purposes (notice how individual pieces of

Figure 3.5

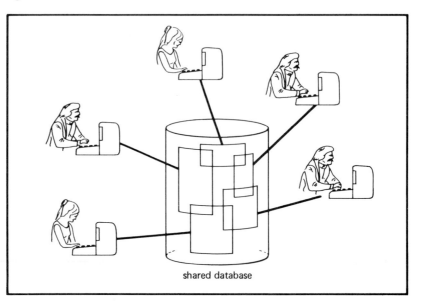

shared database

the database in Fig. 3.5 are being used by different users, presumably for different purposes); it allows new applications to be developed at any time that operate on existing data; and so on. Sharing is crucially important in many installations and will certainly remain so. But notice the assumption that the database is part of a "large system" environment, or at least an environment in which there are multiple users to do the sharing. Historically, database management systems were large themselves and hence were available only on large machines (where, for economic reasons, there were typically many end-users). But the situation is changing rapidly for a variety of reasons, not the least of which is that "small" machines—or, rather, single-user machines—are becoming larger, thanks to the fast-declining cost of electronics. The result is that database facilities are fast becoming available on most single-user systems also.

Now it is true that various additional capabilities are needed in a sharing environment, over and above those that we have already identified as part of the total database management function (data manipulation, data definition, etc.). Those additional capabilities include *concurrency control, integrity control, security control,* and others. What is more, these functions may be perceived as additional advantages, even as overwhelming advantages, in a sharing environment. More precisely, these are the features that many database specialists would claim as the sine qua non of a database system. It is also true that any or all of these features may be missing, and probably will be, in a nonshared system. Despite their importance, however, we defer detailed discussion of these topics to Part II, and content ourselves for now with the following two remarks:

1. Nonshared databases are becoming increasingly important, owing to the rapid spread of microcomputers and minicomputers.

2. Even in a sharing environment, the database system looks (or should look) *to each individual user* exactly as we have described it. In other words, it is a major objective of a shared system to look to each user as if it were *not* shared (as far as possible). The problems of security, concurrency, and so on mentioned above are primarily system problems, not user problems. Since this book is principally concerned with what the system looks like to the user, everything we have said so far is still generally applicable, even in the case of a shared system.

SUMMARY   In this chapter we have discussed what is involved on the part of the machine in performing the functions of database management. From the user's perspective, database management means, primarily, supporting a query language (provided the term "query language" is understood to include formatting, scrolling, data definition, etc.). However, we have taken a look at what the computer has to do to provide these services. A computer consists of a CPU, main storage, secondary storage (disks), a screen and keyboard, and a printer; it operates under the control of a program that resides in main storage during execution. The DBMS is such a program. The DBMS is responsible for reading query language statements from the keyboard, analyzing them, and performing the required operations on the data in the database. Languages for accessing the database range from machine language (lowest level), through programming languages such as COBOL and query languages such as SQL, to (almost) natural languages such as INTELLECT.

We have also touched on data independence—the independence of users from the physical structure of the stored database—and on certain additional DBMS functions that are particularly relevant in a shared environment: integrity, concurrency, security, and others. These latter topics will be discussed in more detail in Part II.

4

A Case Study:
Database Creation
and Sample Queries

INTRODUCTION

In this chapter and the next we discuss a rather more comprehensive example in order to illustrate more fully some of the potential of a database system. Note, however, that the example is still suitable for implementation on a minicomputer or microcomputer. It is based on a real application.

Figure 4.1 represents a system of three private roads (Redwood Road, Creek Road, and Mill Road) located somewhere in the Santa Cruz Mountains of California. Property owners on those roads have banded together to form a Road Association for the purpose of maintaining and repairing the roads as necessary. The sample application concerns the financial accounts of that association.

In this chapter we show an appropriate database for this application and consider some typical queries on that database. In doing so, we will illustrate a number of additional features of the SQL SELECT statement. In Chapter 5 we will consider maintenance operations on the same database.

Figure 4.1

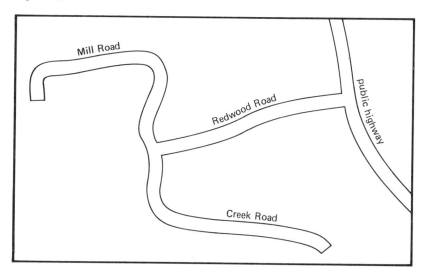

Note 1: The database design shown in the next section is by no means the only one possible. It simply happens to be close to the design actually used in the real application. As indicated in Chapters 1 and 2, the whole question of database design will be discussed in some detail toward the end of this book (Chapters 17 and 18).

Note 2: This database will be used as the basis for almost all examples throughout the next few chapters. It is therefore worth taking the time to make sure you understand it reasonably well.

CREATING THE DATABASE

The database consists of nine tables:

```
PARCELS
OWNERS
PARCEL_ACCOUNTS
SPECIAL_ASSESSMENTS
GENERAL_LEDGER
REDWOOD_LEDGER
CREEK_LEDGER
MILL_LEDGER
LAST_ENTRIES
```

An overview of the structure of these nine tables is given in Fig. 4.2. The corresponding CREATE TABLE statements, plus explanatory comments, are given in paragraphs 1–9 below.

1. CREATE TABLE PARCELS — Contains one row for each piece of property ("parcel") on any one of the three roads

(APN   CHAR(9), — "Assessor's parcel number" (e.g., 93-282-55); uniquely identifies the parcel

  ROAD   CHAR(7), — Road on which parcel is located: 'REDWOOD' or 'CREEK' or 'MILL'

  OWNER   CHAR(20), — Owner's name

  IMPROVED CHAR(1), — 'Y' or 'N' (indicates whether parcel has been "improved" by construction of a dwelling)

  LAST_ENTRY DECIMAL(5), — Entry number of most recent entry for this parcel in the PARCEL_ACCOUNTS table (see paragraph 3)

  BALANCE DECIMAL(7,2)) — Dollar-and-cent balance in that most recent entry (see below)

Figure 4.2

PARCELS table:

APN	ROAD	OWNER	IMPROVED	LAST_ENTRY	BALANCE

OWNERS table:

OWNER	ADDRESS	PHONE

PARCEL_ACCOUNTS table:

APN	ENTRY	DATE	DESCRIPTION	TYPE	AMOUNT	BALANCE

SPECIAL_ASSESSMENTS table:

SAN	ROAD	DATE	TOTAL	PER_PARCEL	EXPLANATION	PAYEE

GENERAL_LEDGER table:

ENTRY	DATE	DESCRIPTION	TYPE	PARTY	AMOUNT	BALANCE

REDWOOD_LEDGER table:

ENTRY	DATE	DESCRIPTION	TYPE	PARTY	AMOUNT	BALANCE

CREEK_LEDGER table:

ENTRY	DATE	DESCRIPTION	TYPE	PARTY	AMOUNT	BALANCE

MILL_LEDGER table:

ENTRY	DATE	DESCRIPTION	TYPE	PARTY	AMOUNT	BALANCE

LAST_ENTRIES table:

ACCOUNT	ENTRY	BALANCE

LAST_ENTRY and BALANCE are included in the PARCELS table in order to simplify subsequent maintenance processing (as will become clear in the next chapter). DECIMAL(7,2) means that the column concerned (here BALANCE) will contain decimal values of the form ddddd.dd, that is, values up to seven digits long, with an assumed decimal point two places from the right. "Assumed" means that if the user sets the BALANCE in a particular row to 6 (say), then that value will be interpreted to mean 6.00 (six dollars and no cents). Some possible BALANCE values are as follows:

12345.67	12345 dollars and 67 cents
29.51	$29.51
6.00	$6.00
6	Same as above
0	$0.00
−342.41	Note that values can be negative

Any of these could be specified as an INSERT or UPDATE value or as a comparison value in a WHERE clause (e.g., WHERE BALANCE = 29.51).

Here is a sample PARCELS row:

APN	ROAD	OWNER	IMPROVED	LAST_ENTRY	BALANCE
93-293-02	MILL	P.J.DEAN	Y	17	120.00

2. CREATE TABLE OWNERS   Contains one row for each person who owns one or more parcels

```
( OWNER     CHAR(20),      Owner's name
  ADDRESS   CHAR(80),      Owner's address
  PHONE     CHAR(12) )     Owner's phone number
```

Sample OWNERS row:

OWNER	ADDRESS	PHONE
P.J.DEAN	23 THE ALBANY	441-296-2015

3. CREATE TABLE PARCEL_ACCOUNTS — Contains a set of rows for each parcel, representing all charges and all credits to that parcel

(APN	CHAR(9),	Assessor's parcel number
ENTRY	DECIMAL(5),	Unique within APN (each parcel has a set of entries —i.e., rows—numbered chronologically 1,2,3,. . .)
DATE	CHAR(6),	Date of entry (YYMMDD)
DESCRIPTION	CHAR(20),	See below
TYPE	CHAR(6),	'CHARGE' or 'CREDIT'
AMOUNT	DECIMAL(7,2),	Amount of charge or credit
BALANCE	DECIMAL(7,2))	New balance owing

DESCRIPTION takes one of a prescribed set of values:

'DUES80'	Annual dues for 1980
'DUES81'	Annual dues for 1981
(etc.)	(etc.)
'PENALTY80'	Penalty imposed in 1980 (20% of balance at YE 1980)
'PENALTY81'	Penalty imposed in 1981 (20% of balance at YE 1981)
(etc.)	(etc.)
'SA1'	Special assessment 1 ⎫ See table
'SA2'	Special assessment 2 ⎬ SPECIAL_ASSESSMENTS
(etc.)	(etc.) ⎭ (paragraph 4)
'DAMAGE FEE'	Charge imposed to pay for road damage caused by construction traffic at time of improvement

Sample PARCEL_ACCOUNTS row:

APN	ENTRY	DATE	DESCRIPTION	TYPE	AMOUNT	BALANCE
93-293-02	17	821016	DAMAGE FEE	CHARGE	500.00	560.00

4. CREATE TABLE SPECIAL_ASSESSMENTS — Contains one row for each "special assessment," that is, each call for funds from Road Association members for some specific purpose (e.g., to pay for some specific repair)

(SAN	DECIMAL(3),	Special assessment number (1,2,3,. . .)
ROAD	CHAR(7),	Road to which assessment applies
DATE	CHAR(6),	Date of assessment

```
TOTAL        DECIMAL(7,2),        Total amount of assessment
PER_PARCEL   DECIMAL(7,2),        Amount due per parcel involved
EXPLANATION  CHAR(40),            Text describing reason for assessment
PAYEE        CHAR(25) )           Party to be paid (e.g., party who did the repair job)
```

Sample SPECIAL_ASSESSMENTS row:

SAN	ROAD	DATE	TOTAL	PER_PARCEL	EXPLANATION	PAYEE
3	CREEK	810522	2460.00	205.00	GRADING	ROAD FIXERS, INC.

```
5. CREATE TABLE GENERAL_LEDGER      Contains one row for each charge or credit to Road
                                    Association general fund
   ( ENTRY       DECIMAL(5),        Uniquely identifies entry (1,2,3,. . .)
     DATE        CHAR(6),           Date of entry
     DESCRIPTION CHAR(80),          See below
     TYPE        CHAR(6),           'CHARGE' or 'CREDIT'
     PARTY       CHAR(25),          APN from which payment received, or other identifica-
                                    tion of party making or receiving payment
     AMOUNT      DECIMAL(7,2),      Amount of charge or credit
     BALANCE     DECIMAL(9,2) )     New balance in hand
```

DESCRIPTION may take any of the values listed under PARCEL_ACCOUNTS above, as well as other values such as 'BANK CHARGES', 'STATIONERY SUPPLIES', 'TRACTOR HIRE', and so on.

Sample GENERAL_LEDGER record:

ENTRY	DATE	DESCRIPTION	TYPE	PARTY	AMOUNT	BALANCE
724	820720	DUES82	CREDIT	93-291-44	120.00	6095.40

The general fund is subdivided into three specific funds, one for each of the three roads. Maintenance on a particular road is paid for out of that road's individual fund. Dues, penalty, and construction fee payments from parcel owners are allocated to individual funds as follows: one-third to Redwood Road (since all members use that road), two-thirds to the road on which the parcel concerned is located. Special assessments are charged only to parcel owners using the road in question, and corresponding payments are allocated entirely to that road. There are thus three further tables:

6. CREATE TABLE REDWOOD_LEDGER

7. CREATE TABLE CREEK_LEDGER

8. CREATE TABLE MILL_LEDGER

These three tables represent charges and credits to the three individual roads. Each has exactly the same structure (same column names, etc.) as the GENERAL_LEDGER table. At any given time the sum of the balances on the three individual ledgers should equal the balance on the general ledger.

9. CREATE TABLE LAST_ENTRIES		Contains one row for the general fund and one for each of the three specific road funds, giving the entry number and balance for the last entry for that fund in the appropriate LEDGER table
(ACCOUNT	CHAR(7),	'GENERAL' or 'REDWOOD' or 'CREEK' or 'MILL'
ENTRY	DECIMAL(5),	Entry number of most recent entry in account identified by ACCOUNT
BALANCE	DECIMAL(9,2))	Balance in that most recent entry

The purpose of the LAST_ENTRIES table, like that of LAST_ENTRY and BALANCE in the PARCELS table, is to simplify certain subsequent processing. Here is a sample set of rows for LAST_ENTRIES (note that the entire table is only four rows long):

ACCOUNT	ENTRY	BALANCE
GENERAL	724	6095.40
REDWOOD	281	977.67
CREEK	113	1618.26
MILL	490	3499.47

LOADING THE DATABASE

Assume for simplicity that the system is being brought into operation on January 1, 1980 ('800101'). The four LEDGER tables and the SPECIAL_ASSESSMENTS table are all initially empty (no activity has yet occurred on any of the four road fund accounts and no special assessments have yet been charged). A series of SQL INSERT statements can be used to load initial data values into the PARCELS, OWNERS, PARCEL__ACCOUNTS, and LAST__ENTRIES tables, as follows.

1. PARCELS

A row must be inserted into PARCELS for each parcel on each road. For example:

```
INSERT INTO PARCELS
            ( APN, ROAD, OWNER, IMPROVED, LAST_ENTRY, BALANCE )
        VALUES ( '93-282-55', 'CREEK', 'I.J.KING', 'Y', 1, 120 )
```

An analogous INSERT is required for each parcel. For an explanation of LAST__ENTRY and BALANCE, see paragraph 3 below. *Note:* It is not necessary to list the column names APN, ROAD, and so on; the system knows what columns the table has from the corresponding CREATE TABLE. It is not wrong to include them, however. We do so for clarity.

2. OWNERS

A row must be inserted into OWNERS for each owner of one or more parcels. For example:

```
INSERT INTO OWNERS ( OWNER, ADDRESS, PHONE )
        VALUES ( 'I.J.KING', '15666 CREEK ROAD' )
```

An analogous INSERT is required for each owner. Notice that no value has been supplied for PHONE in this example. In such a case the system will automatically set PHONE to *null* in the database for the record in question. Null represents "information missing" or "information unknown." It is not the same as blank or zero.

3. PARCEL_ACCOUNTS

One row must be inserted into PARCEL__ACCOUNTS for each parcel, representing the 1980 dues charged to that parcel. Each such row will be entry no. 1 for the parcel in question. For example:

```
INSERT INTO PARCEL_ACCOUNTS
        ( APN, ENTRY, DATE, DESCRIPTION, TYPE, AMOUNT, BALANCE )
        VALUES
        ( '93-282-55', 1, '800101', 'DUES80', 'CHARGE', 120, 120 )
```

An analogous INSERT is required for each parcel. Dues are
$120.00 for improved parcels, $60.00 for unimproved parcels;
hence the initial AMOUNT and BALANCE values for a given parcel account are either both 120 or both 60.

4.   LAST_ENTRIES

This table is initialized with four "dummy" rows, one for each
fund, as follows:

```
INSERT INTO LAST_ENTRIES ( ACCOUNT, ENTRY, BALANCE )
       VALUES ( 'GENERAL', 0, 0 )
INSERT INTO LAST_ENTRIES ( ACCOUNT, ENTRY, BALANCE )
       VALUES ( 'REDWOOD', 0, 0 )
INSERT INTO LAST_ENTRIES ( ACCOUNT, ENTRY, BALANCE )
       VALUES ( 'CREEK', 0, 0 )
INSERT INTO LAST_ENTRIES ( ACCOUNT, ENTRY, BALANCE )
       VALUES ( 'MILL', 0, 0 )
```

Entry no. 0 is a fictitious entry, used just for initialization purposes
(i.e., just to get things going); remember that there are actually no
initial entries in any of the LEDGER tables.

In a really large database, of course, it would be intolerably
tedious to have to load all the data as above, that is, manually, one
row at a time, with a separate INSERT statement for each. In practice, therefore, a variety of techniques for streamlining the process
would normally be provided. However, the manual method is adequate for our purposes.

SAMPLE QUERIES

We now show a variety of typical queries against the Road Association database. Most of these queries (all except 1, 2, and 8)
illustrate further features of the SQL SELECT statement. In each
case the feature illustrated is noted in bold type at the head of the
example for ease of reference.

Note: The examples are in approximate order of increasing
complexity. If you find that they are delving into complications
that you have no interest in, simply go on to the next chapter. It is
certainly not necessary to understand every detail of the present

section in order to understand later material in the book. However, the queries are all "real" in the sense that they all represent genuine queries from the real life application.

The following exercise is strongly recommended:

• Invent some sample data for the nine tables.

• For each of the sample queries, take the SELECT statement shown and execute it by hand on your sample data, and convince yourself that it does in fact produce the right answer.

Furthermore, if you have access to a system of your own, then try creating the nine tables, loading your sample data into them, and running the queries against that data on the machine. (Depending on your system, however, you may wish to defer this exercise until after you have read one or the other of Chapters 8–10.)

1. Basic SELECT–FROM–WHERE

Who is the owner of parcel 93-282-55?

```
SELECT OWNER
FROM   PARCELS
WHERE  APN = '93-282-55'
```

Result:

OWNER

I.J.KING

2. AND in the WHERE clause

What penalty was imposed on parcel 93-282-55 for 1981?

```
SELECT AMOUNT
FROM   PARCEL_ACCOUNTS
WHERE  APN = '93-282-55'
AND    DESCRIPTION = 'PENALTY81'
AND    TYPE = 'CHARGE'
```

Sample result:

AMOUNT

17.35

3. LIKE comparison

List all owners who live in Berkeley.

```
SELECT *
FROM    OWNERS
WHERE   ADDRESS LIKE '%BERKELEY%'
```

Sample result:

OWNER	ADDRESS	PHONE
BILL GREEN	17 AX DR., BERKELEY, CA.	415-636-7227
MARY PATTON	UC BERKELEY	?

The condition ADDRESS LIKE '%BERKELEY%' will select all rows in which the ADDRESS value includes 'BERKELEY' as a *substring*, that is, all rows in which the string 'BERKELEY' appears anywhere within the total string representing the complete ADDRESS value. The percent signs stand for substrings of zero or more other characters; that is, they indicate that 'BERKELEY' can be preceded and/or followed in the total string by any number (possibly zero) of other characters.

4. Arithmetic expressions in the SELECT clause

What will be the number of the *next* GENERAL_LEDGER record?

```
SELECT ENTRY + 1
FROM    LAST_ENTRIES
WHERE   ACCOUNT = 'GENERAL'
```

Sample result:

ENTRY+1
725

This somewhat contrived example shows how you can get the system to retrieve, not only values that are directly stored in the database, but also values that are obtained by performing some kind of arithmetic on those stored values.

5. Built-in functions (SUM)

How much has the association paid (in total) to Road Fixers, Inc.?

In general, there may be many separate payments to this payee. The following SELECT will list all of them:

```
SELECT *
FROM    GENERAL_LEDGER
WHERE   PARTY = 'ROAD FIXERS, INC.'
AND     TYPE = 'CHARGE'
```

The result might be as follows:

ENTRY	DATE	DESCRIPTION	TYPE	PARTY	AMOUNT	BALANCE
147	800904	SA4	CHARGE	ROAD FIXERS, INC.	450.00	6792.04
181	810217	SA4	CHARGE	ROAD FIXERS, INC.	250.00	9081.63
233	811022	SA6	CHARGE	ROAD FIXERS, INC.	1025.00	4227.55

Add these three values. Result = $1725.00.

From this display the total amount can be seen to be $1725.00. However, it is easier to get the system itself to do the arithmetic:

```
SELECT SUM (AMOUNT)
FROM    GENERAL_LEDGER
WHERE   PARTY = 'ROAD FIXERS, INC.'
AND     TYPE = 'CHARGE'
```

Result:

```
SUM(AMOUNT)

  1725.00
```

SUM is an example of a *built-in function*. It is used to add together the values appearing in some column. The WHERE clause can be used (as in the example) to eliminate rows, and hence entries in the column in question, before the sum is computed. Other similar built-in functions include the following:

AVG	To find the average of the values in some column
MAX	To find the largest value in some column
MIN	To find the smallest value in some column
COUNT(*)	To count the number of rows in some table (must be written as shown)

Here are some more examples (6 and 7) of the use of these functions.

6. Built-in functions [COUNT (*)]

How many payments were made on parcel 93-282-55 in 1982?

```
SELECT COUNT (*)
FROM   PARCEL_ACCOUNTS
WHERE  APN = '93-282-55'
AND    TYPE = 'CREDIT'
AND    DATE > '811231'
AND    DATE < '830101'
```

Note: > means "greater than"; < means "less than."

Sample result:

```
COUNT(*)
```

6

7. Built-in functions (MAX)

When was the last time a payment was made on parcel 93-282-55?

```
SELECT MAX (DATE)
FROM   PARCEL_ACCOUNTS
WHERE  APN = '93-282-55'
AND    TYPE = 'CREDIT'
```

Sample result:

```
MAX(DATE)
```

830125

This example raises another problem. What if no payments have *ever* been made on the parcel? (This is regrettably the case for many parcels in the real life application on which our example is based.) The set of DATE values from which we want the MAX would then be *empty*—that is, would not contain any values—and there would therefore not really be a MAX at all (nor would there be a MIN, nor a SUM or AVG, though there would be a COUNT, namely zero). In such a situation, the system considers the result to be *null* (just like a column value that has never been assigned) and will display it on the screen in some distinguishing fashion, such as

```
MAX(DATE)
```

?

The next example illustrates nested SELECTs again.

8. Nested SELECT

Display name, address, and phone number for the owner of parcel 93-282-55.

```
SELECT *
FROM   OWNERS
WHERE  OWNER =
       (SELECT OWNER
        FROM    PARCELS
        WHERE   APN = '93-282-55')
```

Compare the SQL query in Chapter 2 for listing flights from San Francisco to Chicago (that query also involved nested SELECTs). Here the inner SELECT retrieves the OWNER of parcel 93-282-55 (who happens to be I. J. King); the outer SELECT then retrieves (and displays) the record from the OWNERS table for that person. Result:

OWNER	ADDRESS	PHONE
I.J.KING	15666 CREEK ROAD	?

9. IN comparison

What is the total payment made on all parcels owned by John Minski? (Note that the same person may own two or more parcels.)

We can handle this problem in two steps, as follows.

Step 1.   Find all parcels owned by John Minski.

```
SELECT APN
FROM   PARCELS
WHERE  OWNER = 'JOHN MINSKI'
```

Result (say):

APN

```
93-282-50
93-282-51
93-282-54
93-282-58
```

Step 2:   Find total payment made on these parcels.

```
SELECT SUM (AMOUNT)
FROM   PARCEL_ACCOUNTS
WHERE  TYPE = 'CREDIT'
AND    APN IN ('93-282-50', '93-282-51', '93-282-54', '93-282-58')
```

Notice the use of an IN condition here (a new kind of condition for the WHERE clause). Sample result:

SUM(AMOUNT)

```
1495.00
```

As you have probably guessed, however, it is possible to combine the two steps into one, making use of a nested SELECT again:

```
SELECT SUM (AMOUNT)
FROM   PARCEL_ACCOUNTS
WHERE  TYPE = 'CREDIT'
AND    APN IN
       (SELECT APN
        FROM   PARCELS
        WHERE  OWNER = 'JOHN MINSKI')
```

Incidentally, if John Minski has paid nothing at all, the result will display as null, not zero, because we would be asking for the SUM of an empty set.

10. Join

List all special assessments (SAN and EXPLANATION) and, for each one, all parcels (APN) affected by that assessment.

First we show an example of a possible result for this query:

SAN	EXPLANATION	APN
3	GRADING	93-282-55
3	GRADING	93-291-19
7	CULVERTS	93-281-24
7	CULVERTS	93-282-54
7	CULVERTS	93-291-44

The interesting aspect of this query is that the required data comes from two tables: SAN and EXPLANATION are in the SPECIAL_ASSESSMENTS table, but APN is in the PARCELS table. To find the parcels affected by a particular assessment, we must use the ROAD value for that assessment (as given in the SPECIAL_ASSESSMENTS table) to look over in the PARCELS table to find the parcels on that ROAD. So the query looks like this:

```
SELECT SAN, EXPLANATION, APN
FROM    SPECIAL_ASSESSMENTS, PARCELS
WHERE   SPECIAL_ASSESSMENTS.ROAD = PARCELS.ROAD
```

Observe that the FROM clause names the two tables concerned, and the WHERE clause expresses the connection between them. To understand how this works, imagine yourself looking at two rows, one row from each of the two tables—say the two rows shown here:

From SPECIAL_ASSESSMENTS:

SAN	ROAD	···	EXPLANATION	···
3	CREEK	···	GRADING	

From PARCELS:

APN	···	ROAD	···
93-282-55	···	CREEK	

Identical

From these two rows you can see that special assessment 3 applies to parcel 93-282-55. In other words, these two rows will generate the result row:

SAN	EXPLANATION	APN
3	GRADING	93-282-55

Clearly, data is to be selected from the original two rows *if and only if* the ROAD in the SPECIAL_ASSESSMENTS row is the same as the ROAD in the PARCELS row. Hence the form of the WHERE clause:

```
WHERE  SPECIAL_ASSESSMENTS.ROAD=PARCELS.ROAD
```

Another way of thinking about this query is as follows: For each SPECIAL_ASSESSMENTS row, find all PARCELS rows having the same ROAD value (because of the WHERE clause SPECIAL_ASSESSMENTS.ROAD = PARCELS.ROAD), and form a result row by selecting SAN and EXPLANATION from the SPECIAL_ASSESSMENTS row and APN from the PARCELS row.

Notice that it is necessary in this example to *qualify* the column name ROAD by the appropriate table name (SPECIAL_ASSESSMENTS or PARCELS); without such qualification the column name would be ambiguous (in this context). Incidentally, you are free to qualify column names in this manner even when there is no risk of ambiguity, and it is frequently a good idea to do so, for clarity (see the next example).

The operation of combining data from two (or more) tables in a single SELECT is known as a *join;* it is as if the tables concerned were being joined together (on the basis of a *join condition* such as SPECIAL_ASSESSMENTS.ROAD = PARCELS. ROAD) for the duration of the query. Join is so important that we give another example of its use, slightly more complicated.

11. Join

List all improved parcels, with owners' names, addresses, and phone numbers.

```
SELECT PARCELS.APN, OWNERS.OWNER, OWNERS.ADDRESS, OWNERS.PHONE
FROM   PARCELS, OWNERS
WHERE  PARCELS.IMPROVED = 'Y'
AND    PARCELS.OWNER = OWNERS.OWNER
ORDER  BY OWNERS.OWNER, PARCELS.APN
```

Again, to see how the query works, imagine yourself looking at a row from each of the two tables, say the following two rows:

From PARCELS: From OWNERS:

APN	···	OWNER	IMPROVED		OWNER	ADDRESS	
				···			···
93-282-55	···	I.J.KING	Y		I.J.KING	15666 ...	

Identical

Data is to be selected from these two rows if and only if (a) IMPROVED = 'Y' *and* (b) the OWNER in the PARCELS row is equal to the OWNER in the OWNERS row. Hence the structure of the WHERE clause is as shown (notice the qualified column names again). The result row is as follows:

APN	OWNER	ADDRESS	PHONE
93-282-55	I.J.KING	15666 CREEK ROAD	?

We have also shown an ORDER BY clause in this query, just to remind you of the possibility. The ordering we have requested is *ascending parcel number within ascending owner name*. It is also possible to request *descending* order by specifying DESC after the relevant column name. For example:

```
ORDER BY OWNERS.OWNER DESC, PARCELS.APN
```

(which means *ascending* parcel number within *descending* owner name).

12. EXISTS

List parcel number and owner for all parcels on which at least one 1982 dues payment has been made.

This example makes use of another special built-in function, namely EXISTS. EXISTS is used to test whether a row exists in some table satisfying some condition. It appears in a WHERE clause with an associated nested SELECT (to identify the table and the condition to be tested):

```
SELECT APN, OWNER
FROM   PARCELS
WHERE  EXISTS
       (SELECT *
        FROM   PARCEL_ACCOUNTS
        WHERE  APN = PARCELS.APN
        AND    DESCRIPTION = 'DUES82'
        AND    TYPE = 'CREDIT')
```

We can paraphrase this query as follows:

Select APN and owner from the PARCELS table where there exists at least one row in the PARCEL_ACCOUNTS table with the same APN (i.e., with APN = PARCELS.APN) and representing a 1982 dues payment.

Sample result:

APN	OWNER
93-282-55	I.J.KING
93-291-44	BILL GREEN
93-293-02	P.J.DEAN

Though perhaps a little complex, EXISTS is extremely useful, and it is worth making yourself familiar with it. Here is another example (the converse of the previous one).

13. NOT EXISTS

List parcel number and owner for all parcels on which no 1982 dues payment has been made.

```
SELECT APN, OWNER
FROM    PARCELS
WHERE   NOT EXISTS
        (SELECT *
         FROM    PARCEL_ACCOUNTS
         WHERE   APN = PARCELS.APN
         AND     DESCRIPTION = 'DUES82'
         AND     TYPE = 'CREDIT')
```

Paraphrasing:

Select APN and owner from the PARCELS table where there does *not* exist at least one row in the PARCEL_ACCOUNTS table with the same APN (i.e., with APN = PARCELS.APN) and representing a 1982 dues payment.

Sample result:

APN	OWNER
93-282-54	MARY PATTON
93-291-19	KARL HANSEN

14. GROUP BY

List all parties to whom the association has made payments, with total amount paid in each case.

This example is a generalization of example 5 (where we obtained the total amount paid to one specific party). It makes use of another SQL feature, the GROUP BY clause.

```
SELECT PARTY, SUM (AMOUNT)
FROM    GENERAL_LEDGER
WHERE   TYPE = 'CHARGE'
GROUP   BY PARTY
```

This SELECT works as follows. First, rows of the GENERAL_LEDGER table not having TYPE = 'CHARGE' are eliminated (because of the WHERE clause). Next, the remaining rows are arranged into *groups* by values of PARTY such that the first group consists of all rows for party x (say), the second consists of all rows for party y (say), . . ., and the last consists of all rows for party z (say). Then for each *group* the values of PARTY and SUM (AMOUNT) are selected. The result might look something like this:

PARTY	SUM(AMOUNT)
x	2500.00
y	1725.00
.	.
.	.
.	.
z	4160.00

When GROUP BY is used, the items in the SELECT clause must all be "single-valued per group"; that is, each must be *either*

1. A field named in the GROUP BY clause itself, which will have a fixed value throughout each group;

or

2. A reference to a built-in function such as SUM, which will extract a single value out of each group.

15. HAVING

The previous example illustrated the use of GROUP BY to arrange a table into groups (conceptually, at any rate; the table is not really rearranged in the database) before the selection is done.

It is also possible to *eliminate* some of those groups before that final selection by means of a HAVING clause (just as it is possible to eliminate rows by means of the WHERE clause). For example, who owns more than one parcel?

```
SELECT OWNER
FROM   PARCELS
GROUP  BY OWNER
HAVING COUNT(*) > 1
```

Explanation: The PARCELS table is arranged into groups by OWNER. Then any group for which "COUNT(*)"—that is, the number of rows in the group—is not greater than one is eliminated. The OWNER value is then selected from each group that remains. Sample result:

```
OWNER
```
```
JOHN MINSKI
MARY PATTON
```

16.   Finally, we give a very complicated example that shows many of the features of the SQL SELECT statement introduced earlier used in combination.

Query: Who has paid more than $500 this year (1982), and how much have they paid? Remember that one person may make payments on multiple parcels.

```
SELECT PARCELS.OWNER, SUM (PARCEL_ACCOUNTS.AMOUNT)
FROM   PARCELS, PARCEL_ACCOUNTS
WHERE  PARCELS.APN = PARCEL_ACCOUNTS.APN
AND    PARCEL_ACCOUNTS.TYPE = 'CREDIT'
AND    PARCEL_ACCOUNTS.DATE LIKE '82%'
GROUP  BY PARCELS.OWNER
HAVING SUM (PARCEL_ACCOUNTS.AMOUNT) > 500
ORDER  BY PARCELS.OWNER
```

Sample result:

OWNER	SUM(AMOUNT)
ALAN JONES	982.67
I.J.KING	625.00
PETE WILLIAMS	800.00

It is true that this query is quite complex, but think how much work it is doing. If you had to do that work by hand, you would find it extremely tedious (not to mention error-prone). Moreover, a COBOL program to do the same job could easily be eight *pages* long, instead of just eight lines as above. And last, of course, it is a fact that most queries are much simpler than this one in practice; indeed, if you can understand this example, then you can probably understand just about any query you are likely to meet (in SQL or in any language like it).

SUMMARY

In this chapter we have shown how to create and load the database for a realistic sample application. We have also shown a number of typical queries against that database, using the SQL SELECT statement, and in so doing have illustrated almost all of the features of that statement. (The SQL SELECT statement can be regarded as typical of query language retrieval statements in general.) The major features discussed were as follows:

Basic SELECT–FROM–WHERE	Example 1 (also Chapter 2)
AND	Examples 2, 5, 6, 7, 9, 11, 12, 13, 16 (also Chapter 2)
Arithmetic expressions	Example 4
Nested SELECTs	Examples 8, 9, 12, 13 (also Chapter 2)
ORDER BY	Examples 11, 16 (also Chapter 2)
LIKE	Examples 3, 16
Built-in functions: SUM, AVG, etc.	Examples 5, 6, 7, 9, 14, 16
Greater than; less than	Example 6
Null results	Examples 7, 9
IN	Example 9
Join	Examples 10, 11, 16
EXISTS; NOT EXISTS	Examples 12, 13
GROUP BY	Examples 14, 15, 16
HAVING	Examples 15, 16

Some of these examples were quite complicated; in fact, as indicated in Chapter 1, this chapter is in many ways the most difficult in the entire book. If you did not understand it all—or did not even try to—you can take heart from that fact! It is not essential to grasp all of the detail of this chapter in order to appreciate what comes later. In the next chapter we will go on to consider maintenance operations against the same sample database.

EXERCISES

All of the following exercises are based on the Road Association database.

1. List parcel numbers for all parcels that have a negative balance.

2. List owner names and phone numbers for all parcels having a negative balance.

3. What was the average size of payments made to the association in 1982?

4. For each parcel, list APN, ROAD, OWNER, DATE of the last activity (payment or charge) on that parcel, AMOUNT involved in that activity, and BALANCE after that activity. Give the result in APN sequence.

5. List parcel number and owner for all parcels on which at least one payment of $500 or more has been made.

6. List all parcels (APN values) on which more than five charges have been levied since the beginning of 1981.

ANSWERS

1.
```
SELECT  APN
FROM    PARCELS
WHERE   BALANCE < 0
```

2.
```
SELECT  OWNER, PHONE
FROM    OWNERS
WHERE   OWNER IN
        (SELECT OWNER
         FROM    PARCELS
         WHERE   BALANCE < 0)
```

3.
```
SELECT  AVG (AMOUNT)
FROM    GENERAL_LEDGER
WHERE   DATE LIKE '82%'
AND     TYPE = 'CREDIT'
```

4.
```
SELECT  PARCELS.APN, PARCELS.ROAD, PARCELS.OWNER,
        PARCEL_ACCOUNTS.DATE, PARCEL_ACCOUNTS.AMOUNT,
        PARCEL_ACCOUNTS.BALANCE
FROM    PARCELS, PARCEL_ACCOUNTS
WHERE   PARCELS.APN = PARCEL_ACCOUNTS.APN
AND     PARCELS.LAST_ENTRY = PARCEL_ACCOUNTS.ENTRY
ORDER   BY PARCELS.APN
```

Notice that this join involves two join conditions: APN values and entry numbers must both match across the two tables to be joined.

5.
```
SELECT  APN, OWNER
FROM    PARCELS
WHERE   EXISTS
        (SELECT *
        FROM    PARCEL_ACCOUNTS
        WHERE   APN = PARCELS.APN
        AND     TYPE = 'CREDIT'
        AND     AMOUNT > 499.99)
```

6.
```
SELECT  APN
FROM    PARCEL_ACCOUNTS
WHERE   TYPE = 'CHARGE'
AND     DATE > '801231'
GROUP   BY APN
HAVING  COUNT(*) > 5
ORDER   BY APN
```

A Case Study (Continued): Sample Maintenance Operations

INTRODUCTION

As indicated at the end of the previous chapter, this chapter is concerned with the question of *maintaining* the Road Association database. We begin by showing a few elementary examples, using the SQL statements UPDATE, DELETE, and INSERT. The fact is, however, that most real life maintenance operations are too complicated to be handled by a single SQL statement. Thus our later examples will lead us into a discussion of *multistatement updates* and *canned procedures.* But first things first.

1. Single-record UPDATE

Construction has just started on parcel 93–282–51. Update the IMPROVED indicator accordingly.

```
UPDATE PARCELS
SET    IMPROVED = 'Y'
WHERE  APN = '93-282-51'
```

2. Single-record INSERT and DELETE

Parcel 93–282–51 has just been sold by its previous owner (John Minski) to Albert Campion, 12A Bottle Street, Piccadilly, phone number 441–867–3623.

```
UPDATE PARCELS
SET    OWNER = 'ALBERT CAMPION'
WHERE  APN = '93-282-51'
```

If Albert Campion did not previously exist in the OWNERS table, we should enter him as follows:

```
INSERT INTO OWNERS ( OWNER, ADDRESS, PHONE )
       VALUES ('ALBERT CAMPION',
               '12A BOTTLE STREET, PICCADILLY',
               '441-867-3623')
```

And if John Minski no longer owns any property on the road system, we should remove him:

```
DELETE
FROM   OWNERS
WHERE  OWNER = 'JOHN MINSKI'
```

Note that the two "ifs" above could be handled by SQL SE-
LECTs—the first by attempting to SELECT Albert Campion from
the OWNERS table, the second by attempting to SELECT parcels
owned by John Minski from the PARCELS table.

3. Multiple-record UPDATE

It is year-end 1982. Increase the balance owing on each parcel
(as given in the PARCELS table) by 20 percent to reflect the 1982
penalty.

```
UPDATE PARCELS
SET    BALANCE = BALANCE * 1.2
WHERE  BALANCE > 0
```

Note: SQL (in common with most other computer languages) uses the symbol * as a multiplication sign, in order to
avoid possible confusion with the letter X. The UPDATE above
will set the BALANCE value equal to 1.2 times its previous value in
every PARCELS record where the previous value was greater than
zero. (The condition BALANCE > 0 is required to allow for the
fact that some people may have overpaid their accounts and thus
be in credit, i.e., have a negative balance at this time.) Note that
this single UPDATE statement will update multiple records, in general. Note also, however, that updating PARCELS in this way is
just one of several operations that need to be performed on the
database at year-end; it does not do the total year-end processing
job.

EXCEPTIONS

Consideration of update operations leads inevitably into a discussion of errors or *exceptions*. It is obviously possible that some updates, if permitted, would introduce incorrect data into the database. For example, we might try and change a BALANCE value to
a value that is too large (greater than $99999.99), or we might try
to store a character string value in a decimal field, or we might try
to insert a record that already exists (e.g., we might try to INSERT
a PARCELS record for parcel 93–282–55 when that parcel is already represented in the PARCELS table). Most systems will catch
simple errors like these and will reject the erroneous operation: The
database will remain unchanged, and a message such as

```
Field BALANCE - value too large
```

or

```
Field AMOUNT - wrong data type
```

or

```
Table PARCELS, field APN - duplicate value
```

will be displayed.

Different systems have exception-handling facilities of differing degrees of sophistication, as you might expect. Most systems are capable of detecting errors such as those just sketched, but for every system there will be some limit—usually not too difficult to reach—beyond which it is simply the user's responsibility to get things right. As a result, you should generally exercise extreme care when you are updating the database. (This statement is even more applicable in a shared database, where one person's errors can affect some other unfortunate innocent party—though in such an environment the system controls on updating are likely to be more stringent, for precisely that reason. We will take a look at such controls in Part II.)

Note: In this brief discussion of errors, we are of course not referring to simple typing mistakes such as the following:

```
SELRCT * FROM CELLAR
```

Here there is little likelihood of doing any damage to the database. The system will respond to an error of this kind with a message such as

```
Unknown command - SELRCT
```

and you will just have to correct your error and try again. If you have been trying the examples and exercises of this book on a real machine, then no doubt you will have encountered this kind of situation already. You may also have encountered situations such as the following:

```
SELECT *
FROM   CELLAR
WHERE  PRODUCER = 'Mirrasou'
```

The system does not detect the incorrect spelling but merely replies with a message such as

```
NO RECORD(S) FOUND
```

This kind of error is sometimes difficult to spot and can be very annoying!

**MULTISTATEMENT
UPDATES**

Example: The association has just (July 24, 1982) made a payment of $360 to Road Fixers, Inc., for a repair job done on Redwood Road in connection with special assessment SA4. Update the database accordingly.

The necessary updates consist of the following:

- Inserting an entry into the GENERAL__LEDGER table to reflect the payment out of the general fund;

- Inserting a similar entry into the REDWOOD__LEDGER table also;

- Updating the' GENERAL and REDWOOD records in the LAST__ENTRIES table appropriately.

1. Let us deal with the general fund first. First we need to know the current state of that fund:

```
SELECT ENTRY, BALANCE
FROM   LAST_ENTRIES
WHERE  ACCOUNT = 'GENERAL'
```

Suppose the result is

ENTRY	BALANCE
724	6095.40

Then the necessary INSERT to GENERAL__LEDGER is as follows:

```
INSERT INTO GENERAL_LEDGER
       (ENTRY, DATE, DESCRIPTION, TYPE, PARTY, AMOUNT, BALANCE)
VALUES (725,'820724','SA4','CHARGE','ROAD FIXERS, INC.', 360, 5735.40)
```

Previous value plus 1	Special assessment 4		Payee	Payment	

Previous balance minus payment

The corresponding UPDATE to LAST__ENTRIES is as follows:

```
UPDATE LAST_ENTRIES
SET    ENTRY = 725,
       BALANCE = 5735.40
WHERE  ACCOUNT = 'GENERAL'
```

Notice how a single UPDATE statement can update two or more values in the same record (via two or more separate "assignments" within the SET clause).

2. The details for the Redwood Road fund are similar. First, we request the current status of that fund:

```
SELECT ENTRY, BALANCE
FROM   LAST_ENTRIES
WHERE  ACCOUNT = 'REDWOOD'
```

Result (say):

ENTRY	BALANCE
281	977.67

Hence:

```
INSERT INTO REDWOOD_LEDGER
       (ENTRY, DATE, DESCRIPTION, TYPE, PARTY, AMOUNT, BALANCE)
VALUES (282,'820724','SA4','CHARGE','ROAD FIXERS, INC.', 360, 617.67)

UPDATE LAST_ENTRIES
SET    ENTRY = 282,
       BALANCE = 617.67
WHERE  ACCOUNT = 'REDWOOD'
```

Now (at last) we are done. But the example clearly bears out the contention made at the beginning of the chapter, to the effect that most real life maintenance operations are too complex to be handled by a single SQL statement. It is not a particularly complicated example in itself, but look at the database processing it involves. First, three separate tables have to be updated (one of them twice). Second, it is necessary to examine current values in the database (entry numbers and balances) before corresponding new values can be determined. Third, the process of determining those new values involves some arithmetic operations, and those arithmetic operations were performed by the user, not by the system. (Actually, it would be possible to get the system to do the arithmetic, as example 4 of the "Sample Queries" section in the previous chapter illustrates—but it would still be the user's responsibility to copy the results of that arithmetic over to the INSERT and UP-DATE statements correctly.) Thus even in this very simple (but quite realistic) example, the user has to do a significant portion of the work.

Let us consider another example.

Example: Suppose the association has just (July 25, 1982) received the 1982 dues payment ($120) on parcel 93–282–55. Update the database accordingly.

The necessary updates consist of the following:

- Inserting an entry into the GENERAL__LEDGER table to reflect the payment received;
- Inserting an entry into the PARCEL__ACCOUNTS table for this parcel;
- Updating the PARCELS record for this parcel to show the new balance;
- Applying two-thirds of the payment to the appropriate individual road fund;
- Applying one-third of the payment to the Redwood Road fund;
- Updating all applicable entries in the LAST__ENTRIES table.

1. Again we deal with the general fund first:

```
SELECT ENTRY, BALANCE
FROM   LAST_ENTRIES
WHERE  ACCOUNT = 'GENERAL'
```

Result (say):

ENTRY	BALANCE
725	5735.40

Hence:

```
INSERT INTO GENERAL_LEDGER
       (ENTRY, DATE, DESCRIPTION, TYPE, PARTY, AMOUNT, BALANCE)
VALUES (726,'820725','DUES82','CREDIT','93-282-55', 120, 5855.40)

UPDATE LAST_ENTRIES
SET    ENTRY = 726,
       BALANCE = 5855.40
WHERE  ACCOUNT = 'GENERAL'
```

2. Next, we update PARCEL__ACCOUNTS for this parcel, and UPDATE the appropriate PARCELS record to reflect the new balance:

```
SELECT LAST_ENTRY, BALANCE
FROM   PARCELS
WHERE  APN = '93-282-55'
```

Result (say):

LAST_ENTRY	BALANCE
23	120.00

Hence:

```
INSERT INTO PARCEL_ACCOUNTS
       (APN, ENTRY, DATE, DESCRIPTION, TYPE, AMOUNT, BALANCE)
VALUES ('93-282-55',24,'820725','DUES82','CREDIT', 120, 0)

UPDATE PARCELS
SET    LAST_ENTRY = 24,
       BALANCE = 0
WHERE  APN = '93-282-55'
```

3. Now we must add two-thirds of the payment (i.e., $80) to the appropriate road fund. First, we must discover which one that is:

```
SELECT ROAD
FROM   PARCELS
WHERE  APN = '93-282-55'
```

Result:

ROAD
CREEK

Hence:

```
SELECT ENTRY, BALANCE
FROM   LAST_ENTRIES
WHERE  ACCOUNT = 'CREEK'
```

Result (say):

ENTRY	BALANCE
113	1618.26

Hence:

```
INSERT INTO CREEK_LEDGER
       (ENTRY, DATE, DESCRIPTION, TYPE, PARTY, AMOUNT, BALANCE)
VALUES (114,'820725','DUES82','CREDIT','93-282-55', 80, 1698.26)

UPDATE LAST_ENTRIES
SET    ENTRY = 114,
       BALANCE = 1698.26
WHERE  ACCOUNT = 'CREEK'
```

4. Finally, we must add one-third of the payment (i.e., $40) to the Redwood Road fund:

```
SELECT ENTRY, BALANCE
FROM   LAST_ENTRIES
WHERE  ACCOUNT = 'REDWOOD'
```

Result (say):

ENTRY	BALANCE
282	617.67

Hence:

```
INSERT INTO REDWOOD_LEDGER
       (ENTRY, DATE, DESCRIPTION, TYPE, PARTY, AMOUNT, BALANCE)
VALUES (283,'820725','DUES82','CREDIT','93-282-55', 40, 657.26)

UPDATE LAST_ENTRIES
SET    ENTRY = 283,
       BALANCE = 657.26
WHERE  ACCOUNT = 'REDWOOD'
```

And we are done. But what a procedure! There is *far* too much scope for error; steps could be omitted, or mistakes made in the arithmetic, or the user could get confused and apply some update twice. When matters get as complex as this, some improvement is clearly highly desirable.

Now it may be that some improvement can be achieved simply on the basis of the user's own knowledge; that is, some of the SELECTs may be unnecessary (and the overall process thus simplified) if the user already knows the results of those SELECTs. For example, if the user already knows that parcel 93–282–55 is located on Creek Road, it is not necessary to ask the database for that information. In a microcomputer environment, where the database is small, this approach may well be adequate. In a more sophisticated environment, however, it will almost certainly not be. Instead, it will be necessary to find some way to offload more of the work on to the system. The question is, How? The answer is that an appropriate *program* must be created, in which the entire sequence of operations can be pinned down ahead of time and automated, thus eliminating the possible sources of error mentioned above. In the rest of this chapter, therefore, we discuss in outline what is involved in the creation of such a program. If you have no interest in this aspect of the system, skip ahead to the next chapter.

CANNED PROCEDURES

We use the term "canned procedure" to mean a program that has been created to perform some more or less complex task involving (typically) numerous distinct accesses to the database. The user can "invoke" (i.e., request the execution of) such a program by entering a command such as

```
RUN REDWOOD_PAYMENT ( 820724 360 SA4 )
```

at the keyboard. Here REDWOOD__PAYMENT is the name of the program to be invoked (we assume that this program deals with payments made out of the Redwood Road fund, as in the first example in the previous section), and the values in parentheses (820724, 360, and SA4) are input data values, or *parameters*, to be given to that program when it executes. The program will use those values to perform the necessary updates on the database.

How is the REDWOOD__PAYMENT program actually created? At a detail level the answer to this question will depend on the facilities provided by the computer system under consideration and so is beyond the scope of this book. In general, however, the program will first have to be written in some appropriate programming language, say PASCAL or COBOL or PL/I, by a person who is skilled in that language. (Incidentally, it is also possible to create programs that contain multiple SQL statements and nothing else. More usually, however, a program will contain a mixture of SQL statements and programming language statements.)

By way of illustration, we show in outline a PL/I version of REDWOOD__PAYMENT, without, however, going into any detailed explanation of how that program works. (Actually, the details are fairly straightforward in this particular case, and you may be able to piece them together with little further guidance.)

```
REDWOOD_PAYMENT: PROC OPTIONS (MAIN) ;

    DCL GIVEN_DATE        CHAR(6) ;
    DCL GIVEN_AMOUNT      FIXED DECIMAL(7,2) ;
    DCL GIVEN_SAN         CHAR(5) ;
```

```
DCL TEMP_SAN            CHAR(3) ;
DCL DEC_SAN             FIXED DECIMAL(3) ;
DCL ENTRY              FIXED DECIMAL(5) ;
DCL BALANCE            FIXED DECIMAL(9,2) ;
DCL PAYEE             CHAR(25) ;

EXEC SQL INCLUDE SQLCA ;
EXEC SQL WHENEVER NOT FOUND GO TO EXCEPTION ;
EXEC SQL WHENEVER SQLERROR GO TO EXCEPTION ;
EXEC SQL WHENEVER SQLWARNING GO TO EXCEPTION ;

obtain input parameters GIVEN_DATE, GIVEN_AMOUNT, GIVEN_SAN ;
TEMP_SAN = SUBSTR(GIVEN_SAN,3,3) ;
convert TEMP_SAN to decimal and assign result to DEC_SAN ;

EXEC SQL SELECT ENTRY, BALANCE
         INTO    :ENTRY, :BALANCE
         FROM    LAST_ENTRIES
         WHERE   ACCOUNT = 'GENERAL' ;
ENTRY = ENTRY + 1 ;
BALANCE = BALANCE - GIVEN_AMOUNT ;

EXEC SQL SELECT PAYEE
         INTO    :PAYEE
         FROM    SPECIAL_ASSESSMENTS
         WHERE   SAN = :DEC_SAN ;

EXEC SQL INSERT INTO GENERAL_LEDGER
         (ENTRY, DATE, DESCRIPTION, TYPE, PARTY, AMOUNT, BALANCE)
         VALUES
         (:ENTRY, :GIVEN_DATE, :GIVEN_SAN, 'CHARGE', :PAYEE,
          :GIVEN_AMOUNT, :BALANCE) ;

EXEC SQL UPDATE LAST_ENTRIES
         SET     ENTRY = :ENTRY,
                 BALANCE = :BALANCE
         WHERE   ACCOUNT = 'GENERAL' ;

EXEC SQL SELECT ENTRY, BALANCE
         INTO    :ENTRY, :BALANCE
         FROM    LAST_ENTRIES
         WHERE   ACCOUNT = 'REDWOOD' ;
ENTRY = ENTRY + 1 ;
BALANCE = BALANCE - GIVEN_AMOUNT ;
```

```
EXEC SQL INSERT INTO REDWOOD_LEDGER
        (ENTRY, DATE, DESCRIPTION, TYPE, PARTY, AMOUNT, BALANCE)
        VALUES
        (:ENTRY, :GIVEN_DATE, :GIVEN_SAN, 'CHARGE', :PAYEE,
         :GIVEN_AMOUNT, :BALANCE) ;

EXEC SQL UPDATE LAST_ENTRIES
        SET    ENTRY = :ENTRY,
               BALANCE = :BALANCE
        WHERE  ACCOUNT = 'REDWOOD' ;

send message to user 'DATABASE UPDATES COMPLETE' ;
EXEC SQL COMMIT WORK ;
RETURN ;

EXCEPTION:
    display diagnostics, including SQLCA ;
    EXEC SQL ROLLBACK WORK ;

END REDWOOD_PAYMENT ;
```

Once the program has been written, it must be stored away on a disk somewhere in a form ready for execution on demand. The details of this process have nothing to do with the database management system and are again beyond the scope of this text. (Also, we are ignoring the question of testing and debugging, which in practice will probably mean that the cycle of writing the program and storing it away will be repeated many times before the "canned procedure" is finally ready for use.)

Exercises: Here are some more examples of real life maintenance operations on the Road Association database. For each one you might like to work out for yourself the sequence of database operations that a canned procedure would have to go through—possibly even code an appropriate set of SQL statements.

1. Construction has just started on a given parcel. Update the database to indicate that fact and also to reflect the damage fee ($500) assessed against that parcel. (See the first example in the "Introduction" section of this chapter.)

2. A new special assessment has just been charged to the association. Compute the amount charged to each parcel on the road in question and update the database to reflect those individual charges.

3. Update the database to reflect the year-end penalty (20 percent) on all parcels having a positive balance. (*Note:* This exercise involves updating PARCEL__ACCOUNTS as well as PARCELS, not to mention LAST__ENTRIES. See the third example in the "Introduction" section of this chapter.)

4. A charge has been made to the association for miscellaneous items (stationery supplies, postage, beer for the ditch-digging crew, etc.). Such charges are divided equally among the three individual road funds. Update the database accordingly.

APPLICATION GENERATORS

Some systems (especially larger ones) provide *application generators* as well as traditional programming languages such as PL/I. Application generators exploit the fact that application programs tend to fall into a small number of rather stereotyped patterns. For example, the account maintenance programs for bank A are unlikely to differ very significantly from those for bank B. The fact that applications tend to be stereotyped in this manner means that it is feasible to provide *prewritten, generalized* programs (or "modules," i.e., program fragments) to perform commonly required functions such as account maintenance. An application generator (which is itself a program) allows such fragments to be combined and tailored to meet the requirements of some specific application. Thus an application generator, in effect, creates an application program (application *program* generator would be a more apt title) without requiring any application programming per se. (Sometimes the generator may provide an "escape" feature by which some of the fragments in the overall application can be programmed directly in PL/I or some similar language; but the intent is to reduce the need for such programming to a minimum.) Some installations have achieved tenfold or even greater productivity increases through the use of application generators instead of traditional programming languages.

It is not our aim to describe application generators in any detail in this book. We content ourselves with the following observations. In order to get the generator to perform its combining and tailoring of fragments, it is, of course, necessary to enter certain *commands* to tell the generator what to do. (The person doing the application generation is obviously required to be familiar with those commands. It is assumed that this requirement is a less demanding one than the requirement to be familiar with a language such as PL/I.) Those generator commands may well look something like the data definition, formatting, and manipulation commands of a language such as SQL. The DBMS itself may thus be regarded in some lights as a kind of application generator. In other words, the distinction between a DBMS (on the one hand) and an application generator (on the other) is far from clear-cut and probably stems as much as anything from a series of historical accidents. In the future we can expect to see query languages and application generator languages moving closer and closer together, with each absorbing the best characteristics of the other, until ultimately there is no distinction between them.

SUMMARY

We have discussed the question of maintaining the database. Examples of the SQL statements INSERT, DELETE, and UPDATE have been given, including one example in which a single statement operated simultaneously on multiple records in the database. However, it is a fact that most real life update applications require several distinct but related SQL-level operations to be performed on the database, and this fact led us into a discussion of multistatement updates and canned procedures. We showed in outline how a programming language such as PL/I might be used to create a canned procedure; such a procedure can be invoked by a command such as RUN that nominates the program and supplies it with the input values (parameters) it needs to execute. Finally, we gave a brief discussion of application generators.

To conclude this chapter, we should perhaps point out that a typical database is queried far more often than it is updated (a ratio of ten to one for queries over updates is quite usual), and queries can normally be handled quite adequately through the query language without requiring any program or canned procedure to be created. Thus the material of this chapter may be regarded as a little specialized, at least so far as the home computer user is concerned. In the next chapter we will return to query operations and will consider the topic of *report writing*, that is, the problem of obtaining suitably formatted printed reports from the result of a query.

6 Data Display and Report Writing

INTRODUCTION

So far in this book we have said very little about the physical layout of data on the screen or about the format of printed ("hard copy") reports. The simple tabular layout shown in all examples so far is adequate in many cases, of course; but on occasion some more sophisticated arrangement may be necessary. In this chapter we examine these aspects of the system in a little more detail. For consistency we will continue to base our discussions on a SQL system—basically the IBM system SQL/DS—but the principles illustrated are generally applicable.

DATA DISPLAY

A typical computer screen is capable of displaying some 20 rows at a time, with a maximum width of 80 characters. If a query result exceeds these limits in either dimension, then it is obviously possible to see only a portion (one screenful) of that result at any one time. To view the total result, it is necessary to shift the screen around (conceptually speaking), using appropriate *scrolling* commands. For example, consider the following query on the Road Association database:

```
SELECT *
FROM   PARCEL_ACCOUNTS
WHERE  DATE LIKE '82%'
ORDER  BY APN, ENTRY
```

This query might easily return many hundreds of rows. The initial display will show (say) just the first twenty of those rows, as indicated in Fig. 6.1.

Note the effect of the ORDER BY clause. Note also the system message MORE . . ., which tells us that there are more rows to come. To see those additional rows (or at least some of them), we can issue a FORWARD command:

```
FORWARD 20
```

(say). This command will move the screen "forward" over the result so that the next 20 rows (actually fewer, in this particular example) become visible, as shown in Fig. 6.2.

Figure 6.1

APN	ENTRY	DATE	DESCRIPTION	TYPE	AMOUNT	BALANCE
93-281-24	31	820107	DUES82	CHARGE	120.00	120.00
93-281-24	32	820107	SA7	CHARGE	240.00	360.00
93-281-24	33	820408	DUES82	CREDIT	120.00	240.00
93-281-24	34	820408	SA7	CREDIT	240.00	0.00
93-281-24	35	820809	SA8	CHARGE	115.00	115.00
93-281-24	36	821105	SA10	CHARGE	72.00	187.00
93-281-24	37	821231	PENALTY82	CHARGE	37.40	224.40
93-282-54	16	820107	DUES82	CHARGE	60.00	380.00
93-282-54	17	820107	SA7	CHARGE	240.00	610.00
93-282-54	18	821231	PENALTY82	CHARGE	122.00	732.00
93-282-55	40	820107	DUES82	CHARGE	120.00	120.00
93-282-55	41	820107	SA7	CHARGE	240.00	360.00
93-282-55	42	820203	DUES82	CREDIT	120.00	240.00
93-282-55	43	820203	SA7	CREDIT	240.00	0.00
93-291-19	7	820107	DUES82	CHARGE	50.00	190.00
93-291-19	8	820107	SA7	CHARGE	240.00	430.00
93-291-19	9	820809	SA8	CHARGE	115.00	545.00
93-291-19	10	821105	SA10	CHARGE	72.00	617.00
93-291-19	11	821123	SA3	CHARGE	42.50	659.50
93-291-19	12	821231	PENALTY82	CHARGE	131.90	791.40

MORE ...

Figure 6.2

APN	ENTRY	DATE	DESCRIPTION	TYPE	AMOUNT	BALANCE
93-291-44	22	820107	DUES82	CHARGE	120.00	120.00
93-291-44	23	821124	DUES82	CREDIT	60.00	60.00
93-291-44	24	821212	DUES82	CREDIT	60.00	0.00
93-293-02	4	820107	DUES82	CHARGE	60.00	60.00
93-293-02	5	820309	DUES82	CREDIT	60.00	0.00
93-293-02	6	821105	SA10	CHARGE	72.00	72.00
93-293-02	7	821119	SA10	CREDIT	72.00	0.00

RESULT CONTAINS A TOTAL OF 27 ROWS

Any positive integer can be specified in the FORWARD command in place of 20; for example, the command FORWARD 5 (from the top) would cause rows 6–25 to come into view. Similarly, the analogous command

    BACKWARD n

will move the screen backward n rows, where again n is any positive integer. TOP and BOTTOM commands might also be provided to display the top and bottom 20 rows (respectively), regardless of the current position of the screen within the overall result.

Suppose now that the result table is too wide (instead of too long) to fit on a single screen. The initial display will show the first (leftmost) column of the result up against the left-hand side of the screen, and as many columns to the right as will fit. The command

    RIGHT n

will move the screen right n columns (not characters), so that the (n + 1)st column is now at the left-hand side of the screen. Similarly, the command

    LEFT n

will move the screen left n columns.

REPORT WRITING

The term "report writing" means the process of obtaining a hard copy of the result of some query on the printer. The PRINT command is provided for this purpose. For example:

```
SELECT *
FROM    PARCEL_ACCOUNTS
WHERE   TYPE = 'CHARGE'
AND     DATE LIKE '82%'
ORDER   BY APN, ENTRY
```

```
PRINT
```

With the same sample data as shown earlier, this SELECT will produce the result shown in Fig. 6.3 (note that we have now asked for CHARGE entries only).

Figure 6.3

APN	ENTRY	DATE	DESCRIPTION	TYPE	AMOUNT	BALANCE
93-281-24	31	820107	DUES82	CHARGE	120.00	120.00
93-281-24	32	820107	SA7	CHARGE	240.00	360.00
93-281-24	35	820809	SA8	CHARGE	115.00	115.00
93-281-24	36	821105	SA10	CHARGE	72.00	187.00
93-281-24	37	821231	PENALTY82	CHARGE	37.40	224.40
93-282-54	16	820107	DUES82	CHARGE	60.00	380.00
93-282-54	17	820107	SA7	CHARGE	240.00	610.00
93-282-54	18	821231	PENALTY82	CHARGE	122.00	732.00
93-282-55	40	820107	DUES82	CHARGE	120.00	120.00
93-282-55	41	820107	SA7	CHARGE	240.00	360.00
93-291-19	7	820107	DUES82	CHARGE	50.00	190.00
93-291-19	8	820107	SA7	CHARGE	240.00	430.00
93-291-19	9	820809	SA8	CHARGE	115.00	545.00
93-291-19	10	821105	SA10	CHARGE	72.00	617.00
93-291-19	11	821123	SA3	CHARGE	42.50	659.50
93-291-19	12	821231	PENALTY82	CHARGE	131.90	791.40
93-291-44	22	820107	DUES82	CHARGE	120.00	120.00
93-293-02	4	820107	DUES82	CHARGE	60.00	60.00
93-293-02	6	821105	SA10	CHARGE	72.00	72.00

Between the SELECT command and the PRINT command it is possible to issue any number of *FORMAT* commands. The effect of those FORMAT commands is to edit the displayed result in certain ways and thus to arrange it into some more desirable form before it is actually printed. Here are some examples of the FORMAT command.

1.   FORMAT TTITLE 'PARCEL ACCOUNT CHARGES 1982'

This FORMAT will cause the *top title*

PARCEL ACCOUNT DETAILS 1982

to appear (centered) at the top of each page of the printed report. (*Note*: The system will automatically print page numbers.)

2.   FORMAT BTITLE 'REDWOOD – CREEK – MILL ROAD ASSOCIATION'

The specified *bottom title* will appear (again centered) at the foot of each printed page.

3. FORMAT `EXCLUDE TYPE`
    FORMAT `EXCLUDE ENTRY`

These two FORMATs will suppress printing for the TYPE and ENTRY columns (they are not particularly interesting in the context of the required report).

4. FORMAT `COLUMN APN NAME PARCEL`
    FORMAT `COLUMN DESCRIPTION NAME CHARGE`

These two FORMATs will replace the column headings APN and DESCRIPTION by PARCEL and CHARGE, respectively.

5. FORMAT `SEPARATOR ' * '`

Adjacent columns in the report will be separated by the specified string of three characters (a blank, an asterisk, and another blank).

6. FORMAT `TOTAL AMOUNT`

This FORMAT will cause the system to compute the total of all values in the AMOUNT column and to print a final line in the report showing that total.

7. FORMAT `GROUP APN`

This example is a little more complicated. First, remember that the query result in the example was ordered on the basis of APN values (by virtue of the ORDER BY in the SELECT). FORMAT GROUP APN would not make sense otherwise. The effect of the FORMAT GROUP command is to suppress printing for any value in the specified column (APN in the example) that, if it *were* printed, would be the same as the most recently printed value in that column. In other words, a value is printed in the specified column *only when a value change occurs.* See the example in Fig. 6.4. Notice that a blank line is left after each "group." (*Note:* Figure 6.4 also shows the effects of the FORMAT commands in the previous examples.)

8. FORMAT `SUBTOTAL AMOUNT`

This is the last FORMAT example we will give. FORMAT SUBTOTAL can be issued only if FORMAT GROUP has already been issued; it causes the system to compute and print a set of sub-

Figure 6.4

```
1/1/83                 PARCEL ACCOUNT CHARGES 1982                PAGE 1

      PARCEL      *   DATE   *   CHARGE       *   AMOUNT   *   BALANCE
                  *          *                *            *
                  *          *                *            *
      93-281-24   *  820107  *  DUES82        *   120.00   *    120.00
                  *  820107  *  SA7           *   240.00   *    360.00
                  *  820809  *  SA8           *   115.00   *    115.00
                  *  821105  *  SA10          *    72.00   *    187.00
                  *  821231  *  PENALTY82     *    37.40   *    224.40

      93-282-54   *  820107  *  DUES82        *    60.00   *    380.00
                  *  820107  *  SA7           *   240.00   *    610.00
                  *  821231  *  PENALTY82     *   122.00   *    732.00

      93-282-55   *  820107  *  DUES82        *   120.00   *    120.00
                  *  820107  *  SA7           *   240.00   *    360.00

      93-291-19   *  820107  *  DUES82        *    50.00   *    190.00
                  *  820107  *  SA7           *   240.00   *    430.00
                  *  820809  *  SA8           *   115.00   *    545.00
                  *  821105  *  SA10          *    72.00   *    617.00
                  *  821123  *  SA3           *    42.50   *    659.50
                  *  821231  *  PENALTY82     *   131.90   *    791.40

      93-291-44   *  820107  *  DUES82        *   120.00   *    120.00

      93-293-02   *  820107  *  DUES82        *    60.00   *     60.00
                  *  821105  *  SA10          *    72.00   *     72.00
                                                 2269.80

            REDWOOD - CREEK - MILL ROAD ASSOCIATION
```

totals, one for each group as specified by the preceding FORMAT GROUP. In the example the system will print the total AMOUNT for each distinct APN value, as shown in Fig. 6.5. It will also print the grand total of all AMOUNTs, because FORMAT SUBTOTAL always implies a corresponding FORMAT TOTAL (it is not necessary to specify FORMAT TOTAL explicitly if FORMAT SUBTOTAL is specified).

Figure 6.5

```
 1/1/83                    PARCEL ACCOUNT CHARGES 1982                    PAGE 1

        PARCEL     *   DATE    *   CHARGE      *   AMOUNT    *   BALANCE
                   *                           *             *
        93-281-24  *   820107  *   DUES82      *   120.00    *   120.00
                   *   820107  *   SA7         *   240.00    *   360.00
                   *   820809  *   SA8         *   115.00    *   115.00
                   *   821105  *   SA10        *    72.00    *   187.00
                   *   821231  *   PENALTY82   *    37.40    *   224.40
                                                  584.40

        93-282-54  *   820107  *   DUES82      *    60.00    *   380.00
                   *   820107  *   SA7         *   240.00    *   610.00
                   *   821231  *   PENALTY82   *   122.00    *   732.00
                                                  422.00

        93-282-55  *   820107  *   DUES82      *   120.00    *   120.00
                   *   820107  *   SA7         *   240.00    *   360.00
                                                  360.00

        93-291-19  *   820107  *   DUES82      *    50.00    *   190.00
                   *   820107  *   SA7         *   240.00    *   430.00
                   *   820809  *   SA8         *   115.00    *   545.00
                   *   821105  *   SA10        *    72.00    *   617.00
                   *   821123  *   SA3         *    42.50    *   659.50
                   *   821231  *   PENALTY82   *   131.90    *   791.40
                                                  651.40

        93-291-44  *   820107  *   DUES82      *   120.00    *   120.00
                                                  120.00

        93-293-02  *   820107  *   DUES82      *    60.00    *    60.00
                   *   821105  *   SA10        *    72.00    *    72.00
                                                  132.00


                                                 2269.80

                    REDWOOD - CREEK - MILL ROAD ASSOCIATION
```

Many other operations of a formatting nature are possible, but the foregoing should be sufficient to give the general idea. Examples illustrating some of the other possibilities are given in Chapters 9 and 10.

7 The Database Catalog

INTRODUCTION

In Chapter 2 we defined a database as a collection of one or more tables, typically with certain interrelationships among them (such as the interrelationship between the FLIGHTS table and the CITIES table in the flight information database that says that every city code appearing in the FLIGHTS table must also appear in the CITIES table). In fact, any given database will contain, not only user tables—that is, tables created by users to contain user data, such as the FLIGHTS and CITIES tables mentioned above —but also certain *system tables,* whose function is to hold certain data that the system itself needs in order to manage the database for you. Those system tables are collectively referred to as the *database catalog* (or sometimes *database directory*).

An analogy may be helpful here: *The catalog is to the database what the list of contents is to a book.* Thus the catalog for a given database indicates what can be found in that database—what tables exist, what fields they contain, what those fields look like (e.g., whether they contain decimal numbers or character strings), and so on—much as the list of contents for a book shows what can be found in that book. Now, although the catalog is kept by the system primarily for the system's own use, there are occasions when the information in the catalog can be very helpful to the user also. Moreover, an appreciation of the structure of the catalog can help you understand the overall operation of the system a little better. We therefore devote this chapter to a brief explanation of this topic.

AN EXAMPLE

Figure 7.1 represents a possible set of catalog entries for the wine cellar database from Chapter 2. As you can see, the catalog for this database contains two tables, called, respectively, TABLES and COLUMNS.

- The TABLES table is basically a list of all the tables in the database. For each such table it gives the table name, the number of columns, the name of the user who created it (in a shared database different tables may be created by different people), and some additional information (not shown).

Figure 7.1

TABLES table:			COLUMNS table:		
TABNAME	COLCOUNT	CREATOR	TABNAME	COLNAME	TYPE
CELLAR	7	C.J.DATE	CELLAR	BIN	DECIMAL(3)
			CELLAR	WINE	CHAR(25)
			CELLAR	PRODUCER	CHAR(20)
			CELLAR	YEAR	DECIMAL(2)
			CELLAR	BOTTLES	DECIMAL(3)
			CELLAR	READY	DECIMAL(2)
			CELLAR	COMMENTS	CHAR(25)

- The COLUMNS table is a list of all the columns in the database. For each column it gives the name of the table containing that column, the column name (unique within the table), the type of data in that column [e.g., DECIMAL(3)], and some additional information (not shown).

A real catalog would include additional fields in each of these two tables, over and above those shown, and would also include additional tables. Ten or fifteen tables of five to ten fields each might be typical. But there is no need for us to get into further detail here.

Notice, incidentally, that there is an interrelationship between the TABLES and COLUMNS tables that is precisely analogous to the one between the FLIGHTS and CITIES tables—namely, every value (i.e., table name) appearing in the TABNAME column of the COLUMNS table must also appear in the TABNAME column of the TABLES table.

Suppose now for the sake of the example that the FLIGHTS and CITIES tables are kept in the same database as the CELLAR table. Suppose also that these tables were created by a different person, say user F. Hill. Then the catalog might appear as shown in Fig. 7.2.

But the tables as shown are still incomplete. Since TABLES and COLUMNS are themselves tables in the database, they too will have an appropriate set of entries in the catalog (in other words, TABLES and COLUMNS will include entries for themselves). Thus the complete catalog might appear as shown in Fig. 7.3.

The "creator" for the catalog tables is considered to be SYSTEM.

Figure 7.2

TABLES table:

TABNAME	COLCOUNT	CREATOR
CELLAR	7	C.J.DATE
FLIGHTS	5	F.HILL
CITIES	2	F.HILL

COLUMNS table:

TABNAME	COLNAME	TYPE
CELLAR	BIN	DECIMAL(3)
CELLAR	WINE	CHAR(25)
CELLAR	PRODUCER	CHAR(20)
CELLAR	YEAR	DECIMAL(2)
CELLAR	BOTTLES	DECIMAL(3)
CELLAR	READY	DECIMAL(2)
CELLAR	COMMENTS	CHAR(25)
FLIGHTS	FLIGHT	CHAR(6)
FLIGHTS	FROM_CODE	CHAR(3)
FLIGHTS	TO_CODE	CHAR(3)
FLIGHTS	DEP_TIME	CHAR(4)
FLIGHTS	ARR_TIME	CHAR(4)
CITIES	CODE	CHAR(3)
CITIES	CITY	CHAR(20)

Figure 7.3

TABLES table:

TABNAME	COLCOUNT	CREATOR
CELLAR	7	C.J.DATE
FLIGHTS	5	F.HILL
CITIES	2	F.HILL
TABLES	3	SYSTEM
COLUMNS	3	SYSTEM

COLUMNS table:

TABNAME	COLNAME	TYPE
CELLAR	BIN	DECIMAL(3)
CELLAR	WINE	CHAR(25)
CELLAR	PRODUCER	CHAR(20)
CELLAR	YEAR	DECIMAL(2)
CELLAR	BOTTLES	DECIMAL(3)
CELLAR	READY	DECIMAL(2)
CELLAR	COMMENTS	CHAR(25)
FLIGHTS	FLIGHT	CHAR(6)
FLIGHTS	FROM_CODE	CHAR(3)
FLIGHTS	TO_CODE	CHAR(3)
FLIGHTS	DEP_TIME	CHAR(4)
FLIGHTS	ARR_TIME	CHAR(4)
CITIES	CODE	CHAR(3)
CITIES	CITY	CHAR(20)
TABLES	TABNAME	CHAR(31)
TABLES	COLCOUNT	DECIMAL(3)
TABLES	CREATOR	CHAR(31)
COLUMNS	TABNAME	CHAR(31)
COLUMNS	COLNAME	CHAR(31)
COLUMNS	TYPE	CHAR(12)

QUERYING
THE CATALOG

How can the catalog be helpful to the user? Well, since the catalog itself consists of tables, just like ordinary user tables, it can be *queried* using the facilities of the normal query language—for example, by means of SQL SELECT statements, if SQL is the query language in question. Thus, for example, if you want to know what columns the FLIGHTS table contains, you could say:

```
SELECT  COLNAME
FROM    COLUMNS
WHERE   TABNAME = 'FLIGHTS'
```

Result:

COLNAME

FLIGHT
FROM_CODE
TO_CODE
DEP_TIME
ARR_TIME

To find out what user tables exist, you could write:

```
SELECT  TABNAME
FROM    TABLES
WHERE   CREATOR ¬= 'SYSTEM'
```

(The symbol ¬ = means "not equal".) Result:

TABNAME

CELLAR
FLIGHTS
CITIES

Queries like these are obviously helpful if you have not been using the database for a while and cannot remember exactly what it contains. They are also particularly useful in the context of a large and/or shared database. For example, you may be interested in flight information but not know whether the database already contains such information (someone else may or may not have created the appropriate tables). Queries against the catalog can clearly be of assistance in such a situation.

Try the following exercises:

1. Sketch the details of the catalog for the Road Association database (Chapter 4).

2. Write some sample queries against that catalog. For example:

    (a) Which tables include an APN column?

    (b) How many columns are there in the PARCELS table? Write this query in two different ways, one using the COUNT built-in function and one not.

    (c) List the names of all catalog tables (i.e., system tables, as opposed to user tables).

    (d) List the names of all users that have created a table with an APN column, together with the names of the tables concerned.

    As usual, if you have access to a system of your own, it is a good idea to try these queries, or analogous ones, on the machine. SQL versions are given at the end of this chapter.

UPDATING THE CATALOG

We have seen how to *query* the catalog by means of SELECT (or whatever retrieval statement the available query language provides). However, the update statements INSERT, DELETE, and UPDATE should *not* be used to update the catalog. In fact, the system will probably not even allow such operations (you will get an error message if you try). The reason for this rule is that allowing such operations would potentially be very dangerous: It would be far too easy to destroy information (inadvertently or otherwise) in the catalog so that the system could no longer function properly. Suppose, for example, that the statement

```
DELETE
FROM    COLUMNS
WHERE   TABNAME = 'CELLAR'
AND     COLNAME = 'BIN'
```

were allowed. Its effect would be to remove the record

```
( 'CELLAR', 'BIN', 'DECIMAL(3)' )
```

from the COLUMNS table. *As far as the system is concerned, the BIN column in the CELLAR table would now no longer exist—that* is, the DBMS would no longer have any knowledge of that column. Thus attempts to access data on the basis of values of that column—for example,

```
SELECT *
FROM   CELLAR
WHERE  BIN = 4
```

—would fail (the system would produce some error message, such as "illegal column name"). Perhaps worse, attempts to update CELLAR records could go disastrously wrong. For example, inserting a new record might cause the bin number to be taken as the name of the wine, the name of the wine to be taken as the name of the producer, and so on.

How then does the catalog get updated? In particular, how do records such as

```
( 'CELLAR', 'BIN', 'DECIMAL(3)' )
```

get into the catalog in the first place, if not via a regular INSERT operation? The answer is that it is the *data definition* statements—specifically CREATE TABLE—that cause these updates to occur. The CREATE TABLE statement for the CELLAR table, for example—namely,

```
CREATE TABLE CELLAR
     ( BIN       DECIMAL(3),
       WINE      CHAR(25),
       PRODUCER  CHAR(20),
       YEAR      DECIMAL(2),
       BOTTLES   DECIMAL(3),
       READY     DECIMAL(2),
       COMMENTS  CHAR(25) )
```

—causes (a) an entry to be made for CELLAR in the TABLES table and (b) a set of seven entries, for the seven columns of the CELLAR table, to be made in the COLUMNS table. (It also causes some other things to happen, too, which are however of no concern to us here.)

Aside: Perhaps you are wondering how the catalog entries for TABLES and COLUMNS themselves get into the catalog. You do not have to issue CREATE TABLE statements for these tables (nor, of course, for any other catalog tables). Instead, these entries are created automatically by the system itself when the system is first installed on the machine.

You can see, therefore, that CREATE TABLE is in some ways the analog of INSERT for the catalog. (CREATE TABLE inserts a *description* of the table being created into the catalog, and that description is made up of multiple records in multiple catalog tables.) Are there any analogs of DELETE and UPDATE? Is it possible to delete and/or update those descriptions in the catalog? Well, of course, there certainly is an analog for DELETE; it must be possible to get rid of a table from the database when it is no longer needed. The SQL statement

```
DROP TABLE CELLAR
```

(for example) will delete the description of the CELLAR table from the catalog (one row from the TABLES table and seven rows from the COLUMNS table). As for UPDATE, some systems provide analogs of that operation, too. In SQL, for example, it is possible to issue an ALTER TABLE statement to change the description of a table in the catalog. But the details of this statement are a little complicated, and we will not discuss them here.

CATALOG VERSUS DICTIONARY

We have concentrated in this chapter on *table descriptions* (also known as *table descriptors*) as a major component of the catalog, since it is easy to see why the system needs that particular information. But the catalog will also contain a great deal of additional information. It may, for example, include information concerning table interrelationships, such as the one between the FLIGHTS and CITIES tables. It will certainly contain information concerning *indexes* (see Chapter 12). In a multiple-user system it will contain information regarding individual users (such as information indicating which users are allowed to access which parts of the database). All of this information is needed by the DBMS to do its job properly and is therefore maintained by the DBMS.

In large installations the catalog may sometimes be regarded as just part of a larger collection of information called the *dictionary*. Actually, there is not a very clear-cut distinction between the two; but for the purposes of this chapter we reserve "catalog" to mean just the information that is required by the DBMS and use "dictionary" to include *all* the various items of control and descriptive information kept by the installation as a whole, regardless of whether that information is needed by the DBMS. Thus the dictionary (which is itself another database, or perhaps a set of several databases) will include, not just DBMS information such as table descriptors, but also, for example, information about who receives which reports, information concerning the physical equipment used in the computer room, details of the terminal network, and so forth. Since it is a database, the dictionary can also be queried and updated through some appropriate query language (ideally the same language as is used for other databases, though for historical reasons—dictionary systems have typically been developed independently of database systems—the two languages are usually different today).

CONCLUSION

This chapter has described the database catalog. In the next few chapters we will leave SQL for a while and take a brief look at some other systems—Query By Example, NOMAD, and dBASE II—in order to see how other systems handle the problems we have discussed so far using SQL as a vehicle. (SQL certainly does not represent the only possible way a system might look; numerous other styles can be found in other systems, with their own advantages and disadvantages.) In particular, we will see how each of those systems provides access to the database catalog.

ANSWERS

We present some possible SQL queries for exercise 2 at the end of the section "Querying the Catalog."

(a) ```
SELECT TABNAME
FROM   COLUMNS
WHERE   COLNAME = 'APN'
```

(b) ```
SELECT  COLCOUNT
FROM    TABLES
WHERE   TABNAME = 'PARCELS'
```

Or:

```
SELECT  COUNT(*)
FROM    COLUMNS
WHERE   TABNAME = 'PARCELS'
```

(c) ```
SELECT TABNAME
FROM   TABLES
WHERE   CREATOR = 'SYSTEM'
```
```

(d)
```
SELECT CREATOR, TABNAME
FROM    TABLES
WHERE  'APN' IN
       (SELECT COLNAME
        FROM    COLUMNS
        WHERE  COLUMNS.TABNAME = TABLES.TABNAME)
```

Or:

```
SELECT TABLES.CREATOR, TABLES.TABNAME
FROM    TABLES, COLUMNS
WHERE   TABLES.TABNAME = COLUMNS.TABNAME
AND     COLUMNS.COLNAME = 'APN'
```

Or:

```
SELECT CREATOR, TABNAME
FROM    TABLES
WHERE  EXISTS
       (SELECT *
        FROM    COLUMNS
        WHERE   TABNAME = TABLES.TABNAME
        AND     COLNAME = 'APN')
```

8   *Query By Example*

INTRODUCTION

All examples in this book so far have been based on the language SQL. In SQL every command you issue is typed in as a *statement*—in effect, as a *sentence* in a language that can be thought of as a highly stylized and restricted form of written English. Thus being skilled in SQL is somewhat akin to being skilled in the construction of precise written sentences in English. Certainly, it is true that the query language style of which SQL is a typical representative tends to be most attractive to people who are used to thinking in a verbal or word-oriented manner. But many people are more comfortable with a visual or picture-oriented manner of thinking. Such people are likely to find the style of Query By Example somewhat more appealing.

Query By Example (abbreviated QBE) offers a very different approach from that of SQL. Instead of formulating stylized "sentences," as in SQL, the user in QBE operates by filling in blanks in empty tables on the screen (in effect, by filling in forms). For example, consider the query "Who is the owner of parcel 93-282-55?" (example 1 from the section "Sample Queries" in Chapter 4). This query can be represented in QBE as follows:

PARCELS	APN	ROAD	OWNER	IMPROVED	LAST_ENTRY	BALANCE
	93-282-55		P.JACK			

Explanation: First, by pressing a particular key on the keyboard, the user causes the system to display a blank or empty table on the screen:

Then knowing that the answer to the query can be found in the PARCELS table, the user types PARCELS in the table name position (top left) of this empty table. QBE responds by filling in all the column names for PARCELS: APN, ROAD, and so on. (In this particular example the system also has to extend the blank table from four columns to six, incidentally, which it does automatically.) Now the user completes the query by typing entries into two positions in the body of the table, namely 93–282–55 (in the APN position) and P.JACK (in the OWNER position). The "P." stands for "print"; it indicates the target of the query, that is, the values to be displayed. JACK is an *example element*, that is, an example of a possible answer to the query; example elements are indicated by underlining. 93–282–55 (not underlined) is a *constant element*, that is, an actual data value. The entire query may therefore be paraphrased:

> From the PARCELS table, print all OWNER values, such as JACK (say), where the corresponding APN value is 93–282–55.

The user then hits the "enter" key on the keyboard, and QBE responds by displaying the answer to the query on the screen:

PARCELS	OWNER
	I.J.KING

By the way, it is not necessary for JACK to be one of the actual OWNER values; we could equally well have used JILL, PIG, or WHO without changing the meaning of the query.

Notice the comparatively small amount of typing we had to do in this example (certainly less than with SQL). In fact, it can be argued that the amount of information we had to supply is the *minimum possible* for the query, consisting as it does only of the following:

1. The name of the relevant table (PARCELS);

2. An indication of what output the system is to produce (OWNER);

3. An indication of what condition the output has to satisfy (APN must be 93–282–55).

This information is minimal in the sense that anything less would not be enough for the system to be able to tell what it was we were looking for.

The foregoing example is fairly typical of QBE queries and demonstrates very clearly the immediate intuitive attractiveness of the QBE style. As you can see, you do not have to learn and remember certain specific words and phrases (such as SELECT–FROM–WHERE), nor do you have to enter such words and phrases in a certain specific sequence. You just have to supply the minimum necessary to define a complete query; moreover, you have some freedom in the sequence in which you supply that minimum. (In the example it would make no difference which of 93–282–55 and P.JACK was typed first and which second.) It is a fact that comparatively unskilled users can learn enough about QBE to get started on productive work within a very short time—probably less time than is needed for SQL, perhaps even as little as half an hour. Of course, more complicated queries will require more skill on the part of the user and correspondingly more training, but it is still the case that users can become productive very quickly with a system like QBE.

For convenience, in Fig. 8.1 we repeat Fig. 2.1 from Chapter 2, showing (among other things) how retrieval, modification, and so on are expressed in QBE.

Query By Example was originally designed at the IBM Research Laboratory in Yorktown Heights, New York, by M. M. Zloof. A commercial implementation of QBE is available for large machines from IBM. QBE-like systems are also available from other vendors. In the rest of this chapter we will illustrate some of the highlights of QBE by showing several further examples, all based once again on the Road Association database. Again, the purpose of presenting this material is not to teach the specifics of QBE per se but to illustrate another possible style of database ac-

Figure 8.1

	SQL	QBE	NOMAD	dBASE
Retrieval	SELECT	P.	LIST	DISPLAY
Modification	UPDATE	U.	CHANGE	REPLACE
Deletion	DELETE	D.	DELETE	DELETE
Insertion	INSERT	I.	INSERT	APPEND

cess. We will not go into quite as much detail as we did with SQL. The topics we examine are (in order) queries, updates, data definition, and querying the catalog.

QUERIES

1. What penalty was imposed on parcel 93–282–55 for 1981? (Example 2 in the section "Sample Queries" of Chapter 4.)

PARCEL_ACCOUNTS	APN	DESCRIPTION	TYPE	AMOUNT
	93-282-55	PENALTY81	CHARGE	P.<u>XXX</u>

Paraphrasing:

> From the PARCEL__ACCOUNTS table, print the amount, say XXX, where the APN is 93–282–55, the description is PENALTY81, and the type is CHARGE.

You may remember that the PARCEL__ACCOUNTS table actually includes some further columns in addition to those shown here, namely, ENTRY, DATE, and BALANCE. However, those columns are irrelevant to the problem at hand. QBE allows you to suppress such irrelevant columns in the formulation of queries, and we have done so in the example (but we skip the details of the suppression process).

2. How much has the association paid (in total) to Road Fixers, Inc.? (Example 5 in "Sample Queries," Chapter 4.)

GENERAL_LEDGER	TYPE	PARTY	AMOUNT
	CHARGE	ROAD FIXERS, INC.	P.SUM.ALL.<u>XXX</u>

Paraphrasing:

> Print the sum of all amounts from the GENERAL__LEDGER table where the type is CHARGE and the party is ROAD FIXERS, INC.

QBE provides essentially the same set of built-in functions as SQL: CNT, SUM, AVG, MAX, and MIN. The "ALL." is required, for reasons that need not concern us here.

3. Display name, address, and phone number for the owner of parcel 93-282-55. (Example 8 in "Sample Queries," Chapter 4.)

This query involves two tables, PARCELS and OWNERS. The user therefore gets QBE to display both tables on the screen simultaneously and then fills in blanks in both of them, as follows:

PARCELS	APN	OWNER
	93-282-55	JACK

OWNERS	OWNER	ADDRESS	PHONE
	P.JACK	P.JADD	P.JPH

This example shows how to express the procedure of "looking over" from one table to another in QBE, namely, by using the same example element (JACK here) in both tables. The entire query may be paraphrased:

> Let the owner of parcel 93-282-55 be JACK. Print JACK's name, address, and phone number.

A small point: When it is desired to apply "P." to every element of a given row, as in the OWNERS table in this example, a shorthand can be used in which the "P." is applied to the whole *row* rather than to each element individually. For example:

OWNERS	OWNER	ADDRESS	PHONE
P.	JACK	JADD	JPH

And another point: If a given example element is not being used to link across to another entry somewhere, then, in fact, it is not really necessary and can be omitted. Thus JADD and JPH (but not JACK) could be omitted in the example:

PARCELS	APN	OWNER
	93-282-55	JACK

OWNERS	OWNER	ADDRESS	PHONE
P.	JACK		

4. List parcel number and owner for all parcels on which at least one 1982 dues payment has been made. (Example 12 in "Sample Queries," Chapter 4.)

In SQL this query involves the EXISTS function. In QBE it looks like this:

PARCELS	APN	OWNER	PARCEL_ACCOUNTS	APN	DESCRIPTION	TYPE
P.	XYZ			XYZ	DUES82	CREDIT

Paraphrasing:

> Print APN, say XYZ, and corresponding owner, such that a PARCEL_ACCOUNTS record exists for XYZ with description DUES82 and type CREDIT.

5. List parcel number and owner for all parcels on which no 1982 dues payment has been made. (Example 13 in "Sample Queries," Chapter 4.)

This example is, of course, the converse of the previous one, and in SQL it involved prefixing EXISTS by NOT in the previous solution. Similarly, in QBE it involves prefixing a "not" symbol (¬) to the PARCEL__ACCOUNTS row in the previous solution:

PARCELS	APN	OWNER	PARCEL_ACCOUNTS	APN	DESCRIPTION	TYPE
P.	XYZ		¬	XYZ	DUES82	CREDIT

Paraphrasing:

> Print APN, say XYZ, and corresponding owner, such that there does not exist a PARCEL__ACCOUNTS record for XYZ with description DUES82 and type CREDIT.

6. List all special assessments (SAN and EXPLANATION) and, for each one, all parcels (APN) affected by that assessment. (Example 10 in "Sample Queries," Chapter 4.)

This is the first of the join examples from Chapter 4. Since the result is a new table (i.e., not a piece of some existing table in the database, but rather a table that has to be built up out of pieces from two such existing tables), the user must first of all get the system to display *three* empty tables on the screen, one for each of the two existing tables and one for the result. For the result table the user must then type in the table name, say RESULT, *and the col-*

umn names (since the system has no way of knowing those names ahead of time, as this is a new table). Then:

SPECIAL_ASSESSMENTS	SAN	EXPLANATION	ROAD
	SX	EX	RX

PARCELS	APN	ROAD
	AX	RX

RESULT	SAN	EXPLANATION	APN
P.	SX	EX	AX

Paraphrasing:

> Print all combinations of SAN (SX), explanation (EX), and APN (AX), such that SX and EX apply to road RX and AX is located on RX.

The name of the result table (RESULT) is arbitrary.

This completes our set of query examples. We have not illustrated all aspects of query formulation in QBE by any means—in fact, QBE has counterparts to everything in SQL, including, for example, analogs of LIKE, ORDER BY, GROUP BY, and HAVING—but you should have seen enough by now to get the general idea. As an exercise, you might like to take some of the simple SQL queries in Chapter 2 and try casting them into QBE form. Answers are given at the end of this chapter.

Now let us move on to look at some update examples.

UPDATES

Updates are expressed in QBE by the operators "I." (insert), "U." (update), and "D." (delete).

1. Insert a new row into the PARCELS table. (Example 1 in the section "Loading the Database" in Chapter 4.)

PARCELS	APN	ROAD	OWNER	IMPROVED	LAST_ENTRY	BALANCE
I.	93-282-55	CREEK	I.J.KING	Y	1	120

2. Construction has just started on parcel 93-282-51. Update the IMPROVED indicator accordingly. (Example 1 in the section "Introduction" in Chapter 5.)

PARCELS	APN	IMPROVED
	93-282-51	U.Y

Or:

PARCELS	APN	IMPROVED
U.	93-282-51	Y

3. Delete John Minski from the OWNERS table. (Example 2 in "Introduction," Chapter 5.)

OWNERS	OWNER	ADDRESS	PHONE
D.	JOHN MINSKI		

4. Increase the balance owing on each parcel in the PARCELS table by 20 percent. (Example 3 in "Introduction," Chapter 5.)

PARCELS	APN	BALANCE
	XYZ	BAL > 0
U.	XYZ	BAL * 1.2

To update records based on their current value, the user enters two rows into the empty table, one representing the current value and one the new value. The "U." indicates which is the new one. Notice the condition that the current balance must be greater than zero.

At this point you may like to try producing QBE versions of the sample updates from Chapter 2. Answers are given at the end of this chapter.

5. The association has just (July 24, 1982) made a payment of $360 to Road Fixers, Inc., for a repair job done on Redwood Road in connection with special assessment SA4. Update the database accordingly. (First example in the section "Multistatement Updates" in Chapter 5.)

This example required several distinct operations in SQL, and so it does in QBE also—with this difference: It may well be the case that all of those operations can be expressed in QBE *within a single screen.* If so, then to the user it looks much more like a single operation (*all* of the various related updates will be applied simultaneously when, and only when, the user hits the "enter" key on the keyboard). In a sense, therefore, the QBE representation is a little closer to the user's perception of the update in the real world, namely, as a single (complicated) operation.

LAST_ENTRIES	ACCOUNT	ENTRY	BALANCE
	GENERAL	GN	GBAL
U.	GENERAL	GN + 1	GBAL − 360
	REDWOOD	RN	RBAL
U.	REDWOOD	RN + 1	RBAL − 360

GENERAL_LEDGER	ENTRY	DATE	DESCRIPTION	TYPE	PARTY	AMOUNT	BALANCE
I.	GN+1	820724	SA4	CHARGE	ROAD FIXERS, INC.	360	GBAL−360

REDWOOD_LEDGER	ENTRY	DATE	DESCRIPTION	TYPE	PARTY	AMOUNT	BALANCE
I.	RN+1	820724	SA4	CHARGE	ROAD FIXERS, INC.	360	RBAL−360

However, it is still true in QBE, just as it is in SQL, that more complex real world updates will require the creation of canned procedures. As with SQL, such a procedure can consist of database operations (i.e., QBE operations) only, or (more likely) it can involve both QBE operations and statements in some programming language such as PL/I. We will not discuss the details here.

DATA DEFINITION   QBE does not provide any data definition operations as such (there is no CREATE TABLE, for example). Instead, QBE allows you to perform data definition functions by making certain carefully controlled updates directly on the QBE catalog. We show one simple example here (the QBE analog of a CREATE TABLE for the PARCELS table).

Create the PARCELS table. (Example 1 in the section "Creating the Database" in Chapter 4.)

I. PARCELS I.	APN	ROAD	OWNER	IMPROVED	LAST_ENTRY	BALANCE
TYPE I.	CHAR(9)	CHAR(7)	CHAR(20)	CHAR(1)	FIXED	FIXED

Explanation: The first "I." (against the table name) causes an entry to be made for the PARCELS table in the catalog table TABLES. (For simplicity we assume that the QBE catalog consists of a TABLES table and a COLUMNS table, as described in Chapter 7.) The second "I." (against the row of column names) causes a set of six entries to be made in the catalog table COLUMNS. Finally, the third "I." (in the row labeled TYPE) establishes the data types for these six columns in the COLUMNS table.

Note 1: The QBE data type FIXED is used for numeric data such as dollar amounts. Further specifications (beyond the scope of this chapter) are needed to indicate the position of the assumed decimal point in a FIXED column.

Note 2: It is not our intent to describe all possible data types in QBE (after all, we did not do so for SQL either), but one particular data type should be mentioned, namely, the DATE data type. This data type allows you to specify dates directly as (for example) 7/24/82, instead of 820724, which is what SQL requires. A similar TIME data type is also available.

Note 3: Certain other information can also be entered into the catalog to describe any given table. In particular, you can enter certain *formatting* information, such as the format to be used for each column in printed results (e.g.: Should there be a dollar sign? Should leading zeros be printed or not?). Therefore, formats are *permanently* associated with the data. There are no separate report-writing commands as there are in SQL, to enable you to print the same data in different ways at different times.

QUERYING THE CATALOG

1. What tables exist?

There are two possible formulations of this query. One is precisely analogous to the queries you have already seen:

TABLES	TABNAME
	P.

To be able to use this form, of course, you must be aware of the existence of the TABLES table (and of its name). You can obtain the same result without having to know this information by simply typing "P." in the *table name* position of an empty table:

P.				

Either way, the system responds with a list of all table names.

2. What columns does the PARCELS table have?

You already know how to express this query in QBE, namely, by typing PARCELS in the table name position of an empty table. QBE will respond by filling in the column names:

PARCELS	APN	ROAD	OWNER	IMPROVED	LAST_ENTRY	BALANCE

Alternatively, of course, you could issue a regular query on the COLUMNS table (assuming, again, that you are aware of the existence of this table):

COLUMNS	TABNAME	COLNAME
	PARCELS	P.

SUMMARY

We have sketched the facilities of the Query By Example system in a certain amount of detail, since they represent an approach to database access that is significantly different from that of SQL. All operations in QBE are expressed by filling in blanks in empty tables. This is true, not only for data manipulation operations, but also for data definition operations and for the (somewhat limited) formatting operations. For straightforward interactions QBE possesses some very attractive features and is probably rather easier to use than SQL and other word-oriented (as opposed to picture-oriented, or, perhaps more accurately, forms-oriented) systems. It is, however, not clear that QBE retains all of its attractiveness when interactions become more complex. Also, of course, some people prefer words to pictures! It is a safe bet that both styles will be around for some considerable time to come.

ANSWERS

We give QBE versions of some of the SQL examples from Chapter 2. For ease of comparison we give the SQL version in each case, too.

1. SQL:

    ```
    SELECT *
    FROM    CELLAR
    ```

    QBE:

CELLAR	BIN	WINE	PRODUCER	YEAR	BOTTLES	READY	COMMENTS
P.							

2. SQL:

    ```
    SELECT *
    FROM    CELLAR
    WHERE   WINE = 'Chardonnay'
    ```

    QBE:

CELLAR	BIN	WINE	PRODUCER	YEAR	BOTTLES	READY	COMMENTS
P.		Chardonnay					

3. SQL:

    ```
    SELECT BIN, PRODUCER, READY, BOTTLES
    FROM    CELLAR
    WHERE   WINE = 'Chardonnay'
    ```

QBE:

CELLAR	BIN	WINE	PRODUCER	YEAR	BOTTLES	READY	COMMENTS
	P.	Chardonnay	P.		P.	P.	

4. SQL:

```
SELECT *
FROM   FLIGHTS
WHERE  FROM_CODE =
       (SELECT CODE
        FROM   CITIES
        WHERE  CITY = 'San Francisco')
AND    TO_CODE =
       (SELECT CODE
        FROM   CITIES
        WHERE  CITY = 'Chicago')
```

QBE:

FLIGHTS	FLIGHT	FROM_CODE	TO_CODE	DEP_TIME	ARR_TIME
P.		FFF	TTT		

CITIES	CODE	CITY
	FFF	San Francisco
	TTT	Chicago

5. SQL:

```
UPDATE CELLAR
SET    BOTTLES = 4
WHERE  BIN = 3
```

QBE:

CELLAR	BIN	BOTTLES
	3	U.4

6. SQL:

```
DELETE
FROM    CELLAR
WHERE   BIN = 2
```

QBE:

CELLAR	BIN	WINE	PRODUCER	YEAR	BOTTLES	READY	COMMENTS
D.	2						

7. SQL:

```
INSERT
INTO    CELLAR
VALUES (53, 'Pinot Noir', 'Franciscan',76,1,83,'present from Joan')
```

QBE:

CELLAR	BIN	WINE	PRODUCER	YEAR	BOTTLES	READY	COMMENTS
I.	53	Pinot Noir	Franciscan	76	1	83	present from Joan

9   *NOMAD*

INTRODUCTION

In this chapter we take a look at another system, NOMAD, to illustrate some further possibilities in regard to the style of a query language. First, we repeat once again, in Fig. 9.1, the summary table from Chapter 2.

Like SQL, NOMAD is word-oriented rather than picture- or forms-oriented. However, it differs from SQL in a number of respects, of which the following are some of the most significant:

1. Query, data definition, and formatting operations are more tightly interwoven than they are in SQL. Furthermore, results can be produced in a wide variety of graphic forms (pie charts, bar charts, line graphs, scatter graphs), as well as simply being displayed or printed in some kind of tabular form.

2. Update operations follow a pattern that more closely resembles the manner in which you would work with files on paper. To be specific, such operations typically involve two steps: First, you find the record you want to change (using a special LOCATE statement) then you make the actual change (using some kind of CHANGE statement). SQL, by contrast, works in a kind of out-of-the-blue fashion: You say UPDATE . . . WHERE, and it is the WHERE clause that identifies the record(s) to be changed—there is no notion of finding the record(s) first. QBE resembles SQL in this regard.

Figure 9.1

	SQL	QBE	NOMAD	dBASE
Retrieval	SELECT	P.	LIST	DISPLAY
Modification	UPDATE	U.	CHANGE	REPLACE
Deletion	DELETE	D.	DELETE	DELETE
Insertion	INSERT	I.	INSERT	APPEND

3. A wide variety of statistical functions (basic statistics, chi-square test, polynomial regression, and others) is provided in addition to the usual SUM, AVG, and so on.

4. Security and integrity features are provided. (SQL and QBE also provide good security features but are currently rather weak in the area of integrity.) These topics will be addressed in Part II of this book.

5. The NOMAD language is a complete *programming* language in its own right, as well as being a query language. Thus even when it becomes necessary to create a canned procedure, that procedure can be written entirely in NOMAD; there is no need to cross over into (say) COBOL or PL/I. Moreover, functions are provided for the creation, storage, and display of predefined screen forms and for program manipulation of such forms. This facility allows canned procedures to be written in such a way that the process of supplying the input parameters to those programs can be made highly user-friendly. For example, the REDWOOD__PAYMENT procedure (see Chapter 5) might begin by displaying a "form" (screen) as shown in Fig. 9.2. Note the cursor positioned ready for

Figure 9.2

```
               *** REDWOOD PAYMENT ***

    This procedure assumes that a payment has just been made
    out of the Redwood Road fund. Its purpose is to update the
    database appropriately to reflect that payment.


    Please supply the following information:


        DATE OF PAYMENT = > _
        AMOUNT PAID = >
        PARTY TO WHOM PAYMENT MADE = >


    After you have typed in these three pieces of information,
    please hit ENTER.
```

input following the <u>DATE OF PAYMENT</u> prompt. Text on the form can be made to blink, can be underlined (as in the example), can be displayed in half or full brightness, in normal or reverse lettering (e.g., green on black or black on green), and so on. The form can display initial values for particular fields (specified in the definition of the form) and/or values extracted from the database.

Similar techniques can also be used in the production of displayed reports and output messages, of course.

The current version of NOMAD is called NOMAD2. We will continue to refer to the product simply as NOMAD, however. NOMAD and NOMAD2 are registered trademarks of National CSS Inc., Wilton, Connecticut 06897.

Let us take a look at some examples of NOMAD, once again using the Road Association database as a basis.

DATA DEFINITION
1. Create the PARCELS table. (Example 1 in the section "Creating the Database" in Chapter 4.)

```
MASTER PARCELS INSERT KEYED(APN)
  ITEM APN          A9          HEADING 'PARCEL'
  ITEM ROAD         A7
  ITEM OWNER        A20
  ITEM IMPROVED     A1
  ITEM LAST_ENTRY   99999       HEADING 'LAST:ENTRY'
  ITEM BALANCE      99999.99
```

Tables and columns are called *masters* and *items*, respectively, in NOMAD. "INSERT KEYED(APN)" means two things: (a) No two parcels can have the same parcel number; (b) the PARCELS table will be kept in the database in parcel number order. Note the NOMAD method of specifying data types. For instance, "A9" is the NOMAD equivalent of CHAR(9), and "99999.99" is the NOMAD equivalent of DECIMAL(7,2). Other possible data types include DATEs (as in QBE) and NAMEs. NAMEs are basically just character strings, but strings that have a very sophisticated set of possible *formats* associated with them to handle middle initials, titles (such as Ms. or Dr.), and similar details peculiar to names. Finally, the HEADING clause specifies the heading to be used for this item when it appears in a report. APN items will be printed with a heading of PARCEL. LAST_ENTRY items will be printed with a heading that appears as follows:

```
LAST
ENTRY
```

(The colon in the HEADING clause indicates a new line.) All other items will be printed under their own name, since no other heading has been specified for them.

Incidentally, any formatting information specified in the table definition (such as HEADING) can always be overridden at the time a report is actually produced, as we will see later (example 2 in the next section).

2. Create the PARCELS table. (This example is an extended version of the previous example to illustrate virtual items.)

```
MASTER PARCELS INSERT KEYED(APN)
    ITEM APN          A9          HEADING 'PARCEL'
    ITEM ROAD         A7
    ITEM OWNER        A20
    DEFINE ADDRESS    AS EXTRACT'ADDRESS FROM OWNERS USING OWNER'
    DEFINE PHONE      AS EXTRACT'PHONE   FROM OWNERS USING OWNER'
    ITEM IMPROVED     A1
    ITEM LAST_ENTRY   99999       HEADING 'LAST:ENTRY'
    ITEM BALANCE      99999.99
```

A *virtual item* is an item that does not really exist in the database but looks to the user as if it did. It is derived in some way from some real item that does exist. For example, the virtual item ADDRESS in the PARCELS table here is derived from the real item ADDRESS in the OWNERS table; similarly, the virtual item PHONE in the PARCELS table is derived from the real item PHONE in the OWNERS table. (We could have used different item names if we had wished.) The PARCELS table does not really include these items, but *to the user* it is as if it did. What actually happens when you retrieve a PARCELS record is this: First, NOMAD uses the OWNER value in that PARCELS record to find the record for that owner in the OWNERS table. It then extracts the address and phone number from that OWNERS record and passes them back to you together with the data from the original PARCELS record. For example:

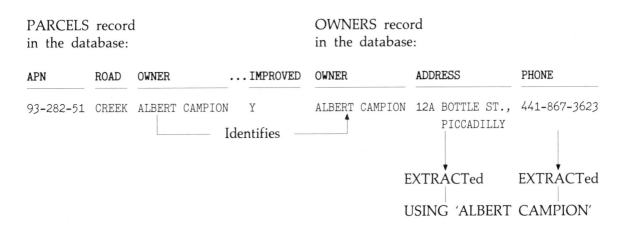

PARCELS record
in the database:

OWNERS record
in the database:

APN	ROAD	OWNER	...IMPROVED	OWNER	ADDRESS	PHONE
93-282-51	CREEK	ALBERT CAMPION	Y	ALBERT CAMPION	12A BOTTLE ST., PICCADILLY	441-867-3623

Identifies

EXTRACTed   EXTRACTed

USING 'ALBERT CAMPION'

PARCELS record returned to user:

APN	ROAD	OWNER	ADDRESS	PHONE	IMPROVED	. . .
93-282-51	CREEK	ALBERT CAMPION	12A BOTTLE ST., PICCADILLY	441-867-3623	Y	

◄——— Virtual ———►

In effect, you can think of DEFINE . . . EXTRACT as causing NOMAD to perform a *predefined join* for you. More precisely, the DEFINE clause

```
DEFINE . . . EXTRACT . . . FROM master USING item
```

works by matching "item" (i.e., OWNER from the PARCELS table, in the example) with the item specified in the KEYED clause in the definition of "master" (i.e., the OWNER item in the OWNERS table, in the example).

It is also possible to define a virtual item as the result of some arithmetic expression involving several real items. For example, an ORDER_LINE record might include a virtual item COST that is

defined as the product of the two real items PRICE and QUAN-
TITY:

```
MASTER ORDER_LINE
   ITEM PRICE . . .
   ITEM QUANTITY . . .
        .
        .
        .
   DEFINE COST   99999.99 EXPR PRICE * QUANTITY
```

QUERY AND FORMATTING OPERATIONS

1. Who is the owner of parcel 93–282–55? (Example 1 in "Sample
Queries," Chapter 4.)

```
FROM  PARCELS
LIST  OWNER
WHERE APN = '93-282-55'
```

The FROM clause could be omitted if the item name OWNER were
unique across the entire database (but it is not).

The above example is only one of several ways of expressing
this query in NOMAD. However, LIST is the command that is
normally used to query the database and produce a report. An alternative to LIST, PLOT, is used to produce the results in some
graphic form (e.g., PLOT BAR . . . will produce a bar chart). Details of the PLOT command are beyond the scope of this text.

To list all of the fields in the record (the NOMAD analog of
SQL "SELECT *"), we can say

```
LIST SEGMENT PARCELS
```

For our purposes we can regard SEGMENT as synonymous with
MASTER. Note that no FROM is required (it would obviously be
superfluous).

2. List all charges made in 1982, and:

- Print the results in ascending order by entry number within
  parcel number.

- Include a top title 'PARCEL ACCOUNT CHARGES 1982'.

- Include a bottom title 'REDWOOD—CREEK—MILL ROAD
  ASSOCIATION'.

- Suppress printing for the TYPE and ENTRY columns.

- Rename the APN and DESCRIPTION columns as PARCEL and CHARGE, respectively, in the report.

- Suppress repetition of parcel numbers.

- Include AMOUNT subtotals and total.

(Examples in the section "Report Writing" in Chapter 6.)

```
FROM PARCEL_ACCOUNTS
LIST
  BY APN HEADING 'PARCEL'
  BY ENTRY NOPRINT
    DATE
    DESCRIPTION HEADING 'CHARGE'
    AMOUNT SUBTOTAL TOTAL
    BALANCE
    WHERE TYPE = 'CHARGE' AND DATE BETWEEN ('820101', '821231')
  TITLE 'PARCEL ACCOUNT CHARGES 1982'
  FOOTING 'REDWOOD-CREEK-MILL ROAD ASSOCIATION'
```

Explanation:

- By APN . . . BY ENTRY causes the report to be printed in ascending ENTRY sequence within ascending APN sequence. It also automatically causes suppression of repeated values.

- HEADING 'PARCEL' overrides the default heading specified for APN in the definition of the PARCEL__ACCOUNTS table (whatever that default was). Similarly for HEADING 'CHARGE' on DESCRIPTION.

- NOPRINT in the BY ENTRY clause suppresses printing for the ENTRY column.

- Printing is suppressed for the TYPE column by virtue of the fact that TYPE is simply never mentioned at all.

- AMOUNT SUBTOTAL TOTAL is self-explanatory.

- TITLE and FOOTING are also self-explanatory.

Notice the use of BETWEEN in the WHERE clause, incidentally. A similar BETWEEN comparison is available in SQL also, though we did not show it in any of our SQL examples.

This example illustrates very clearly how query, data definition, and formatting are all interwoven in NOMAD. Of course, if no particular formatting is specified explicitly in a given query (as in example 1 above), NOMAD will automatically apply certain default formats, and these may be quite satisfactory in many situations.

3. List all parties to whom the association has made payments, with total amount paid in each case. (Example 14 in "Sample Queries," Chapter 4.)

```
FROM GENERAL_LEDGER
LIST
  BY PARTY
     SUM (AMOUNT)
```

Notice how the BY clause combines the functions of both ORDER BY and GROUP BY, in SQL terms. Adding the condition

```
WHERE PARTY = 'ROAD FIXERS, INC.'
```

to the foregoing LIST would reduce it to a NOMAD equivalent of example 5 in "Sample Queries," Chapter 4. (BY PARTY could then be dropped, though it would not be wrong to include it.)

4. When was the last time a payment was made on parcel 93–282–55? Show the amount paid at that time. (This example is an extended version of example 7 in "Sample Queries," Chapter 4.)

```
FROM PARCEL_ACCOUNTS
LIST
  MAX(DATE) WITH AMOUNT
  WHERE APN = '93-282-55'
```

NOMAD finds the account record for parcel 93–282–55 having the most recent date, then prints that date *and the associated amount* (by virtue of the WITH clause). This extended version of the original query is quite awkward in SQL:

```
SELECT DATE, AMOUNT
FROM    PARCEL_ACCOUNTS
WHERE   APN = '93-282-55'
AND     DATE =
        (SELECT MAX (DATE)
         FROM    PARCEL_ACCOUNTS
         WHERE   APN = '93-282-55')
```

5. Display name, address, and phone number for the owner of parcel 93–282–55. (Example 8 in "Sample Queries," Chapter 4.)

We show two solutions to this problem. First, suppose ADDRESS and PHONE have been defined as virtual items in the PARCELS table, as in example 2 in the previous section. The solution is then almost trivial:

```
FROM PARCELS
LIST
   OWNER
   ADDRESS
   PHONE
   WHERE APN = '93-282-55'
```

Alternatively, suppose that those virtual items were *not* included in the PARCELS table. Then we can simply define such virtual items by means of appropriate DEFINE commands *dynamically* at the time we need the report:

```
FROM PARCELS
DEFINE ADDRESS AS EXTRACT'ADDRESS FROM OWNERS USING OWNER'
DEFINE PHONE   AS EXTRACT'PHONE   FROM OWNERS USING OWNER'
LIST
   OWNER
   ADDRESS
   PHONE
   WHERE APN = '93-282-55'
```

6. List all improved parcels, with owners' names, addresses, and phone numbers. (Example 11 in "Sample Queries," Chapter 4.)

We show a solution that does not make any use of virtual items.

```
FROM PARCELS
LIST
   BY OWNER
      APN
      IF IMPROVED = 'Y'
         FROM OWNERS
         EXTRACT
            MATCHING OWNER
            ADDRESS
            PHONE
```

Explanation: At first glance this command may appear overwhelmingly complex. However, it is basically nothing more than a variation on the familiar *join* function. NOMAD in fact provides several different kinds of join, represented by several different key words, of which one (EXTRACT) is shown in the example. The two tables to be joined here are

- that subset of the PARCELS table having IMPROVED = 'Y' (specified by the clause FROM PARCELS . . . IF IMPROVED = 'Y');

- the OWNERS table (specified by the clause FROM OWNERS).

The join is taken over the OWNER column of the PARCELS table (because of the clause BY OWNER following FROM PARCELS LIST) and the OWNER column of the OWNERS table (because of the clause MATCHING OWNER following FROM OWNERS EXTRACT). The items OWNER, APN, ADDRESS, and PHONE are then listed from the result of the join (in OWNER sequence, because of the clause BY OWNER).

Note: The IF clause (which expresses the restriction on the PARCELS table that IMPROVED must be 'Y') is similar to a WHERE clause, but applies only to the set of records identified by that portion of the query going back as far as the last BY or MATCHING clause. A single (complicated) query can have multiple IF clauses, each one applying to a different set of records, but only one WHERE clause, which applies to the overall result.

As indicated above, NOMAD provides several different kinds of join. The various possibilities are as follows.

- **EXTRACT**

  See the foregoing example.

- **EXTRACT ALL**

  EXTRACT without ALL will select at most one record (the first) from the MATCHING table for each record from the BY table. EXTRACT ALL, by contrast, will select *all* MATCHING records corresponding to each BY record. (Of course, if there can only be one matching record, as in the example above, then EXTRACT without ALL is perfectly adequate.)

- **SUBSET**

    EXTRACT (with or without ALL) will select all records from the BY table, regardless of whether they have any matches in the MATCHING table. SUBSET, by contrast, will eliminate BY records that have no match. In example 6 we could have used either SUBSET or EXTRACT, since we know that every parcel is guaranteed to have an owner.

- **SUBSET ALL**

    SUBSET ALL is to SUBSET what EXTRACT ALL is to EXTRACT.

- **REJECT**

    REJECT will select only records from the BY table that have no match in the MATCHING table (no data from the MATCHING table will appear in the result at all).

- **MERGE**

    MERGE will select all records from the BY table with their matches in the MATCHING table, together with BY records that have no corresponding MATCHING record, together with MATCHING records that have no corresponding BY record.

    It cannot be claimed that the operations have particularly obvious or self-explanatory names! Figure 9.3 may help you to understand them better. In each of the four pairs of tables in that figure, the left table is the BY table and the right table is the MATCHING table. The overlap indicates where matches exist between the two. Shading indicates the records that will be selected. We have not attempted to distinguish between the ALL and nonALL versions of EXTRACT and SUBSET.

Figure 9.3

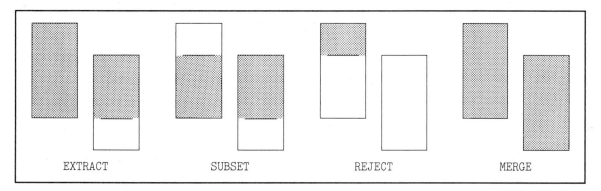

EXTRACT   SUBSET   REJECT   MERGE

We give three further examples of the use of these operations.

7. List all special assessments (SAN and EXPLANATION) and, for each one, all parcels (APN) affected by that assessment. (Example 10 in "Sample Queries," Chapter 4.)

```
FROM SPECIAL_ASSESSMENTS
LIST
   BY ROAD NOPRINT
      SAN
      EXPLANATION
      FROM PARCELS
         EXTRACT ALL
         MATCHING ROAD
         APN
```

EXTRACT ALL (or SUBSET ALL) is required here because each special assessment applies to multiple parcels.

8. List parcel number and owner for all parcels on which at least one 1982 dues payment has been made. (Example 12 in "Sample Queries," Chapter 4.)

```
FROM PARCELS
LIST
   BY APN
      OWNER
      FROM PARCEL_ACCOUNTS
      SUBSET
         MATCHING APN
         IF DESCRIPTION = 'DUES82' AND TYPE = 'CREDIT'
```

ALL is not necessary here (it would not be wrong).

9. List parcel number and owner for all parcels on which no 1982 dues payment has been made. (Example 13 in "Sample Queries," Chapter 4.)

```
FROM PARCELS
LIST
   BY APN
      OWNER
      FROM PARCEL_ACCOUNTS
      REJECT
         MATCHING APN
         IF DESCRIPTION = 'DUES82' AND TYPE = 'CREDIT'
```

We have now illustrated some of the major features of the NOMAD LIST command—enough to give you some appreciation of the power, versatility, and flexibility of that command, even though there are still numerous aspects that we have not even touched on. (The NOMAD *Reference Manual* devotes over sixty pages to this one command, more than is given to any other single topic.) Now let us go on to see how NOMAD handles the problems of database maintenance.

UPDATE OPERATIONS

NOMAD provides numerous different update operations with somewhat overlapping capabilities. We show only the most important ones here, which are as follows:

- INSERT: Inserts data one record at a time.

- PROMPT: Inserts a record one item at a time.

- DELETE: Deletes a single record (the "current" record).

- DELETE WITHIN DB: Deletes all records satisfying some condition.

- CHANGE: Changes a single record (the "current" record).

- CHANGE WITHIN DB: Changes all records satisfying some condition.

Let us look at some examples.

1. Insert a new row into the PARCELS table. (Example 1 in the section "Loading the Database" in Chapter 4.)

```
INSERT PARCELS
        APN = '93-282-55'
        ROAD = 'CREEK'
        OWNER = 'I.J.KING'
        IMPROVED = 'Y'
        LAST_ENTRY = 1
        BALANCE = 120
```

There are several ways to simplify the use of INSERT. For example, if you need to INSERT several records, one after another, such that some particular item within those records has the same value in all of them, then you can establish the value of that item

once and for all before you do the INSERTs. Suppose, for example,
that several PARCELS records are to be inserted in sequence, and
suppose they all have a BALANCE of 120:

```
&BALANCE = 120


INSERT PARCELS
        APN = . . .
                .
                .
                .
        LAST_ENTRY = . . .


INSERT PARCELS
        APN = . . .
                .
                .
                .
        LAST_ENTRY = . . .
    .
    .
    .


INSERT PARCELS
        APN = . . .
                .
                .
                .
        LAST_ENTRY = . . .
```

The assignment statement &BALANCE = 0 sets the value of
the "ampersand variable" corresponding to BALANCE to 120 (it
will stay at 120 until another such statement sets it to some different value). This value will be used as the value for the BALANCE
item in an INSERT whenever no other value is specified for that
item. Thus the clause "BALANCE = 120" can be *omitted* from all
the following INSERTs, and the value 120 will be taken by default.
Note, however, that it is possible to override the 120 for any specific record by simply including an appropriate "BALANCE = value"
clause in the relevant INSERT.

If you have difficulty remembering exactly what items are included in the record you want to insert (or if you just want to save yourself some work), then you will probably find it more convenient to use PROMPT instead of INSERT, as in example 2 below.

2. Insert a new row into the PARCELS table (same as the previous example).

```
PROMPT PARCELS
APN=>93-282-55
ROAD=>CREEK
OWNER=>I.J.KING
IMPROVED=>Y
LAST_ENTRY=>1
BALANCE=>120
```

The command PROMPT PARCELS causes NOMAD to respond with a series of prompts, one for each item in the PARCELS table. For each prompt you can then enter the value you want. When all values have been supplied, NOMAD will then automatically insert the new record into the table.

3. Construction has just started on parcel 93-282-51. Update the IMPROVED indicator accordingly. (Example 1 in the section "Introduction" in Chapter 5.)

```
TOP PARCELS

LOCATE APN = '93-282-51'

CHANGE IMPROVED = 'Y'
```

Explanation: There are three commands here. TOP PARCELS positions you in front of the first record of the PARCELS table. The LOCATE then searches through the table from that initial position, looking for the first (actually the only) record having APN equal to 93-282-51. The record found becomes the *current* record. Finally, the CHANGE updates that current record by setting the indicated item in that record (IMPROVED) to the indicated value ('Y').

This example illustrates the normal technique for updating an individual record in NOMAD (though in fact there are several ways of achieving the same effect)—namely, by locating the record concerned, thus making it "current," and then issuing a CHANGE for that record. Incidentally, it is always possible to display the current record by issuing a PRINT command. Issuing PRINT after the LOCATE—CHANGE sequence above would cause NOMAD to display the newly updated record.

Single-record deletion is very similar to single-record update, as the next example illustrates.

4. Delete John Minski from the OWNERS table. (Example 2 in "Introduction," Chapter 5.)

```
TOP OWNERS

LOCATE OWNER = 'JOHN MINSKI'
```

   DELETE OWNERS

5. Increase the balance owing on each parcel in the PARCELS table by 20 percent. (Example 3 in "Introduction," Chapter 5.)

One way of handling this problem is as follows:

```
TOP PARCELS

LOCATE BALANCE > 0
CHANGE BALANCE = BALANCE * 1.2

LOCATE BALANCE > 0
CHANGE BALANCE = BALANCE * 1.2
```

(Repeat LOCATE—CHANGE sequence until LOCATE indicates "end of table")

The foregoing sequence will work: Each time the LOCATE is executed, it moves on from the current position, looking for the next record satisfying the specified condition and making that record current in turn when it finds it. But the following sequence is preferable:

```
TOP PARCELS

CHANGE BALANCE = BALANCE * 1.2 WHERE BALANCE > 0
                                WITHIN DB
```

The WITHIN DB clause causes NOMAD to apply the specified change to all records following the current position that satisfy the WHERE condition.

DELETE . . . WITHIN DB is analogous.

Exercises:

1. Give NOMAD versions of the simple SQL queries and up-
    dates from Chapter 2. Answers are given at the end of the
    chapter.

2. Give a NOMAD version of the first example from the section
    "Multistatement Updates" in Chapter 5. (You will quickly see
    that canned procedures are still desirable with NOMAD. As
    suggested in the introduction to this chapter, the NOMAD
    facilities for creating such procedures are very powerful, but
    the details are beyond the scope of this book.)

QUERYING THE CATALOG

The special command SLIST is used to query the catalog in
NOMAD. SLIST stands for "schema list": NOMAD uses the term
schema to refer to what we have been calling the catalog. Here are
some examples of SLIST:

*   SLIST MASTERS

    This command will list the names of all tables in the database.

*   SLIST PARCELS

    This SLIST will display the complete description of the PAR-
    CELS table, more or less in the form in which it was originally
    entered (see the section "Data Definition" earlier in this chap-
    ter).

*   SLIST

    SLIST without any further specification will produce a listing
    of the entire schema, that is, a description of every table in the
    database.

SUMMARY

We have sketched some of the principal features of NOMAD very
briefly. NOMAD is an extremely powerful, self-contained database management system. By "self-contained" here we mean that
all functions of the system—data definition, data manipulation,
report writing, graphics, screen form handling, statistics, and

others—are provided within a single uniform system. It is even possible to create canned procedures without having to leave the NOMAD environment, that is, without having to make use of other languages such as COBOL, though we have not discussed this aspect of the system in any detail. NOMAD can thus make fair claim to being one of the most sophisticated systems around, at least in terms of the amount of function it provides to the user and the degree to which that function is made available through a single, well-integrated language. On the other hand, there is no denying that some of the NOMAD commands—particularly the LIST command, in its more complex manifestations—can be quite difficult to understand on occasion.

ANSWERS

For ease of comparison we give the SQL version in each case, too.

1. SQL:

   ```
   SELECT *
   FROM   CELLAR
   ```

   NOMAD:

   ```
   LIST SEGMENT CELLAR
   ```

2. SQL:

   ```
   SELECT *
   FROM   CELLAR
   WHERE  WINE = 'Chardonnay'
   ```

   NOMAD:

   ```
   LIST SEGMENT CELLAR
   WHERE WINE = 'Chardonnay'
   ```

3. SQL:

   ```
   SELECT BIN, PRODUCER, READY, BOTTLES
   FROM   CELLAR
   WHERE  WINE = 'Chardonnay'
   ```

   NOMAD:

   ```
   FROM CELLAR
   LIST BIN PRODUCER READY BOTTLES
   WHERE WINE = 'Chardonnay'
   ```

4. SQL:

```
SELECT *
FROM   FLIGHTS
WHERE  FROM_CODE =
        (SELECT CODE
         FROM   CITIES
         WHERE  CITY = 'San Francisco')
AND    TO_CODE =
        (SELECT CODE
         FROM   CITIES
         WHERE  CITY = 'Chicago')
ORDER  BY DEP_TIME
```

NOMAD:

```
FROM FLIGHTS
    DEFINE FROM_CITY AS EXTRACT'CITY FROM CITIES USING FROM_CODE'
    DEFINE TO_CITY   AS EXTRACT'CITY FROM CITIES USING TO_CODE'
    LIST FLIGHT
        FROM_CODE
        TO_CODE
        BY DEP_TIME
        ARR_TIME
    WHERE FROM_CITY = 'San Francisco'
    AND   TO_CITY   = 'Chicago'
```

5. SQL:

```
UPDATE CELLAR
SET    BOTTLES = 4
WHERE  BIN = 3
```

NOMAD:

```
TOP    CELLAR
CHANGE BOTTLES = 4 WHERE BIN = 3 WITHIN DB
```

6. SQL:

```
DELETE
FROM  CELLAR
WHERE BIN = 2
```

NOMAD:

```
TOP    CELLAR
DELETE CELLAR WHERE BIN = 2 WITHIN DB
```

7.   SQL:

```
INSERT
INTO    CELLAR
VALUES (53,'Pinot Noir','Franciscan',76,1,83,'present from Joan')
```

NOMAD:

```
INSERT CELLAR
    BIN = 53
    WINE = 'Pinot Noir'
    PRODUCER = 'Franciscan'
    YEAR = 76
    BOTTLES = 1
    READY = 83
    COMMENTS = 'present from Joan'
```

10   *dBASE II*

INTRODUCTION

The last of the systems we describe in any detail is dBASE II. Unlike the systems discussed so far, namely SQL, QBE, and NOMAD, dBASE II is already available on a wide variety of microcomputers, which is the principal reason for including it in this book. We do not, of course, mean to imply that dBASE II is the *only* system available for micros; on the contrary, there are many such systems (and what is more, at least one company has already announced a microcomputer implementation of SQL, though at the time of writing—early 1983—that system is not yet available). But dBASE II does possess a number of interesting characteristics that are not shared by all such systems. It is available from Ashton-Tate, 9929 West Jefferson Boulevard, Culver City, California. dBASE II is a trademark owned by Ashton-Tate.

Note: In what follows, we will abbreviate dBASE II to simply dBASE (as indeed the dBASE II documentation does, much of the time).

The major query statements of dBASE are summarized in Fig. 10.1, our by now familiar comparison table.

Like NOMAD, which it resembles in some ways, dBASE is a self-contained system. The dBASE language provides all the necessary facilities (including screen-handling capabilities) to allow you to create canned procedures without having to cross over into some other language such as COBOL. However, you will still re-

Figure 10.1

	SQL	QBE	NOMAD	**dBASE**
Retrieval	SELECT	P.	LIST	DISPLAY
Modification	UPDATE	U.	CHANGE	REPLACE
Deletion	DELETE	D.	DELETE	DELETE
Insertion	INSERT	I.	INSERT	APPEND

quire some programming expertise if you are going to create canned procedures of your own. Fortunately, the interactive facilities of the system will usually be adequate for what you need to do in most situations; but for interest we do include in this chapter a brief introduction to the dBASE canned procedure language, and we show an example of a procedure written in that language. You can skip that section if you have no interest in creating canned procedures of your own.

The aspects of dBASE that distinguish it from the other systems discussed earlier—apart from its availability on micros, of course—are as follows:

- **Text-editor updating**

  Data can be easily entered, deleted, and modified by direct manipulation on the screen, much as text is manipulated in a typical text-editing system. (But it is also possible to use more indirect operations as in, e.g., SQL or QBE or NOMAD.)

- **Detailed prompting**

  Automatic prompts are provided for most operations at a very fine level of detail. (This facility is similar to the PROMPT command of NOMAD, but it applies to other operations in addition to data entry.) To put it another way, we might describe dBASE as a "hyperinteractive" system.

We therefore concentrate on these two aspects of the system in what follows.

DATA DEFINITION AND LOADING

1. Create the PARCELS table. (Example 1 in "Creating the Database," Chapter 4.)

```
. CREATE PARCELS
ENTER RECORD STRUCTURE AS FOLLOWS:
FIELD   NAME,TYPE,WIDTH,DECIMAL PLACES
001     APN,C,9
002     ROAD,C,7
003     OWNER,C,20
004     IMPROVED,C,1
005     LAST_ENTRY,N,5
006     BALANCE,N,10,2
007     (enter)

INPUT NOW? Y
```

When dBASE is ready to accept a command, it displays a *prompt dot.* In the example the user then enters the command CREATE PARCELS. dBASE responds with a message indicating how the user is to define the fields of the PARCELS table, together with a 001 to identify the first field. The user then supplies the name (APN), data type (C), and width (9) for that field; dBASE responds with 002, and the process repeats, until the user indicates that the definition is complete by hitting "enter" instead of typing another field name. At this point dBASE asks whether the user now wishes to enter data into the new table, and the user answers Y (yes). Notice, incidentally, that the width for BALANCE must be specified as 10, not 9, to include room for the decimal point.

2.   Insert a row into the PARCELS table. (Example 1 in "Loading the Database," Chapter 4.)

Following the user's Y response to the question "INPUT NOW?", dBASE displays the number of the next record in the table (which is 1, since, of course, the table is initially empty), and then prompts for each field in turn:

```
RECORD 00001
APN          :93-282-55
ROAD         :CREEK
OWNER        :I.J.KING
IMPROVED     :Y
LAST_ENTRY   :1
BALANCE      :120


RECORD 00002
APN          :(enter)
```

When record 1 is filled, dBASE stores it away on the disk and starts prompting for record 2. The user indicates that loading is complete by simply hitting "enter."

QUERIES

1.   Who is the owner of parcel 93-282-55? (Example 1 in "Sample Queries," Chapter 4.)

```
. USE PARCELS
. DISPLAY OWNER FOR APN = '93-282-55'
```

Most dBASE commands are applied to the "table currently in USE." A table is established as the one in USE by means of a USE command, as in the example here. Once established, the table remains in USE until the next USE command.

Another way of handling this same query is as follows:

```
. USE PARCELS
. LOCATE FOR APN = '93-282-55'
RECORD : 00028     (say)
. DISPLAY OWNER
```

The LOCATE command searches the table in USE for the first record satisfying the condition specified in the FOR clause. That record becomes the *current* record; dBASE will automatically display its record number (28 in the example). The subsequent DISPLAY command (without a FOR clause) will then display the specified field(s) from that current record.

If no fields are explicitly nominated in the DISPLAY command, the entire record will be displayed. For example, if "OWNER" were omitted from either of the DISPLAY commands above, then dBASE would display the entire PARCELS record (fields APN, ROAD, OWNER, IMPROVED, LAST_ENTRY, and BALANCE).

It is also possible to display an entire table, for example, as follows:

```
. USE PARCELS
. DISPLAY ALL
```

2. What penalty was imposed on parcel 93-282-55 for 1981? (Example 2 in "Sample Queries," Chapter 4.)

```
. USE PARCEL_ACCOUNTS
. DISPLAY AMOUNT FOR APN = '93-282-55'
            .AND. DESCRIPTION = 'PENALTY81'
            .AND. TYPE = 'CHARGE'
```

Note that "AND" must be surrounded by two dots, as shown.

3. List all owners who live in Berkeley. (Example 3 in "Sample Queries," Chapter 4.)

```
. USE OWNERS
. DISPLAY FOR 'BERKELEY' $ ADDRESS
```

The $ sign is a *substring inclusion* operator; "string1 $ string2" is *true* if and only if string1 is a substring of (that is, is included in) string2. Thus, for example,

```
    'CAT' $ 'EDUCATED'
```

is true, whereas

```
    'DOG' $ 'EDUCATED'
```

is not.

4. How much has the Road Association paid (in total) to Road Fixers, Inc.? (Example 5 in "Sample Queries," Chapter 4.)

```
. USE GENERAL_LEDGER
. SUM AMOUNT FOR PARTY = 'ROAD FIXERS, INC.'
          .AND. TYPE = 'CHARGE'
```

The *commands* SUM and COUNT are the dBASE versions of the usual SUM and COUNT *functions.* There are no analogs of AVG, MAX, and MIN.

5. Display name, address, and phone number for the owner of parcel 93-282-55. (Example 8 in "Sample Queries," Chapter 4.)

```
. USE PARCELS
. DISPLAY OWNER FOR APN = '93-282-55'
```

(dBASE displays I. J.KING.)

```
. USE OWNERS
. DISPLAY FOR OWNER = 'I.J.KING'
```

6. List all special assessments (SAN and EXPLANATION) and, for each one, all parcels (APN) affected by that assessment. (Example 10 in "Sample Queries," Chapter 4.)

```
. SELECT SECONDARY
. USE SPECIAL_ASSESSMENTS
. SELECT PRIMARY
. USE PARCELS
. JOIN TO RESULT FIELDS SAN, EXPLANATION, APN
              FOR ROAD = S.ROAD
. USE RESULT
. DISPLAY ALL
```

In addition to the normal ("primary") USE table, dBASE allows you to work with a "secondary" USE table, as in this example. SELECT PRIMARY or SELECT SECONDARY establishes the primary or secondary table (as specified) as the *current* USE table.

References to fields in the other USE table can be made by means of "P." or "S." prefixes (standing for primary and secondary, respectively). Thus the JOIN statement above creates a new table called RESULT by joining the current USE table (PARCELS, in the primary area) to the other USE table (SPECIAL__ASSESSMENTS, in the secondary area) on the basis of matching ROAD values and then picking out the SAN, EXPLANATION, and APN fields from that join. Then we issue USE RESULT and DISPLAY ALL to display the entire RESULT table.

If we wanted to display the result of this query in APN order, we could issue the commands

```
. SORT ON APN TO RESULTX
. USE RESULTX
```

between the USE RESULT and the final DISPLAY ALL. (The SORT command creates a new table called RESULTX, containing the same records as RESULT but in APN order. The USE RESULTX then ensures that the final DISPLAY refers to this new table.)

UPDATE OPERATIONS

Like NOMAD, dBASE provides numerous different update operations with somewhat overlapping capabilities. Probably the easiest ones to use are those that operate in a kind of text-editing manner, as suggested at the beginning of the chapter. Basically, what you do is the following: First, you need to know the relative position of the record you want to update within its containing table (i.e., record 00001 or record 00002 or whatever it is). One way of discovering this information is by means of a LOCATE command (see the second solution to example 1 in the previous section); another is by means of an appropriate DISPLAY command (DISPLAY displays record numbers as well as data values). Then you can issue the EDIT command, specifying the appropriate record number. EDIT will then let you "edit" the record; that is, it will let you use control keys on the keyboard to do any of the following:

- Type over (and so replace) existing data in any field;

- Insert characters anywhere within an existing value (characters following the inserted data are moved right);

- Delete characters anywhere within an existing value (characters following the deleted data are moved left);

- Insert a new field into the record (fields following the new field are moved right);

- Delete a field from the record (fields following the deleted field are moved left);

- Delete the entire record;

- Recall or "undelete" a deleted record;

- Put the current record back in the database and step to the next or previous record.

It is a little difficult to illustrate these operations on the printed page, but they are largely common sense once you have become moderately familiar with the use of the keyboard. We show one EDIT example, then a few examples using more traditional kinds of update operation.

1. Construction has just started on parcel 93-282-51. Update the IMPROVED indicator accordingly. (Example 1 in "Introduction," Chapter 5.)

```
. USE PARCELS
. LOCATE FOR APN = '93-282-51'
RECORD : 00013  (say)
. EDIT 13
RECORD 00013
APN        :93-282-51
ROAD       :CREEK
OWNER      :ALBERT CAMPION
IMPROVED   :(change N to Y by overtyping)
LAST_ENTRY :    24
```

The foregoing example looks much more complicated on the page than it really is. What is happening is the following: First, we discover the record number for the record we are interested in (assume it is 13, for the sake of the example). We issue EDIT 13. dBASE responds by displaying all fields of record 13, with their current values. We then make the change(s) we want on the screen, and leave EDIT mode by hitting an appropriate combination of keys on the keyboard. dBASE then makes the same change in the actual database on the disk.

2. Construction has just started on parcel 93-282-51. Update the IMPROVED indicator accordingly (same as the previous example but without using EDIT mode).

```
. USE PARCELS
. REPLACE IMPROVED WITH 'Y'
                    FOR APN = '93-282-51'
```

This looks much simpler than the previous solution but may not be so in practice!

3. Insert Albert Campion into the OWNERS table. (Example 2 in "Introduction," Chapter 5.)

The command for adding new records is APPEND. Its operation is very similar to that of the "INPUT NOW?" option on CREATE:

```
. USE OWNERS
. APPEND
RECORD 00027   (suppose there are currently 26 records in OWNERS)
OWNER          :ALBERT  CAMPION
ADDRESS        :12A  BOTTLE  STREET,  PICCADILLY
PHONE          :441-867-3623


RECORD  00028
OWNER          :(leave APPEND mode by hitting an
                appropriate  key  combination)
```

4. Delete John Minski from the OWNERS table. (Example 2 in "Introduction," Chapter 5.)

```
. USE OWNERS
. DELETE FOR OWNER = 'JOHN MINSKI'
```

DELETE does not really delete the record, it merely "marks it for deletion." If you were to display the table, you would see all "deleted" records still there but marked with an asterisk. As a consequence, it is possible to "undelete" a deleted record, using the RE-CALL command:

```
. USE OWNERS
. DELETE FOR OWNER = 'JOHN MINSKI'
. RECALL
```

RECALL erases the deletion marker on the current record. It is also possible to RECALL ALL deleted records in the table in USE, or to RECALL some specific record by giving its record number. This is a very convenient method of recovering from inadvertent errors!

There is another command, PACK, which is the real delete operation. PACK physically erases all records in the table that are currently marked for deletion:

```
. USE OWNERS
. DELETE . . .
       .
       .
       .
. DELETE . . .
       .
       .
       .
. PACK
```

After PACK, deleted records can no longer be recalled.

5. Increase the balance owing on each parcel in the PARCELS table by 20 percent. (Example 3 in "Introduction," Chapter 5.)

```
. USE PARCELS
. REPLACE ALL BALANCE WITH BALANCE * 1.2
                    FOR BALANCE > 0
```

Exercise: Give dBASE versions of the simple SQL queries and updates from Chapter 2. Answers are given at the end of the chapter.

CANNED PROCEDURES

It is if you are a microcomputer user, using a system such as dBASE, that you are most likely to be faced with the problem of creating canned procedures of your own. (In other environments there is probably some expert you can call on to do the job for you, if necessary.) In this section, therefore, we give some idea as to what is involved in the creation of such a procedure in dBASE. The example we show is, of course, very simple (although not unrealistically so); you should be aware that we are ignoring numerous facilities that can be used in the construction of more sophisticated procedures. Also (as usual), we are simplifying a few details.

Example: Create a canned procedure for the Redwood payment problem (see the first example in the section "Multistatement Updates" in Chapter 5).

The procedure for this example will consist of a set of dBASE commands, stored in a disk file called (say) REDWOOD_PAYMENT.CMD (CMD for "command"). This file can be created using the normal file creation facilities of your computer system, whatever those may be; alternatively, you can use dBASE's own full-screen editor (invoked via the command MODIFY COMMAND), which is specifically intended for the creation and subsequent editing of text files such as CMD files. In our particular example the contents of the file (i.e., the dBASE commands) might be as follows; the lines have been numbered to facilitate the subsequent explanations.

```
 1 ACCEPT 'DATE OF PAYMENT' TO GIVEN_DATE
 2 INPUT 'AMOUNT PAID' TO GIVEN_AMOUNT
 3 INPUT 'SPECIAL ASSESSMENT NUMBER' TO GIVEN_SAN


 4 USE LAST_ENTRIES
 5 LOCATE FOR ACCOUNT = 'GENERAL'
 6 STORE ENTRY + 1 TO NEW_GENERAL_ENTRY
 7 STORE BALANCE - GIVEN_AMOUNT TO NEW_GENERAL_BALANCE
 8 REPLACE ENTRY WITH NEW_GENERAL_ENTRY,
 9         BALANCE WITH NEW_GENERAL_BALANCE


10 USE SPECIAL_ASSESSMENTS
11 LOCATE FOR SAN = GIVEN_SAN
12 STORE PAYEE TO PARTY_PAID


13 USE GENERAL_LEDGER
14 APPEND BLANK
15 REPLACE ENTRY WITH NEW_GENERAL_ENTRY,
16         DATE WITH GIVEN_DATE,
17         DESCRIPTION WITH 'SA' + CHR(GIVEN_SAN),
18         TYPE WITH 'CHARGE',
19         PARTY WITH PARTY_PAID,
20         AMOUNT WITH GIVEN_AMOUNT,
21         BALANCE WITH NEW_GENERAL_BALANCE
```

```
22 USE LAST_ENTRIES
23 LOCATE FOR ACCOUNT = 'REDWOOD'
24 STORE ENTRY + 1 TO NEW_REDWOOD_ENTRY
25 STORE BALANCE - GIVEN_AMOUNT TO NEW_REDWOOD_BALANCE
26 REPLACE ENTRY WITH NEW_REDWOOD_ENTRY,
27         BALANCE WITH NEW_REDWOOD_BALANCE

28 USE REDWOOD_LEDGER
29 APPEND BLANK
30 REPLACE ENTRY WITH NEW_REDWOOD_ENTRY,
31         DATE WITH GIVEN_DATE,
32         DESCRIPTION WITH 'SA' + CHR(GIVEN_SAN),
33         TYPE.WITH 'CHARGE',
34         PARTY WITH PARTY_PAID,
35         AMOUNT WITH GIVEN_AMOUNT,
36         BALANCE WITH NEW_REDWOOD_BALANCE

37 ERASE
38 @ 0,0 SAY 'DATABASE UPDATES COMPLETE'
39 RETURN
```

Using the procedure: To invoke this canned procedure, enter the dBASE command

```
. DO REDWOOD_PAYMENT
```

The procedure will then prompt for its parameters. Respond to the prompts appropriately—for example, as follows:

```
DATE OF PAYMENT:820724
AMOUNT PAID:360
SPECIAL ASSESSMENT NUMBER:4
```

The procedure will now perform its database processing. Then the screen will clear, and the message

```
DATABASE UPDATES COMPLETE
```

will appear in the top left corner.

Explanations:

Line 1: The ACCEPT command causes the specified prompt (DATE OF PAYMENT) to be displayed, followed by a colon, and waits for the user to enter a value. The required parameter is assumed to be a character string (no quotes required). When entered, the specified value will be saved in main storage under the name GIVEN_DATE. Notice that commands in a command file do not start with the dBASE prompt dot.

Lines 2–3: These lines are similar to line 1, except that INPUT is used instead of ACCEPT. INPUT allows you to enter numbers as well as character strings (character strings require quotes in this case).

Line 4: Establish LAST_ENTRIES as the table in USE.

Line 5: Find the LAST_ENTRIES record for the general ledger and make it current.

Line 6: Take a copy of the ENTRY value in that record, add 1 to it, and STORE the result (i.e., save it) in main storage under the name NEW_GENERAL_ENTRY.

Line 7: This line is similar to line 6.

Lines 8–9: Update the LAST_ENTRIES record for the general ledger appropriately.

Lines 10–12: Find the name of the party paid under the given special assessment and store it in main storage under the name PARTY_PAID.

Line 13: Establish GENERAL_LEDGER as the table in USE.

Line 14: Insert a blank (empty) record into that table.

Lines 15–21: Now update that blank record with appropriate nonblank values. Line 17 requires a little additional explanation: We need to set DESCRIPTION to the *character string* value 'SA4' (say), but GIVEN_SAN has the *numeric* (decimal) value 4. It is therefore necessary to convert 4 to 'SA4' by taking the characters 'SA' and *concatenating* to them (this is the meaning of the plus sign in this context) the result of applying the CHR built-in function to the value of GIVEN_SAN, namely 4. The effect of CHR is to take a decimal value and to yield the corresponding character string representation of that value.

Lines 22–27: These are analogous to lines 4–9, but they apply to the LAST_ENTRIES record for the Redwood ledger instead of the general ledger.

Lines 28–36: These are analogous to lines 13–21, but they apply to REDWOOD_LEDGER instead of GENERAL_LEDGER.

Line 37: Clears the screen.

Line 38: Displays the message DATABASE UPDATES COMPLETE at row 0, column 0 (i.e., top left corner) of the screen.

Line 39: Returns control to dBASE (the canned procedure is finished).

Although it is not our purpose in this book to give a full tutorial on the features of dBASE canned procedures, we sketch below some further commands that can be used in the creation of such procedures. If you have no background in programming, however, you may want to jump ahead to the following section ("Report Writing").

1. DO filename

Just as our example procedure was invoked by the user via the command "DO REDWOOD_PAYMENT," so it is possible for one canned procedure, while it is executing, to invoke another (inner) procedure via an appropriate DO command. The inner procedure will then return control to the outer procedure when it is done (via the RETURN in that inner procedure), instead of all the way back to dBASE itself. And, of course, the inner procedure in turn can invoke a lower-level procedure, and so on.

2. IF . . . ELSE . . . ENDIF

The structure of the REDWOOD_PAYMENT procedure is extremely simple, consisting as it does of nothing more than a set of commands to be executed straight through from top to bottom, each command being executed exactly once (a straight-line procedure). The IF command allows *conditional* execution of other commands, and hence the construction of procedures that are more complex than straight-line procedures. For example:

```
IF GIVEN_AMOUNT > 199
   DO SUBPROC_A
ENDIF

IF GIVEN_AMOUNT < 400 .AND. GIVEN_SAN > 6
   DO SUBPROC_B
   DO SUBPROC_C
   ERASE
   @ 0,0 SAY 'HAVE DONE B AND C'
ELSE
   DO SUBPROC_D
   ERASE
   @ 0,0 SAY 'HAVE DONE D'
ENDIF
```

Any command can be embedded within an IF . . . ELSE . . . ENDIF, including, in particular, another IF . . . ELSE . . . ENDIF.

3. DO WHILE . . . ENDDO

DO WHILE . . . ENDDO allows you to execute a set of commands repeatedly (i.e., to loop) while some specified condition remains true. When the condition becomes false, dBASE continues with the command following the ENDDO. For example:

```
INPUT 'N' TO N
STORE 0 TO X
STORE 0 TO NSUM
DO WHILE X < N + 1
   STORE X + 1 TO X
   STORE NSUM + X TO NSUM
ENDDO
@ 0,0 SAY 'NSUM =' + CHR(NSUM)
```

This set of commands will compute and display the sum of the first n natural numbers 1, 2, . . ., n (where n is a user-supplied parameter). No database access is involved at all in this example. Here is another (slightly more realistic) example that does involve such access:

```
USE PARCEL_ACCOUNTS
LOCATE FOR APN = '93-282-55'
DO WHILE .NOT. EOF
   process this PARCEL_ACCOUNTS record
   CONTINUE
ENDDO
```

This loop will process all PARCEL__ACCOUNTS records for APN 93-282-55. EOF is a built-in function that is set to "false" when a given table is established as the table in USE and is set to "true" when the end-of-file position is reached on that table. CONTINUE causes the search specified in the last LOCATE to be repeated starting from the current position, looking for the next record that satisfies the condition specified in that LOCATE.

Any command can be embedded within a DO WHILE . . . ENDDO, including, in particular, another DO WHILE . . . ENDDO.

Exercises: Write dBASE procedures (command files) for the following problems.

1. The Road Association has just (July 25, 1982) received the 1982 dues payment on parcel 93-282-55. Update the database accordingly. (Same as the second example from the section "Multistatement Updates" in Chapter 5.)

2. List all improved parcels, with owners' names, addresses, and phone numbers, in parcel number order within owner. (Same as example 11 in "Sample Queries," Chapter 4.) [*Note:* You will need to use the SORT command to do the ordering. The SORT command is described in the next section of this chapter ("Report Writing").]

3. Write a dBASE procedure to compute the sum of the squares of the first n natural numbers (not a database example).

4. List parcel number and owner for all parcels on which no 1982 dues payment has been made. (Same as example 13 in "Sample Queries," Chapter 4.)

5. Who has paid more than $500 this year (1982), and how much have they paid? Remember that one person may make payments on multiple parcels. (Same as example 16 in "Sample Queries," Chapter 4.)

REPORT WRITING

The dBASE approach to report writing differs in a number of respects from that of SQL and NOMAD. We present a single detailed example.

List all charges made in 1982, and:

*   Print the results in ascending order by entry number within parcel number.

*   Include a top title 'PARCEL ACCOUNT CHARGES 1982'.

*   Suppress printing for the TYPE and ENTRY columns.

*   Rename the APN and DESCRIPTION columns as PARCEL and CHARGE, respectively, in the report.

*   Include AMOUNT subtotals and total.

(This example is a modified version of the example from the section "Report Writing" in Chapter 6.)

The overall operation requires a number of separate steps. First, we need a table to hold the result of the basic query. Let us call that table TEMP.

```
. CREATE TEMP
ENTER RECORD STRUCTURE AS FOLLOWS:
 FIELD    NAME,TYPE,WIDTH,DECIMAL PLACES
 001      APN,C,9
 002      ENTRY,N,5
 003      DATE,C,6
 004      DESCRIPTION,C,20
 005      TYPE,C,6
 006      AMOUNT,N,8,2
 007      BALANCE,N,10,2
 008      (enter)
INPUT NOW? N
```

Next, we switch to TEMP as the table in USE:

```
. USE TEMP
```

Now we can load the desired records into TEMP by means of an APPEND FROM statement:

```
. APPEND FROM PARCEL_ACCOUNTS FOR TYPE = 'CHARGE'
                        .AND. DATE > '811231'
                        .AND. DATE < '830101'
```

Note that APPEND FROM is a multiple-record insert; it takes copies of all records from PARCEL_ACCOUNTS satisfying the specified FOR clause and places them into the table in USE.

Aside: For tutorial reasons we have shown the steps so far as a series of three separate operations (CREATE TEMP, USE TEMP, APPEND FROM PARCEL_ACCOUNTS), one of which (CREATE TEMP) is itself a collection of many suboperations. But in fact the same effect could have been achieved much more simply with the following two operations:

```
. USE PARCEL_ACCOUNTS
. COPY TO TEMP FOR TYPE = 'CHARGE'
              .AND. DATE > '811231'
              .AND. DATE < '830101'
```

The COPY command will create a new table called TEMP with the same structure as the table in USE (i.e., table PARCEL_ACCOUNTS) and will then copy the desired records into that new table. This is obviously preferable to our previous approach. However, it has nothing to do with our main topic of report writing per se. Let us get back to that topic.

At this point we have in TEMP exactly the data records we want (regardless of which approach we used to get them there). The next step is to sort those records into the desired sequence. This involves *two* SORT commands, one to sort on ENTRY values and then one to sort the result of the first SORT on APN values. The final result is in table TEMP2.

```
. SORT ON ENTRY TO TEMP1
. USE TEMP1
. SORT ON APN TO TEMP2
```

Now we indicate that we wish to produce a report from the data in TEMP2. To do so, we ask dBASE to create a *report form*, which we will call CHARGE82. dBASE will start prompting for details of that report form. After the form is complete, dBASE will automatically create the report in accordance with that form, display it, and (because of the TO PRINT clause) also produce a hard copy on the printer.

```
. USE TEMP2
. REPORT FORM CHARGE82 TO PRINT

PAGE HEADING? (Y/N) Y
ENTER PAGE HEADING: PARCEL ACCOUNT CHARGES 1982
ARE TOTALS REQUIRED? (Y/N) Y
SUBTOTALS IN REPORT? (Y/N) Y
ENTER SUBTOTALS FIELD: APN
ENTER SUBTOTAL HEADING: CHARGES FOR PARCEL
COL    WIDTH,CONTENTS
001    9,APN
ENTER HEADING: PARCEL;---------
002    3,' * '
ENTER HEADING: * ; *
003    6,DATE
ENTER HEADING: DATE;------
```

```
004    3,' * '
ENTER HEADING: * ; *
005    20,DESCRIPTION
ENTER HEADING: CHARGE;--------------------
006    3,' * '
ENTER HEADING: * ; *
007    8,AMOUNT
ENTER HEADING: AMOUNT;--------
ARE TOTALS REQUIRED? (Y/N) Y
008    3,' * '
ENTER HEADING: * ; *
009    10,BALANCE
ENTER HEADING: BALANCE;----------
ARE TOTALS REQUIRED? (Y/N) N
010    (enter)
```

Most of the foregoing is self-explanatory. The line beginning 001 specifies that APN values are to occupy nine character positions on the printed page (i.e., nine characters from the APN field in the database). The next line indicates that those APN values are to appear under a heading that looks like this:

```
PARCEL
---------
```

—that is, a heading consisting of two lines (the semicolon means "new line"), the first consisting of the word PARCEL and the second consisting of nine dashes. The first is centered above the second, as near as possible.

The next two lines (beginning 002 and ENTER . . .) indicate that a constant data value consisting of a blank, an asterisk, and another blank is to appear under a heading that looks like this:

```
b*b
b*b
```

(where b stands for a blank space). That constant value is fixed for every row of the report.

The rest of the report is specified in a similar manner. The final output is as shown in Fig. 10.2 (except that we have had to reduce the width of the CHARGE column for reasons of space).

As stated earlier, the effect of the REPORT command is not only to produce the report as shown, but also to save the report form (CHARGE82) on the disk somewhere. Subsequently, we can

Figure 10.2

```
PAGE NO. 00001
DATE 10/12/83
                         PARCEL ACCOUNT CHARGES 1982


        PARCEL  *  DATE  *   CHARGE    *  AMOUNT  *  BALANCE
                *        *              *          *
     ─────────── * ───── * ──────────── * ──────── * ─────────
     * CHARGES FOR PARCEL 93-281-24
     93-281-24 * 820107 * DUES82      *  120.00 *    120.00
     93-281-24 * 820107 * SA7         *  240.00 *    360.00
     93-281-24 * 820809 * SA8         *  115.00 *    115.00
     93-281-24 * 821105 * SA10        *   72.00 *    187.00
     93-281-24 * 821231 * PENALTY82   *   37.40 *    224.40
     ** SUBTOTAL **

                                          584.40

     * CHARGES FOR PARCEL 93-282-54
     93-282-54 * 820107 * DUES82      *   60.00 *    380.00
     93-282-54 * 820107 * SA7         *  240.00 *    610.00
     93-282-54 * 821231 * PENALTY82   *  122.00 *    732.00
     ** SUBTOTAL **

                                          422.00

     * CHARGES FOR PARCEL 93-282-55
     93-282-55 * 820107 * DUES82      *  120.00 *    120.00
     93-282-55 * 820107 * SA7         *  240.00 *    360.00
     ** SUBTOTAL **

                                          360.00

     * CHARGES FOR PARCEL 93-291-19
     93-291-19 * 820107 * DUES82      *   50.00 *    190.00
     93-291-19 * 820107 * SA7         *  240.00 *    430.00
     93-291-19 * 820809 * SA8         *  115.00 *    545.00
     93-291-19 * 821105 * SA10        *   72.00 *    617.00
     93-291-19 * 821123 * SA3         *   42.50 *    659.50
     93-291-19 * 821231 * PENALTY82   *  131.90 *    791.40
     ** SUBTOTAL **

                                          651.40

     * CHARGES FOR PARCEL 93-291-44
     93-291-44 * 820107 * DUES82      *  120.00 *    120.00
     ** SUBTOTAL **

                                          120.00

     * CHARGES FOR PARCEL 93-293-02
     93-293-02 * 820107 * DUES82      *   60.00 *     60.00
     93-293-02 * 821105 * SA10        *   72.00 *     72.00
     ** SUBTOTAL **

                                          132.00

     ** TOTAL **

                                         2269.80
```

use that stored form to generate new reports from the table in USE at any time by simply referring to the form by name:

```
. USE . . .
        .
        .
        .
. REPORT FORM CHARGE82 TO PRINT
```

(Of course, for this REPORT to make any sense, the table in USE must have the same kind of structure as TEMP2. That is, it must consist of fields APN, ENTRY, DATE, DESCRIPTION, TYPE, AMOUNT, and BALANCE, and the records must be in order by ENTRY within APN.)

It is also possible to produce *selective* reports using a stored form. For example:

```
. REPORT FORM CHARGE82 FOR APN = '93-282-55'
```

which will produce just that portion of the foregoing report that applies to parcel 93-282-55 (assuming that the table in USE is TEMP2, where TEMP2 is as defined earlier).

QUERYING THE CATALOG

Two forms of the DISPLAY command are provided in dBASE for querying the catalog. We give one example of each.

```
. DISPLAY FILES
```

This command will list the names, number of records, and date of last update for every table known to dBASE.

```
. USE PARCELS
. DISPLAY STRUCTURE
```

This DISPLAY will give a complete description of the PARCELS table, in the following format:

```
STRUCTURE FOR FILE: PARCELS
NUMBER OF RECORDS:  31    (say)
DATE OF LAST UPDATE: 07/24/82
FLD     NAME      TYPE    WIDTH    DEC
001     APN        C      009
002     ROAD       C      007
003     OWNER      C      020
004     IMPROVED   C      001
005     LAST_ENTRY N      005
006     BALANCE    N      010      002
..  TOTAL                 00053
```

The total in the last line is the number of bytes required for each record of the PARCELS table. (A byte is the amount of storage needed to hold one character. The same term is used in almost all systems, not just in dBASE.) The total includes one byte that is used by dBASE itself for control information (i.e., not for a user data value).

SUMMARY

This brings us to the end of our discussion of dBASE and to the end of our detailed system descriptions. By now you should have gained (a) a general understanding of the kind of function provided by a typical modern database management system and (b) an appreciation of the fact that each system has its own distinct style and way of doing things. To summarize, the major DBMS functions (from the user's perspective) are as follows:

- Table creation
- Retrieval
- Insertion
- Deletion
- Update
- Creation of canned procedures
- Report writing
- Catalog access

In the next few chapters we will take a look at some additional aspects of a typical DBMS—aspects that generally do not (or at least should not) have any direct effect on the user as such, but nevertheless are very definitely part of the overall database system.

ANSWERS

For ease of comparison we give the SQL version in each case, too.

1. SQL:
    ```
    SELECT *
    FROM   CELLAR
    ```
    dBASE:
    ```
    . USE CELLAR
    . DISPLAY ALL
    ```

2.   SQL:

```
SELECT *
FROM    CELLAR
WHERE   WINE = 'Chardonnay'
```

dBASE:

```
. USE CELLAR
. DISPLAY FOR WINE = 'Chardonnay'
```

3.   SQL:

```
SELECT BIN, PRODUCER, READY, BOTTLES
FROM    CELLAR
WHERE   WINE = 'Chardonnay'
```

dBASE:

```
. USE CELLAR
. DISPLAY BIN, PRODUCER, READY, BOTTLES
          FOR WINE = 'Chardonnay'
```

4.   SQL:

```
SELECT *
FROM    FLIGHTS
WHERE   FROM_CODE =
        (SELECT CODE
         FROM    CITIES
         WHERE   CITY = 'San Francisco')
AND     TO_CODE =
        (SELECT CODE
         FROM    CITIES
         WHERE   CITY = 'Chicago')
```

dBASE:

```
. USE CITIES
. DISPLAY CODE FOR CITY = 'San Francisco'
```

(dBASE displays SFO)

```
. DISPLAY CODE FOR CITY = 'Chicago'
```

(dBASE displays ORD)

```
. USE FLIGHTS
. DISPLAY FOR FROM_CODE = 'SFO'
          .AND.  TO_CODE = 'ORD'
```

5. SQL:

```
UPDATE CELLAR
SET    BOTTLES = 4
WHERE  BIN = 3
```

dBASE:

```
. USE CELLAR
. REPLACE BOTTLES WITH 4 FOR BIN = 3
```

6. SQL:

```
DELETE
FROM    CELLAR
WHERE   BIN = 2
```

dBASE:

```
. USE CELLAR
. DELETE FOR BIN = 2
. PACK
```

7. SQL:

```
INSERT
INTO    CELLAR
VALUES (53,'Pinot Noir','Franciscan',76,1,83,'present from Joan')
```

dBASE:

```
. USE CELLAR
. APPEND
RECORD 00019    (say)
BIN         :53
WINE        :Pinot Noir
PRODUCER    :Franciscan
YEAR        :76
BOTTLES     :1
READY       :83
COMMENTS    :present from Joan
```

PART II

Database Design and Control

11   *Introduction to Part II*

In the first part of this book we concentrated on the primary purpose of a database system—that is, we addressed the question of how you actually go about storing and accessing data in such a system. As promised in Chapter 1, we now turn to a variety of further topics, topics that are less directly relevant to the functions of simple data access and maintenance, but are nonetheless important when it comes to the overall operation of the system. The topics in question can conveniently be collected together under the general heading of *database design and control.* The major topics we consider are as follows:

- Indexing

- Views

- Security

- Integrity

- Locking

- Database design

The last of these topics is rather different in kind from the rest, since it affects what the user does rather than the way the system behaves. The other topics all require specific system support. The remarks that follow apply more specifically to those other topics.

In principle, most of the topics in the list—actually all except locking—could apply to both shared and nonshared systems. In practice, however, only shared systems, and large ones at that, support everything in the list; nonshared systems typically provide only indexing support and a limited amount of integrity support. Partly this is because, while the other concepts *could* be significant in a nonshared system, they are much more so in a sharing environment; partly also it is because system support for these facilities requires a lot of machine resources, which implies in turn that the system is probably large and the database therefore probably shared. Once again, however, this situation is likely to change with time.

Despite the foregoing, it is still worth trying to acquire a broad understanding of these ideas, even if your system is of the single-user variety, just as it is a good idea to have some general awareness of how the computer works even though you do not really need that knowledge just to use the system. Although your current system may be single-user, you may find yourself using a shared system someday, or your present system may be upgraded to provide support for some of the foregoing concepts, or your single-user system may be enhanced to include some of those additional functions.

What, then, are the major differences between a shared and a nonshared system from the point of view of the user? Here are some of them. In a shared system:

1.   You may be limited to *read-only access* (in SQL terms, you may be allowed to use SELECT statements but no update statements and no data definition statements). Someone else, the *database administrator* (DBA), will probably have done the database design, created all the tables and loaded them, and taken responsibility for all maintenance operations. This division of responsibility is quite common in large organizations. The general idea is that many people may need to take information out of the system, but precisely because of that first point (i.e., precisely because the data is important to so many people), only a few appropriately skilled users are allowed to put information in.

2.   Your keyboard and screen will probably no longer be "tightly coupled" to the computer itself but will be one of many remote terminals, connected to the computer via some kind of communications channel such as a telephone line. Alternatively, you may be able to hook your entire (micro)computer via such a communications link into some public system such as The Dow Jones News/Retrieval Service. (The Dow Jones News/Retrieval Service is a publicly available system that provides a variety of financial information. "The Dow Jones News/Retrieval Service" is a registered trademark of Dow Jones and Company, Inc.) Your machine will then serve as an "intelligent terminal"—that is, a terminal that includes its own computation facilities—and will provide read-only access to that public system.

3.   You must be prepared for a variety of additional possible exception messages from the system, because the system is applying the additional controls that are the subject of the next few chapters.

For example, you may get a message indicating that you are attempting to access data you are not authorized to see; or (if you are allowed to issue maintenance operations) you may be told that your attempted update failed because it was attempting to introduce some obviously incorrect data into the database (such as a PARCEL_ACCOUNTS record for a nonexistent parcel).

By and large, however, as stated in Chapter 3, the fact that the database is shared should be "transparent" to the user and can usually be ignored.

STRUCTURE

The structure of Part II is as follows: In Chapter 12 we introduce the idea of *indexes*. Unlike most of the topics in this part of the book, indexes are very definitely relevant to nonshared as well as shared databases even today, so you should make sure you understand this concept (not that it is at all difficult).

Chapter 13 is concerned with *views*. Views provide a means for enabling an individual user to see the database the way he or she wants to see it rather than the way it may really be. In particular, views allow you to screen out pieces of the database that for some reason you have no interest in.

Chapter 14 covers *authorization* and *security*. In a shared environment it is obviously likely that not every user needs to see, or should be allowed to see, every piece of data in the database. A shared database will typically include information of varying levels of sensitivity, and different users will be authorized to see just those portions of the database that they need to do their own particular job. In a manufacturing organization, for example, the database might include product-planning information relating to future products, and such information would typically be restricted to users in the product-planning and product development departments. Thus some kind of "authorization mechanism" (part of the DBMS) is clearly needed in such an environment to control who is able to get access to what. Equally clearly, however, such a mechanism has no place in a single-user system, where all the data is the property of that single user. (But we do not mean to imply that the concept of security is totally irrelevant in a single-user environment; see Chapter 14.)

Chapter 15 discusses the problem of *integrity*—that is, the problem of ensuring that the data in the database is correct. In theory, the idea of controlling the integrity of the database (like the concept of indexing) is just as relevant to a nonshared system as it is to a shared one. In practice, however, few systems today, and those typically of the shared variety, actually provide much support in this area at all. But this situation is likely to change rapidly.

Chapter 16 discusses *locking*. Locking is used in a multiple-user system to ensure that the operations of one user do not interfere with those of another. (It has nothing to do with *security*, incidentally, despite the name.) For example, locking can be used to make sure that two users do not change the same record at the same time.

Finally, Chapters 17 and 18 discuss the question of *database design* and present a design procedure that is suitable for "large" databases.

The book concludes with an Afterword, which discusses some possible future directions for the database field, and two appendixes: one on the relational model and one giving some guidelines on further reading.

12 *Indexes*

INTRODUCTION

A good way to introduce the topic of indexing is by analogy. Suppose you need to look up some information in a book. Suppose, for example, you want to find every entry in this book concerning data independence. Then there are two things you can do:

1. You can search the entire book page by page, from beginning to end, looking for every occurrence of the term "data independence"—a *sequential scan* operation; or

2. You can look up "data independence" in the index and hence go directly to the page(s) you want—an *index lookup* operation.

Of course, some books do not have an index, in which case you are stuck with sequential scanning as your only real option.

Now, looking something up in the database is rather like looking something up in a book. If you ask for some particular data from some particular table (using, for example, a SQL SELECT statement), then the system has basically the same two options: It can do a sequential scan or it can do an index lookup—assuming, in the second case, that the table in question does in fact have an index (not all tables do, just as not all books do). And an index lookup will usually be faster than a sequential scan, unless the table is very small, say less than a hundred records or so.

So what exactly is an index, in the database context? The foregoing analogy gives the general idea, but like most analogies it can become misleading if pushed too far. Let us look at a concrete example. Figure 12.1 represents an index, called XAPN, on the APN field of the PARCEL__ACCOUNTS table. (See the Road Association database from Part I. For simplicity we show only part of the table, and therefore only part of the index, in this figure.)

Explanation: First you should know that the total storage space on a disk is divided up into units called *blocks* or (by analogy with a book) *pages.* We will generally stay with the term "page."

Figure 12.1

		PARCEL_ACCOUNTS table:				
		APN	ENTRY	DATE	...	BALANCE

XAPN index:

APN	page
.	.
.	.
.	.
93-281-24	213
93-282-54	213
93-282-54	214
93-282-55	214
93-282-55	215
93-291-19	215
93-291-44	215
.	.
.	.
.	.
93-292-60	277
93-293-02	277
93-293-02	278
.	.
.	.
.	.

PARCEL_ACCOUNTS table detail:

page	APN	ENTRY	DATE		BALANCE
	.	.	.		.
	.	.	.		.
	.	.	.		.
page 213	93-281-24	31	820107	...	120.00
	93-281-24	32	820107	...	360.00
	93-281-24	37	821231	...	224.40
	93-282-54	16	820107	...	380.00
page 214	93-282-54	17	820107	...	610.00
	93-282-54	18	821231	...	732.00
	93-282-55	40	820107	...	120.00
	93-282-55	41	820107	...	360.00
page 215	93-282-55	42	820203	...	240.00
	93-282-55	43	820203	...	0.00
	93-291-19	7	820107	...	190.00
	93-291-44	22	820107	...	120.00
	.	.	.		.
	.	.	.		.
	.	.	.		.
page 277	93-292-60	23	821124	...	60.00
	93-292-60	24	821212	...	0.00
	93-293-02	4	820107	...	60.00
	93-293-02	5	820309	...	0.00
page 278	93-293-02	6	821105	...	72.00
	93-293-02	7	821119	...	0.00
	.	.	.		.
	.	.	.		.
	.	.	.		.

Each page has its own *page number,* unique with respect to all the pages on the disk, and each page typically contains several database records (a page is typically 1000 or 2000 bytes in size; remember that a byte is the amount of storage needed to hold a single character of data). To read any given record into main storage, the system actually has to read the entire page containing that record and then has to search through that page in main storage to find the given record. (The page is "the unit of I/O"—i.e., it is the amount of data transferred between disk and main storage in a single input/output operation. See Chapter 3.)

Now you should be in a position to understand Fig. 12.1. We have assumed in that figure that each page contains four records and that the PARCEL__ACCOUNTS table is stored on the disk on pages 213, 214, 215, . . ., 277, 278, ... *The index (XAPN) is also a table* and is also stored on the disk; its function is to indicate, for each value of the *indexed field* (namely, the APN field in the PAR-CEL__ACCOUNTS table), which pages records having that particular value of that field happen to be stored on. An index record such as

```
( 93-282-55, 214 )
```

(for example) says that at least one PARCEL__ACCOUNTS record having an APN value of 93-282-55 can be found on page 214. Hence to find all PARCEL__ACCOUNTS records for APN 93-282-55, the DBMS can do a sequential scan of the *index*, find all index records for that APN, and then go directly to the required PARCEL__ACCOUNTS records (or, rather, to the pages containing those records) without having to scan the whole data table. If the index is much smaller than the indexed table, which it normally will be, then this index lookup procedure will be much faster than a sequential scan of the data table. (Specifically, it will be faster because it involves fewer I/O operations.)

One further point about the example: Page numbers in an index are often referred to as *pointers*, since they "point" to the corresponding data records (or, more accurately, to the pages containing those data records). We often therefore draw indexes in a slightly more symbolic style, as shown in Fig. 12.2.

DIRECT ACCESS VERSUS SEQUENTIAL ACCESS

Indexes actually provide two methods of access to the indexed data, *direct access* and *sequential access*:

1. *Direct access* refers to the ability to locate data records having a specific value for the indexed field "directly" (i.e., without having to scan the entire data table), as in our introductory example.

Figure 12.2

PARCEL__ACCOUNTS table:

APN	ENTRY	DATE	...	BALANCE
.	.	.		.
.	.	.		.
.	.	.		.
93-281-24	31	820107	...	120.00
93-281-24	32	820107	...	360.00
93-281-24	37	821231	...	224.40
93-282-54	16	820107	...	380.00
93-282-54	17	820107	...	610.00
93-282-54	18	821231	...	732.00
93-282-55	40	820107	...	120.00
93-282-55	41	820107	...	360.00
93-282-55	42	820203	...	240.00
93-282-55	43	820203	...	0.00
93-291-19	7	820107	...	190.00
93-291-44	22	820107	...	120.00
.	.	.		.
.	.	.		.
.	.	.		.
93-292-60	23	821124	...	60.00
93-292-60	24	821212	...	0.00
93-293-02	4	820107	...	60.00
93-293-02	5	820309	...	0.00
93-293-02	6	821105	...	72.00
93-293-02	7	821119	...	0.00
.	.	.		.
.	.	.		.

XAPN index:

APN	pointer
.	.
.	.
.	.
93-281-24	•
93-282-54	•
93-282-54	•
93-282-55	•
93-282-55	•
93-291-19	•
93-291-44	•
.	.
.	.
.	.
93-292-60	•
93-293-02	•
93-293-02	•
.	.
.	.
.	.

2. *Sequential access* refers to the ability to access all of the records in the data table in the sequence defined by the index—that is, the sequence defined by values of the indexed field—rather than in the sequence in which the data records are actually stored on the disk (which is called "physical sequence"). For example, index XAPN allows the system to access the PARCEL__ACCOUNTS table in APN order, *even if the table is not physically stored in that order.*

Figure 12.3

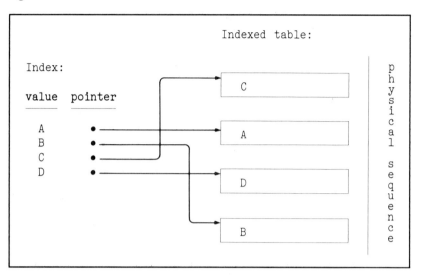

To illustrate this latter point, let us take a simpler example (see Fig. 12.3). Here the system can retrieve data records A, B, C, and D, *in that order*, despite the fact that they are not physically stored in that order, by going through the index records in sequence and following the pointer from each index record in turn to the corresponding data record. Note that "sequence" in this sentence refers to the physical sequence in which the *index* records are stored. Note, too, that there may even be records of other tables stored interspersed among records C, A, D, and B on the disk. Thus the records of a given table may be physically scattered all over the disk, even though logically they are all grouped together. This distinction between physical and logical structure is another aspect of *data independence* (see the discussion of this topic in Chapter 3).

Going back to our first example (Fig. 12.1), index XAPN will allow the system to use *direct access* in responding to a query such as

```
SELECT  . . .
FROM    PARCEL_ACCOUNTS
WHERE   APN = '93-282-55'
```

(the system can look up the required records directly, without having to do a sequential scan of the PARCEL__ACCOUNTS table).

Similarly, the APN index will allow the system to use *sequential access* in responding to a query such as

```
SELECT . . .
FROM    PARCEL_ACCOUNTS
WHERE   . . .
ORDER   BY APN
```

Note carefully, however, that neither of these queries actually mentions the index explicitly. When you issue queries such as these, it is the *system's* responsibility to look around and see whether there is a suitable index that can be of help. If there is, then the system will use it; otherwise, it will have to do a sequential scan of the data. But either way, it *will* respond to the query; the only difference you may see in the two cases is one of "response time" (it may take longer to get the result if there is no index). The point is, there does not *have* to be an index for the query to work. This is yet another aspect of data independence (again, see Chapter 3): The presence or absence of indexes is a system concern, not a user concern, generally speaking.

To put this another way, indexes may be thought of as system tables, just as the tables in the catalog are system tables; but they are system tables that should be "transparent" to the user (unlike the catalog tables, which are very definitely something that the user should be aware of and should be able to get access to, as explained in Chapter 7).

FURTHER CONSIDERATIONS

There are a number of additional considerations concerning the use of indexes. We sketch these additional points briefly in this section.

1. Multiple indexes per table

A given table can have *any number* of indexes, including, of course, zero. (This is where the analogy with a book breaks down.) For example, consider the CELLAR table from Chapter 2. It would be quite possible to have (say) one index on the WINE field, in which the entries are for Chardonnay, Pinot Noir, and so on, and another on the PRODUCER field, in which the entries are for Buena Vista, Mirassou, and so forth (though in fact the CELLAR table is not really big enough to need any indexes at all). The first of these indexes would help with queries such as

```
SELECT . . .
FROM   CELLAR
WHERE  WINE = 'Chardonnay'
```

and the second with queries such as

```
SELECT . . .
FROM   CELLAR
WHERE  PRODUCER = 'Mirassou'
```

2. Multiple-field indexes

All the indexes we have discussed so far have been on a single field. It is also possible to construct an index over a *combination* of multiple fields. Such an index would include entries for every combination of values occurring in the relevant fields in the indexed table. It is as if those multiple fields were strung together to form a single, wider field, so far as the index is concerned. For example, consider the flight information database from Chapter 2. An index over the combination (FROM_CODE,TO_CODE) from the FLIGHTS table could have helped with the query

```
SELECT *
FROM   FLIGHTS
WEHRE  FROM_CODE = 'SFO'
AND    TO_CODE = 'ORD'
```

("Find all flights from San Francisco to Chicago.")

3. Multilevel indexes

The main purpose of an index, as already indicated, is to speed up access to the indexed table, by reducing the need for physical sequential scan operations on that table. Note, however, that physical sequential scans are still required for the *index*. If the indexed table is very large, then the index also can get to be quite sizable, and sequentially scanning the index can therefore itself get to be quite time-consuming. The solution to this problem is the same as before—namely, we treat the index as if it were a data table and build an index to it (an index to the index). Now we have a *two-level index*. Figure 12.4 shows an example of such an index. Access to a given data record (say data record P) via that index involves the following sequence of steps:

Figure 12.4

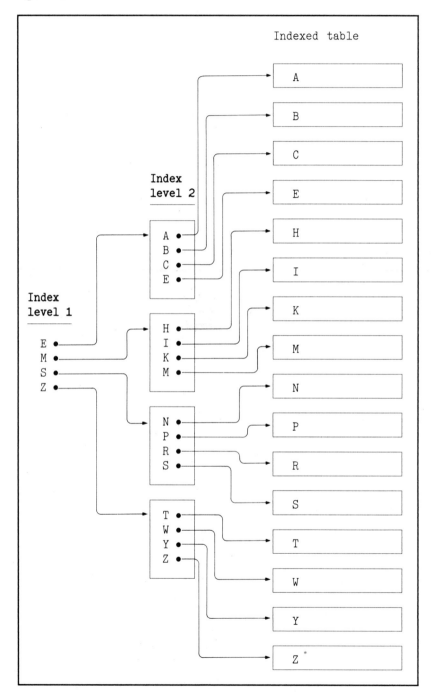

(a) Read pages sequentially from the first level of the index and scan them (in main storage) until the entry is found that points to the appropriate page of entries at the second level. For data record P this is the S entry (because P is greater than M and less than S).

(b) Next, follow the pointer from that entry to that page of second-level entries and read it. Scan that page (in main storage) for the specific second-level entry required (namely, the entry for P in our example).

(c) Finally, follow the pointer from that specific second-level entry to the page containing the required data record and read it. Scan that page (in main storage) for the required data record.

In some situations it might be necessary to expand the index to three levels, or even more. However, in all cases it is the system that decides how many levels are needed; no matter how many levels are involved, the entire index is transparent to the user, who can always think in terms of the data table alone.

4. Index maintenance

Indexes are not static. If an indexed table is updated, any indexes on that table may need to be updated too in order to remain "in synch" with the table. For example, suppose a new record is inserted into the PARCEL_ACCOUNTS table for parcel 93-282-55, and suppose that record is stored on page 273. Then a new index record

(93-282-55, 273)

will also have to be inserted into index XAPN. Once again, however, this problem is a system problem, not a user problem; the system will *automatically* apply any necessary maintenance operations to the index in order to keep it "in synch" with the indexed table. But users should be aware that their update operations may trigger this additional activity on the part of the system; a comparatively innocuous-seeming update may actually be causing a large number of operations to occur under the covers and thus may take a significant time to complete. This fact is also an argument against having too many indexes, for the more indexes there are, the longer updates will take, in general.

SYSTEM EXAMPLES   All of the systems discussed in the first part of this book (SQL, QBE, NOMAD, and dBASE) support indexes in one form or another. In SQL, for example, an index can be created at any time by means of a statement such as

```
CREATE INDEX XAPN ON PARCEL_ACCOUNTS (APN)
```

(Note the similarity to the SQL "CREATE TABLE" statement.) Once created, the index will be used by the system (when appropriate) and maintained by the system (when necessary), without further involvement on the part of the user at all.

It is also possible to get rid of an unwanted index:

```
DROP INDEX XAPN
```

An index may become "unwanted" if, for example, it is causing unacceptable delays in the processing of update operations.

Note: In a shared system it is likely that index creation (and destruction) will be the responsibility of the database administrator, not of ordinary users (just as table creation and destruction in such an environment will probably also be handled by the DBA, and for similar reasons). The system's authorization mechanism may even be used to *prevent* ordinary users from performing such operations.

The dBASE facilities are somewhat similar to those of SQL, though less sophisticated. The statement

```
. INDEX ON APN TO XAPN
```

will build an index on the table in USE (presumably PARCEL_ACCOUNTS) and store that index as a system table called XAPN. Subsequently, the user can issue the command

```
. USE PARCEL_ACCOUNTS INDEX XAPN
```

(say) which will mean that subsequent LOCATE statements (etc.) will operate in terms of the sequence defined by XAPN. A special FIND statement is available for searching for a particular record according to that sequence. Update operations will update the XAPN index appropriately, too (by virtue of the INDEX clause on the USE statement). However, any other indexes on PARCEL_ACCOUNTS will *not* automatically be updated; to get such updates applied, the user will have to drop those indexes and rebuild them.

The facilities of NOMAD and QBE are a little different in style, though not fundamentally different in function. In both cases indexing is specified as part of the definition of the table to be indexed: in NOMAD, as part of the MASTER definition; in QBE, via a special row (analogous to the TYPE row, see the section "Data Definition" in Chapter 8) in the table that defines the table in question. To create an index at some later time, after the database has already been in use for a while, it is necessary to *alter* the original table definition. Details of the alteration process are beyond the scope of this book.

SUMMARY

We have discussed indexing, a technique for improving the system's response time for certain queries. The most important features of indexes from the user's point of view are as follows: (a) They are "transparent"; (b) they may improve retrieval time but they may also increase update time; (c) they will of course take up space on the disk, and that space might possibly be better used for some other purpose.

In conclusion, we should mention the fact that indexes are only one of numerous techniques that can be used for improving system performance. We discuss them because they are by far the most commonly used technique in practice and because they are quite adequate in many situations. (Every system known to this writer provides indexing as a performance enhancement technique, and several provide no others.) However, the more complex systems do provide a range of other techniques in addition to indexing, and in some applications these other techniques may provide better performance than indexing. But it is generally true that indexing represents the best overall approach to the performance problem, and it is certain that it will remain an important technique for the foreseeable future.

13 Views

In the previous chapter we introduced indexes, which are tables that actually exist in the database but are not directly visible to the user. In this chapter we investigate *views*, which are tables that do not actually exist in the database but *are* visible to the user! A view is a *virtual* table. In other words, it is a table that is derived in some way from one or more "real" tables, that is, tables that are physically stored in the database. (There is an analogy here with the virtual items or virtual fields discussed in Chapter 9.) For example, consider PARCEL_ACCOUNTS once again (which is a real table). Suppose we are interested only in PARCEL_ACCOUNTS records for parcel 93-293-02 for the year 1982; that is, we wish to issue a series of operations, both retrievals and updates, against that portion of the table for which the APN value is 93-293-02 and the date is between 811231 and 830101 (exclusive). One thing we could do, of course, is to specify an appropriate set of conditions in every single one of those operations:

```
SELECT   . . .
FROM     PARCEL_ACCOUNTS
WHERE    . . .
AND      APN = '93-293-02'
AND      DATE > '811231'
AND      DATE < '830101'

UPDATE PARCEL_ACCOUNTS
SET      . . .
WHERE    . . .
AND      APN = '93-293-02'
AND      DATE > '811231'
AND      DATE < '830101'

DELETE
FROM     PARCEL_ACCOUNTS
WHERE    . . .
AND      APN = '93-293-02'
AND      DATE > '811231'
AND      DATE < '830101'
```

and so on. (Once again we use SQL as the basis for our initial examples.)

Alternatively, we can create a *view* of the PARCEL_ACCOUNTS table in which just those records we want are visible:

```
CREATE VIEW WANTED_RECS
    AS SELECT *
        FROM    PARCEL_ACCOUNTS
        WHERE   APN = '93-293-02'
        AND     DATE > '811231'
        AND     DATE < '830101'
```

When you create a view, the SELECT in that CREATE VIEW is *not* executed. Instead, it is simply stored away in the catalog and remembered by the system. But now you can use the view name (WANTED_RECS in the example) *just as if it were the name of a real table;* you can issue SELECTs, UPDATEs, INSERTs, and so on, just as if there really were a table with that name containing the data you are interested in. The system will accept those operations and will convert them into *equivalent* operations on the real table (PARCEL_ACCOUNTS in the example) that underlies that view. For example, the operation

```
SELECT *
FROM    WANTED_RECS
WHERE   TYPE = 'CREDIT'
ORDER   BY DATE
```

will be converted by the system into the operation

```
SELECT *
FROM    PARCEL_ACCOUNTS
WHERE   TYPE = 'CREDIT'
AND     APN = '93-293-02'
AND     DATE > '811231'
AND     DATE < '830101'
ORDER   BY DATE
```

The conversion is done, in effect, by *merging* the SELECT issued by the user with the SELECT that was saved in the catalog. From the catalog, the system knows that FROM WANTED_RECS really means FROM PARCEL_ACCOUNTS; it also knows that any selection FROM PARCEL_ACCOUNTS must be further qualified by the WHERE condition APN = '93-293-02' AND DATE > '811231' AND DATE < '830101'. Hence it is able to convert the original SELECT on the *virtual* table WANTED_RECS into an equivalent SELECT on the *real* table PARCEL_ACCOUNTS—equivalent in the sense that the effect of executing that SELECT on the real table PARCEL_ACCOUNTS is as if there really were a real table called WANTED_RECS and you had executed the original SELECT on that. In other words, the view WANTED_RECS acts as a kind of "window" into the PARCEL_ACCOUNTS table, through which you can see only those PARCEL_ACCOUNTS records that satisfy the conditions specified in the definition of that "window." See Fig. 13.1.

Figure 13.1

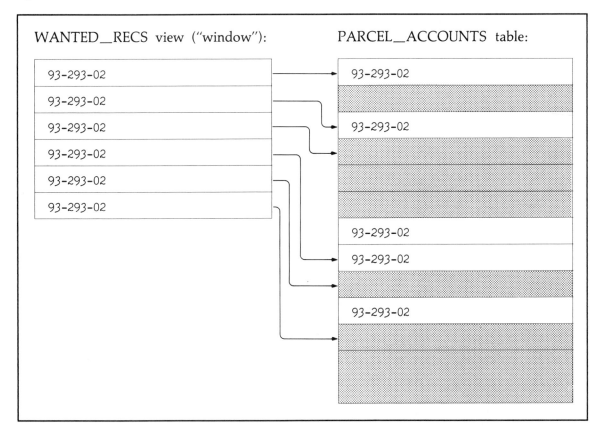

Update operations are treated in a similar manner. For example, the operation

```
UPDATE  WANTED_RECS
SET     TYPE = 'CHARGE'
WHERE   DESCRIPTION = 'DUES82'
```

will be converted by the system into

```
UPDATE  PARCEL_ACCOUNTS
SET     TYPE = 'CHARGE'
WHERE   DESCRIPTION = 'DUES82'
AND     APN = '93-293-02'
AND     DATE > '811231'
AND     DATE < '830101'
```

Again, the effect of executing the second of these UPDATEs on the real table PARCEL__ACCOUNTS is as if there really were a real table called WANTED__RECS and you had executed the first of these UPDATEs on that.

Exercise: Show the converted forms for the statements

```
DELETE
FROM    WANTED_RECS
WHERE   TYPE = 'CHARGE'
```

and

```
INSERT INTO WANTED_RECS
       ( APN, ENTRY, DATE, DESCRIPTION, TYPE, AMOUNT, BALANCE )
VALUES ('93-282-55', 47, '820101', 'DUES82', 'CHARGE', 120, 120 )
```

FURTHER EXAMPLES   Anything you can SELECT in a retrieval operation you can alternatively define as a view, if you want to. Thus a view is not restricted to being just a simple subset of the rows of the real table, as in the case of WANTED__RECS above; it can also consist of a subset of the *columns* of the real table (see examples 1 and 2 below), or it can involve virtual fields (examples 3 and 4), or it can be a *join* of two or more real tables (example 5), and so on.

1.   **Column subset**

```
CREATE VIEW ASSESSMENTS
    AS SELECT SAN, ROAD, TOTAL, PAYEE
       FROM   SPECIAL_ASSESSMENTS
```

This view picks out just the SAN, ROAD, TOTAL, and PAYEE columns from the real table SPECIAL_ASSESSMENTS, thus omitting the DATE, PER_PARCEL, and EXPLANATION columns.

2. Row-and-column subset

```
CREATE VIEW IMPROVED_PARCELS
    AS SELECT APN, ROAD, OWNER
        FROM   PARCELS
        WHERE  IMPROVED = 'Y'
```

Through this "window" the user can see the APN, ROAD, and OWNER fields (only) of those PARCELS records for which the IMPROVED value is 'Y' (only).

3. Virtual field

```
CREATE VIEW CHARGES (APN, DATE, OLDBAL, NEWBAL)
    AS SELECT APN, DATE, BALANCE - AMOUNT, BALANCE
        FROM   PARCEL_ACCOUNTS
        WHERE  TYPE = 'CHARGE'
```

Field NEWBAL in this view corresponds to field BALANCE in the underlying table; field OLDBAL is *virtual* and represents the difference between the BALANCE and AMOUNT fields in the underlying table. Notice that we have to specify field names for the view in this example, since in the case of OLDBAL, at least, there is no obvious name that it can inherit from the underlying table.

4. Virtual field, involving a built-in function

```
CREATE VIEW TOTAL_PAYMENTS (APN, TOTAL)
    AS SELECT APN, SUM (AMOUNT)
        FROM   PARCEL_ACCOUNTS
        WHERE  TYPE = 'CREDIT'
        GROUP  BY APN
```

TOTAL is a virtual field.

5. Join

```
CREATE VIEW ASSESSED_PARCELS
    AS SELECT SAN, EXPLANATION, APN
        FROM   SPECIAL_ASSESSMENTS, PARCELS
        WHERE  SPECIAL_ASSESSMENTS.ROAD = PARCELS.ROAD
```

This join is the same as that illustrated in Chapter 4, section "Sample Queries," example 10. See that example if you need to refresh your memory on the details of how the join works.

Exercises:

1.   Invent some sample SELECTs against the views shown above and give the equivalent SELECTs actually executed by the system in each case.

2.   (More difficult.) Repeat exercise 1 for UPDATE, INSERT, and DELETE statements. (*Note:* For technical reasons that are beyond the scope of this text, most systems will not permit update operations on views involving virtual fields or joins. If you attempt this exercise, you will probably realize why this is so.)

NOMAD FACILITIES

All the examples in this chapter so far have been expressed in terms of SQL. Of the systems discussed in this book, QBE and dBASE do not currently provide any kind of view support at all. NOMAD does not really support views either, but it does provide certain analogous facilities, which we now briefly discuss. Those facilities fall into two broad categories: definitional facilities and manipulative facilities. Each of these two categories has in fact already been touched on in Chapter 9.

1.   **Definitional facilities**

Within the definition of a table ("master"), it is possible to include virtual fields ("items") by means of suitable DEFINE entries. A virtual item can be defined as the result of some arithmetic expression. For example:

```
MASTER ORDER_LINE . . .
   ITEM PRICE . . .
   ITEM QUANTITY . . .
         .
         .
         .
DEFINE COST 99999.99 EXPR PRICE * QUANTITY
```

Alternatively, a virtual item can be an item that is extracted from some other master. For example:

```
MASTER PARCELS . . .
  ITEM APN . . .
  ITEM ROAD . . .
  ITEM OWNER . . .
  DEFINE ADDRESS  AS EXTRACT'ADDRESS FROM OWNERS USING OWNER'
  DEFINE PHONE    AS EXTRACT'PHONE   FROM OWNERS USING OWNER'
  ITEM IMPROVED . . .
  ITEM LAST_ENTRY . . .
  ITEM BALANCE . . .
```

See Chapter 9 for more details and explanation of these two examples. Note that in both cases here we are not really creating a view per se, but only virtual fields that are, as it were, appended on to real tables.

2.   Manipulative facilities

There are two relevant manipulative facilities. The first we discuss is the DEFINE *command* (contrast the DEFINE *entry* in a MASTER definition), which can be used to define virtual items dynamically (i.e., in the middle of your manipulative processing). For example:

```
FROM PARCELS
DEFINE ADDRESS AS EXTRACT'ADDRESS FROM OWNERS USING OWNER'
DEFINE PHONE   AS EXTRACT'PHONE   FROM OWNERS USING OWNER'
LIST
  OWNER
  ADDRESS
  PHONE
  WHERE PARCEL = '93-282-55'
```

Here we are assuming that the PARCELS master does not already contain the two virtual items. For more details of this facility, again see Chapter 9.

The other manipulative facility, the SELECT command, has not been mentioned before in this book. The NOMAD SELECT (not to be confused with the SQL SELECT or the dBASE SELECT) is used to establish a "screen" in terms of which subsequent com-

mands are interpreted. For example, consider the following sequence of commands:

```
FROM PARCEL_ACCOUNTS
SELECT APN = '93-293-02'
    AND DATE > '820101'
    AND DATE < '821231'
            .
            .
            .

LIST
    BY DATE
        ENTRY
        DESCRIPTION
        AMOUNT
        BALANCE
        WHERE TYPE = 'CREDIT'
```

(Compare with the SQL SELECT on WANTED_RECS in the introduction to this chapter.) The LIST command here will be applied, not to the entire PARCEL_ACCOUNTS table, but only to
that subset of it satisfying the screening established in the preceding
SELECT command. Again we have not really created a view as
such, but the overall effect is somewhat similar.

ADVANTAGES OF VIEWS

The principal purpose of views, as our examples have implied, is to
simplify the user's perception of the database and thereby to simplify the user's job. For example, if the database contains two
tables A and B that are frequently used together in the form of a
join, then we can define that join once and for all as a view C and
from that point on use the view C instead of the real tables A and B
whenever we need the join. But there are a number of corollary advantages also, which we now briefly sketch.

● **The same data can be seen by different users in different ways.**

Since any number of distinct views can be defined over the
same real tables, there is no reason why everyone should have to
perceive the database in exactly the same way. This consideration
is obviously important in the environment of a large shared database.

- **Users can be shielded from changes in the structure of the real tables.**

For example, suppose the database administrator decides to move field F from table X to table Y. A user of the old table X can be given a *view* in which the new X is joined with field F from the new Y, thus making it look to that user as if F were still in X. (This is still another aspect of data independence, incidentally, though it is somewhat different in kind from those aspects discussed previously in this book.)

- **Views provide an automatic measure of security for hidden data.**

"Hidden data" refers to tables and fields not included in the views available to some given user. For that user hidden data is clearly unavailable and hence secure from all access. Thus, forcing users to access the database via views is a simple but effective mechanism for authorization control. We will have more to say on this topic in the next chapter.

This brings our discussion of the view mechanism to a close. In conclusion, let us recap the basic point of that mechanism: It allows users to concentrate on just the data they are interested in and to ignore the rest. However, it must be clearly understood that views are "windows" into the real data, not separate copies of that data, and hence that operations on views are really operations on the underlying data. In particular, the user must realize that making any changes via a view will cause the real data to change underneath.

14 *Security*

INTRODUCTION

In a single-user system the entire database is presumably the property of a single person, who therefore should obviously be allowed to do anything to that database that he or she pleases. In a shared system, by contrast, different pieces of the database will typically belong to different people, and individual owners may be quite concerned as to who is allowed access to their particular piece. It therefore becomes very important in such an environment to control exactly who is allowed to do what. Just because some particular person is able to sign on to the system in the first place does not necessarily mean that that person should be entitled to unrestricted access to everything in the database.

The principal reason for this state of affairs is, of course, *confidentiality*. Most data is confidential to a greater or lesser degree. For example:

- Individuals have a right to privacy (such a right is even guaranteed by law in some countries). Thus personal information such as income sources and amounts, medical records, criminal offenses, even phone numbers in some situations, should not be freely disseminated but should be restricted to people having a legitimate "need to know."

- In a commercial or industrial environment, data is a significant and valuable corporate asset and may require extremely careful protection against, for example, industrial espionage. In a high-technology industry such as computer manufacture, for instance, the design data for a new product such as a new disk drive can be worth literally millions of dollars to the company. At a more mundane level, marketing strategies, sales projections, survey results, and similar information all represent a significant dollar investment on the part of the corporation and deserve commensurate protection.

- Military secrets and similar items of national or international interest provide even more obvious examples of cases where stringent controls are necessary.

Breach of confidentiality is, of course, not the only problem. Breach of confidentiality implies merely that people are able to see data that was not intended for them. Matters are even worse if they are able to *change* that data. A well-known (or at least well-publicized) illustration is provided by the so-called *electronic crimes* of recent years. In the absence of suitable controls a skilled operator in a banking system, for instance, can steal more money electronically in a few hours than a conventional thief could steal in a lifetime. The scope is orders of magnitude greater than with conventional crime, as several organizations have discovered to their cost.

So it is necessary in a shared system to protect the database against both illegal retrievals and illegal updates. For if such protection is not provided, then users will simply (and quite rightly) not entrust their data to the system if it is in any way sensitive. The term "security" is used to refer to that necessary protection. More precisely, it is used to mean *the protection of the database against unauthorized disclosure, alteration, or destruction.* The component of the system that is responsible for the provision of security in this sense is referred to as the *authorization mechanism* (or authorization subsystem). In this chapter we examine some of the principles underlying such an authorization mechanism. Once again we use SQL as the basis for most of our discussions, though the principles illustrated are in fact quite generally applicable.

Note: Even in a single-user system, it may be desirable to protect the database *as a whole* against intruders (just as it may be desirable to keep valuables such as money or jewelry under lock and key, and for much the same reason). A password scheme can be used to provide this level of protection. Most probably, such a scheme would be an all-or-nothing proposition: Either you can do everything (if you know the password) or you can do nothing (otherwise). However, it might also be possible to require, for example, one password for retrieval and another for update, or different passwords for different tables. Passwords are discussed in more detail in the final section of this chapter.

GRANTING AUTHORITY

The general principle behind the approach to security in SQL (and it is a good one) is that *you cannot do anything you are not explicitly authorized to do.* The default is that you are *not* allowed to do it, whatever "it" is. If you try to do something illegal—say SELECT data from a table you are not authorized to see—your command will be rejected and you will get an error message telling you why.

In outline, the SQL mechanism works as follows. When the system is first installed, some specially privileged user is identified to the system as having "database administrator authority" (DBA authority). DBA authority allows the holder to perform any valid operation in the system, including, in particular, the operation of granting authority to other users. Initially, then, the DBA can do everything, and nobody else can do anything at all.

Following initial installation of the system, the DBA can selectively grant authority for specific operations to specific users, using a special SQL statement called GRANT. For example:

```
GRANT SELECT ON PARCEL_ACCOUNTS TO JUDY
```

User Judy is now allowed to perform SELECT operations (but no others) on the PARCEL__ACCOUNTS table.

```
GRANT UPDATE, DELETE ON MILL_LEDGER TO DOUG
```

User Doug can perform UPDATE and DELETE operations (but no others) on the MILL__LEDGER table.

```
GRANT SELECT, UPDATE (ADDRESS, PHONE) ON OWNERS TO SANDY
```

User Sandy can SELECT anything from the OWNERS table but can UPDATE only the ADDRESS and PHONE fields.

```
GRANT CREATE TO BARBARA
```

User Barbara is allowed to create new tables. (The actual SQL formulation of this GRANT is not quite as shown, but that is a detail that need not concern us here.) What is more, if Barbara in fact does create a table called, say, BREX, then she automatically has full rights over that table, and no one else has any rights over it at all—expect (of course) the DBA, who always has full rights over everything. In particular, Barbara has the right to grant authority on BREX to other users, just as if she *were* the DBA as far as that table is concerned. For example:

```
GRANT SELECT ON BREX TO DOUG
```

```
GRANT SELECT, INSERT ON BREX TO JUDY
```

and so on.

Authorizations are recorded in the database catalog and hence can be queried like everything else. For instance, the statement

```
SELECT  USERNAME
FROM    TABLE_AUTHORITIES
WHERE   TABNAME = 'MILL_LEDGER'
AND     AUTHORITY = 'SELECT'
```

might be used to list all users with SELECT authority on the MILL_LEDGER table. Of course, this query will only work if the user has SELECT authority on the TABLE_AUTHORITIES table itself! Access to the catalog tables is controlled by the security mechanism, just as it is for all other tables. In some databases, in fact, the catalog tables may be the most highly protected of all.

Incidentally, the true SQL formulation of the foregoing query would be slightly different from the version we show, for reasons that are not important for our purposes.

VIEWS AND AUTHORIZATION

As indicated at the end of the previous chapter, views provide a simple but effective measure of security "for free." To be specific, views can be used to *hide sensitive data* from users who are not authorized to access that data. Of course, even to access a view, you still need the appropriate authorization, which can be given to you by means of a GRANT statement in the usual way. For example:

```
CREATE VIEW IMPROVED_PARCELS
    AS SELECT APN, ROAD, OWNER
        FROM    PARCELS
        WHERE   IMPROVED = 'Y'
                    .
                    .
                    .
```

```
GRANT SELECT ON IMPROVED_PARCELS TO SANDY
```

User Sandy can perform SELECT operations (only) on fields APN, ROAD, and OWNER (only) of records from the PARCELS table for which the IMPROVED value is 'Y' (only).

Any of the following cases of authorization can easily be handled through the view mechanism:

1.   Authority to access some records of a table but not others;

2.   Authority to access some columns of a table but not others;

3. Combination of 1 and 2 (the case illustrated by the IMPROVED_PARCELS example above);

4. Authority to see summary information only, not detailed information. For example, some user might be allowed to see the average dues amount paid per parcel, say, but no individual payments. A view could be defined to provide this function. (As an exercise, define such a view.)

REVOKING
AUTHORITY

A system like SQL that provides a means (the GRANT statement) for selectively granting authority to users must also provide a means for revoking such grants. That facility is provided in SQL in the form of the REVOKE statement. For instance, if user Barbara has previously issued the statement

```
GRANT SELECT, INSERT ON BREX TO JUDY
```

(as shown earlier), she can now issue the statement

```
REVOKE INSERT ON BREX FROM JUDY
```

to revoke Judy's INSERT authority (only) on table BREX. Judy still has SELECT authority on that table.

Just as GRANT causes new entries to be made in the database catalog, so REVOKE causes those entries to be deleted again.

QBE FACILITIES

As you will probably have come to expect by now, the Query By Example analog of a GRANT operation is expressed by filling in blanks in an empty table. For example, here is a QBE equivalent of the second of the SQL GRANTs shown earlier:

MILL_LEDGER	ENTRY	DATE	DESCRIPTION	TYPE	PARTY	AMOUNT	BALANCE
I.AUTH(U.,D.) DOUG							

The effect of this specification is to insert an *authorization constraint* (indicating that user Doug can issue "U." and "D." operations on table MILL_LEDGER) into the QBE catalog.

QBE does not support views. To hide sensitive data, therefore, it is necessary to be more specific in the expression of the authorization constraint. In fact, what you do is indicate in that constraint those portions of the table that are *not* to be hidden. For example, the QBE equivalent of the first of the examples in the section "Views and Authorization" might look like this:

PARCELS	APN	ROAD	OWNER	IMPROVED
I.AUTH(P.) SANDY				Y

User Sandy has no access at all to fields LAST_ENTRY and BALANCE of the PARCELS table (because they are not included in the table on the screen) and has read-only access ("P.") to the remaining fields (APN, ROAD, OWNER, and IMPROVED) only where the IMPROVED value is 'Y'.

Authorization constraints in the catalog can be queried ("printed"), updated, and deleted in QBE in a similar manner.

OTHER ASPECTS OF SECURITY

Views and the authorization mechanism are by no means the end of the security story. In this section we briefly sketch a number of other relevant considerations.

1. User identification

An implicit assumption underlying the whole authorization mechanism is that the system knows who users are. It is no good permitting access to some table T to user A and denying it to user B if user B can access that table T by simply pretending to be user A. In other words, the system should require any user who claims to be user A to prove the truth of that claim. "Proving the truth of the claim" is normally done by supplying a *password* that is (in principle) known only to the user concerned. For example:

User enters	JUDY
System responds	HELLO JUDY. PLEASE ENTER YOUR PASSWORD:
User enters password but makes an error	(System suppresses display.)
System responds	PASSWORD INCORRECT. PLEASE TRY AGAIN:
User enters password correctly	(System suppresses display.)
System responds	PASSWORD ACCEPTED. PLEASE ENTER COMMAND:

And so on.

A common use of passwords with which you are certainly familiar is for controlling access to personal bank accounts via a cash-issuing terminal.

2. Additional uses for passwords

In the example above a password was used to control access to the overall system. It is also possible to apply password protection at finer levels of control. In NOMAD, for example, different passwords can be used to control access to different databases, to different tables ("masters") within a database, or even to different *row subsets* within a single table. For instance, it would be possible to arrange matters (via a NOMAD facility known as a "retrieval procedure," or RPROC) such that each user of the PARCEL_ACCOUNTS table would have to supply a different password to access that table; and the effect of the password would be to allow the user concerned to see just the records that applied to that user's own account and no others.

Note: This latter facility amounts to a restricted form of view support. But it is clear from the NOMAD documentation that it is intended as a security feature rather than as any kind of general view mechanism.

3. Auditing

It is important not to assume that the security system is perfect. A would-be infiltrator who is sufficiently determined will usually find a way of breaking through the controls, especially if the payoff for doing so is high. In situations where the data is sufficiently sensitive, therefore, or where the processing performed on the data is sufficiently critical, an *audit trail* becomes a necessity. If, for example, data discrepancies lead to a suspicion that an embezzler has been at work, the audit trail can be used to examine what has been going on and to verify that matters are under control (or if they are not, to help pinpoint the wrongdoer).

An audit trail can be thought of as a special file or database in which the system automatically keeps track of all operations performed by users on the regular database. A typical entry in the audit trail might contain the following information:

Operation (UPDATE, say);
Terminal from which the operation was invoked;
User who invoked the operation;
Date and time of the operation;
Database, table, record, and field affected;
Old value of field;
New value of field.

Using the information in the audit trail, an impartial auditor should be able to reconstruct the sequence of events leading up to the state of the database at any particular time. The very fact that an audit trail is being maintained may be sufficient in itself to deter some would-be infiltrators.

4.   Encryption

Another level of security can be provided by *data encryption.* The idea here is that data can be physically stored on the disk in a scrambled or encrypted form, so that anyone who tries to access it other than through the official channels (e.g., via a program of their own making instead of via the DBMS) will see just an unintelligible jumble of bits.

Data encryption requires the use of an *encryption key.* The encryption process takes the data to be encrypted and combines it in some more or less complicated fashion with the encryption key, thus generating the corresponding encrypted form. As a trivial example, suppose the data to be encrypted is the decimal number

    427 961 022 517

Suppose also that the encryption key is 6, and the encryption process consists of replacing each digit of the data by the sum of that digit and the encryption key (if that sum is greater than 9, then just ignore the tens part):

    427 961 022 517
    666 666 666 666
    ─────────────────
    083 527 688 173

The encrypted form

    083 527 688 173

is stored on the disk. To retrieve the original value, the user must supply the encryption key again, and the system can then go through an appropriate *decryption* process.

Exercise: Decrypt the encrypted value shown above.

Note that the encryption key itself is not stored anywhere in the database; if it is lost or forgotten, then to all intents and purposes the encrypted data becomes totally irretrievable.

An encryption scheme along the lines just illustrated (but of course much more sophisticated) is provided in NOMAD.

We conclude this chapter by remarking that technical safeguards such as those we have been discussing are not the whole story. First of all, the decisions as to who can do what are, of course, *human* decisions. Some external agent (typically, the database administrator) has to make those decisions; all the system can do is enforce them when they are made. There is no way it can ensure that those decisions are the right ones. Second, physical controls on the database (e.g., locks and alarms on the computer room door) may be just as important as the technical controls we have been describing, or even more so. It is, unfortunately, all too easy to do a good job on one aspect of security but neglect some other equally important aspect. I used to work in a technical laboratory at which a variety of confidential research and development activities were carried out. Access to the laboratory was via a computer-controlled locked gate. To open the gate, you had to insert a machine-readable badge into a badge reader standing just outside the gate. However, although there was a gate, there was no *wall*—it was perfectly possible just to walk round the side of the gate. Admittedly, you would then have to cross a flower bed, and few people ever did; but the moral is clear.

15   *Integrity*

INTRODUCTION

We use the term "integrity" to refer to the accuracy, correctness, or validity of the data in the database. Maintaining database integrity is of paramount importance, for obvious reasons. To maintain such integrity, it is necessary to check all update operations (INSERTs, DELETEs, and UPDATEs) to make sure that they are valid—for example, to check an INSERT operation on the PARCELS table to ensure that the new APN value is of the correct form, namely 99-999-99 (where each 9 stands for an arbitrary digit in the range 0 to 9).

Integrity is frequently confused with security, and indeed the two concepts do have certain features in common. We can distinguish between them as follows:

- *Security* involves ensuring that users are *allowed* to do the things they are trying to do.

- *Integrity* involves ensuring that the things they are trying to do are *correct*.

To put it rather glibly: Security means protecting the database against unauthorized users; integrity means protecting it against authorized users. Indeed, integrity, unlike security, is applicable even in a single-user system (it is always desirable to avoid errors); however, it is far *more* relevant when the system is shared. The reason is that in a shared environment one person's mistakes can affect other people. Each user is dependent to some extent on the correctness of other people's actions. (In a single-user system, if things go wrong, you have only yourself to blame.) However, as stated in Chapter 11, the fact is that few systems today, shared or otherwise, provide very much in the way of integrity support (except inasmuch as users can always provide such support for themselves by creating appropriate canned procedures).

INTEGRITY CONSTRAINTS

Let us consider the APN example quoted above in a little more detail. Suppose we are using NOMAD. Then the fact that APN values are required to conform to a specific pattern can be specified by means of a MASK clause within the definition of the APN field (or "item"):

```
MASTER PARCELS INSERT KEYED(APN)
    ITEM APN       A9      HEADING 'PARCEL'   MASK '99-999-99'
```

NOMAD will now check all INSERTs and CHANGEs on the PARCELS table to ensure that APN values do in fact conform to this pattern.

The MASK clause in this example is a simple example of an *integrity constraint.* What is needed in a general system is a means for specifying arbitrary constraints, plus an enforcement mechanism to monitor update operations and reject any that would cause any of those specified constraints to be violated. In practice, however, no system commercially available today provides such a general facility; instead, systems typically support just a few important special cases, such as the case illustrated in the example above. In fact, most systems are really quite weak in this area at the time of writing.

It is not my aim to describe a completely general facility in this book. However, I do wish to cover a few important special cases, four of them to be precise, which is more than are supported by any of the systems described in this book (though NOMAD comes close). Therefore, I will discuss each of the special cases in general terms first, then indicate briefly how that case is supported (if at all) in specific implemented systems. The four special cases are as follows:

- Primary keys;
- Foreign keys;
- Format constraints;
- Range constraints.

PRIMARY KEYS

Every table should have a primary key. The primary key of a table is a field of that table—or perhaps a combination of several fields of that table—that can be used as a *unique identifier* for the records in that table. For example, APN is the primary key for the PARCELS table: Every parcel has its own unique parcel number, and that parcel number can be used to identify the parcel and to distinguish it from all others.

Primary keys should be a very familiar concept to you. Some everyday examples are listed below:

Social security numbers   Bank account numbers
Employee serial numbers   Credit card numbers
Vehicle license numbers   Latitudes and longitudes
Purchase order numbers   Dates and times
Driver's license numbers   Chemical element symbols
Telephone numbers   Musical opus numbers
Flight numbers   Policy numbers

An example of a primary key involving more than one field is provided by the PARCEL__ACCOUNTS table. We show the column headings and a sample row of this table below:

APN	ENTRY	DATE	DESCRIPTION	TYPE	AMOUNT	BALANCE
93-293-02	17	821016	DAMAGE FEE	CHARGE	500.00	560.00

The unique identifier (primary key) here is the combination (APN, ENTRY): Each row requires a parcel number together with an entry number within that parcel in order to identify it uniquely.

Of the systems discussed in this book, only NOMAD and QBE support primary keys directly. In NOMAD, for example, the MASTER definition includes an INSERT KEYED clause—for example,

```
MASTER PARCELS INSERT KEYED(APN)
    ITEM APN . . .
```

The INSERT KEYED(APN) specification guarantees that no new PARCELS record will be accepted for insertion if it has the same APN value as some existing PARCELS record. It also guarantees that no existing PARCELS record will be updated in such a way that its APN value becomes the same as that in some other existing PARCELS record. As a matter of fact, it will prevent the regular CHANGE command from being used at all on the APN field; the special command *CHANGE KEY* must be used instead if you need to change an APN value. The intent of this latter restriction is to make users think twice before changing a primary key value. Such changes should not be undertaken lightly, because those primary keys may be referenced—via *foreign* keys (see the next section)—from elsewhere in the database.

In QBE primary keys can be specified as illustrated in the following example:

PARCELS	APN	ROAD	OWNER	IMPROVED	LAST_ENTRY	BALANCE
KEY U.	Y	N	N	N	N	N

The result of this specification is to create an entry in the QBE catalog indicating that, of the fields of the PARCELS table, APN *is* part of the primary key for that table (because of the Y, meaning YES) and fields ROAD, OWNER, . . ., BALANCE are not (because of the N, meaning NO). The reason "U." is specified, rather than "I." as you might have expected, is that QBE assumes by default that *every* field in the table is part of the primary key. Thus you are actually updating an existing (default) row in the catalog (one that specifies 'Y' for every field), not inserting a new row.

As for SQL, primary keys as such are not recognized by the SQL system. However, we can achieve the required uniqueness guarantee by creating a *UNIQUE index* over the field or field combination concerned. For example:

```
CREATE TABLE PARCELS
        (APN . . .,
            . . . )
```

CREATE UNIQUE INDEX APNPK ON PARCELS (APN)

See Chapter 12 for a discussion of the CREATE INDEX statement. The UNIQUE specification is of course what informs SQL of the required uniqueness constraint.

FOREIGN KEYS

Some tables will include one or more *foreign keys* in addition to the primary key. A foreign key is a field or field combination in one table whose values are required to match those of the primary key in some other table. For example, every APN value in the PARCEL_ACCOUNTS table must match the APN value in some record of the PARCELS table (because every account record must apply to some known parcel). See Fig. 15.1.

Field APN of PARCEL_ACCOUNTS is a foreign key matching the primary key of PARCELS. (It also happens to be a component of the primary key of PARCEL_ACCOUNTS, but that fact

Figure 15.1

```
      PARCELS  table:

      primary
      key APN      ROAD      OWNER       IMPROVED   LAST_ENTRY   BALANCE

  ┌─► 93-293-02   MILL      P.J.DEAN    Y                 17    120.00
  │     ...        ..        ...         ...             ...     ...

      PARCEL__ACCOUNTS  table:

      foreign
      key APN      ENTRY     DATE       DESCRIPTION   TYPE     AMOUNT    BALANCE

  ├── 93-293-02      16      820107     DUES82        CHARGE    60.00     60.00
  └── 93-293-02      17      821016     DAMAGE FEE    CHARGE   500.00    560.00
        ...         ...        ..        .....         ..       ...       ...
```

is of no consequence in the present context.) You can think of a foreign key (very loosely) as "pointing to" the matching primary key (as Fig. 15.1 suggests). However, it is not really a pointer like a pointer in an index, because its values are real data values (APN values in the example), not just page numbers on a disk. Incidentally, there is no requirement that a foreign key and the matching primary key have the same name, but it is generally a good idea if they do.

A limited form of support for foreign keys is provided in NOMAD (no support at all is provided in SQL, QBE, or dBASE). The PARCEL__ACCOUNTS example would look like this in NOMAD:

```
MASTER PARCELS INSERT KEYED(APN)                        [Primary key] ◄─┐
   ITEM APN     . . .                                                   │
      .                                                                 │
      .                                                                 │
      .                                                                 │
MASTER PARCEL_ACCOUNTS INSERT KEYED(APN,ENTRY)                          │
   ITEM APN . . . MEMBER'PARCELS'                        [Foreign key] ─┘
   ITEM ENTRY . . .
```

The clause MEMBER'PARCELS' on the definition of the APN item in PARCEL__ACCOUNTS says that this item is a foreign key matching the primary key of the PARCELS master. NOMAD will check INSERT and CHANGE operations on PARCEL__AC-COUNTS to ensure that every APN value entered into that table already exists as an APN value in PARCELS. (We should strictly say CHANGE KEY operations, rather than CHANGE operations, since APN happens also to be part of the *primary* key of PAR-CEL__ACCOUNTS, and ordinary CHANGE operations would not be allowed anyway.) Note, however, that NOMAD will *not* check DELETE operations on PARCELS. Thus, for example, it would be possible to delete a given PARCELS record and leave some PARCEL__ACCOUNTS records referring to a now nonexistent parcel. A more general mechanism would either prohibit such a DELETE or would automatically "cascade" it to delete the matching PARCEL__ACCOUNTS records as well (depending on what had been specified in the schema, i.e., the definition of the database). Similar remarks apply to CHANGE KEY operations on PARCELS; these operations also are not monitored, but should be.

We will have more to say on the topic of foreign keys (and primary keys) in Chapters 17 and 18.

FORMAT CONSTRAINTS

Format constraints are used to ensure that the values of a given field conform to some specific pattern. The MASK clause of NOMAD is used to specify such constraints (and once again NOMAD is the only system of those we discuss that provides any support in this area). We therefore take the NOMAD facility as typical of format constraints in general.

Note first that the field in question must be a character string field (format constraints would make no sense for a numeric field). The MASK clause for a character string field takes the form

```
MASK 'sequence-of-n-characters'
```

(there must be exactly n characters in the mask, where n is the length of the character string field in question). The first character in the mask corresponds to the first character of the field, the

Figure 15.2

If the Mask Character Is	Then the Corresponding Character in the Field Value Must Be
A	Alphabetic (A-Z) or blank
9	Numeric (0-9)
X	Alphabetic, numeric, or blank
*	Anything

Figure 15.3

Mask	Good Value	Bad Value
99-999-99	93-282-55	123456789
AAAA	GOOD	A123
XXXX	A123	X+Y
A99	D35	35D
A****	X+Y+Z	4+Y+Z
UK***	UK	USA

second to the second, and so on. Four mask characters (A, 9, X, and *) have special meanings, as shown in Fig. 15.2. Any other mask character represents itself; that is, the corresponding character in the field must be exactly that character. Figure 15.3 gives some examples.

RANGE CONSTRAINTS

A range constraint is a constraint that every value of a given field must lie within some prescribed range. An example of such a constraint is one that states that the ROAD field in the PARCELS table can take only three different values, namely 'CREEK', 'MILL', or 'REDWOOD'. The prescribed set may be specified as a collection of discrete values, as in this example, or as a collection of one or more ranges of values (indicated by lower and upper limits), or as a mixture of both. Range constraints are specified in NOMAD by means of a LIMITS clause for the item in question. Here are some examples:

1. ITEM ROAD   A7   LIMITS ('CREEK', 'MILL', 'REDWOOD')

2. ITEM IMPROVED A1   LIMITS ('Y', 'N')

    IMPROVED must be 'Y' or 'N'.

3. ITEM AMOUNT 99999.99   LIMITS (0:99999.99)

    AMOUNT must be greater than or equal to 0 and less than or equal to $99999.99. In other words, AMOUNT must not be negative.

4. ITEM APN   A9   LIMITS (NOTNAV)

    APN must not be null (in NOMAD, NAV stands for "not available" or null; NOTNAV therefore means *not* not available" or not null). SQL also supports this particular range constraint, via the specification NOT NULL in the definition of the field within the applicable CREATE TABLE statement. For example:

    ```
    CREATE TABLE PARCELS
          (APN . . . NOT NULL,
             . . . )
    ```

    QBE supports this same constraint automatically (i.e., without any further explicit specification) in the case of primary key fields but not for any other fields. It is a good idea always to insist that primary keys not be null, incidentally (see Chapter 17).

    Finally, we give one more (very contrived) NOMAD example.

5. ITEM FAKE   A1   LIMITS (NOTNAV, 'A':'H', 'K', 'T':'X')

    FAKE cannot be null and must take one of the values A, B, C, D, E, F, G, H, K, T, U, V, W, X.

CONCLUSION

We have discussed four important special cases of integrity constraints: primary key constraints, foreign key constraints, format constraints, and range constraints. NOMAD supports all of these cases, except that its support of foreign key constraints is still somewhat deficient (it does not apply any checks on DELETE or CHANGE KEY operations on the table *referenced* by the foreign key). QBE supports primary keys but none of the other cases (except for the "no nulls" constraint on primary key fields). And SQL supports a uniqueness constraint, via CREATE UNIQUE INDEX, and the "no nulls" constraint, via a NOT NULL specification within CREATE TABLE; but these constraints are applicable to any field, at the user's discretion, not just to primary keys (SQL has no knowledge of primary keys as such).

We repeat that there are other kinds of constraint that could be useful in practice. For example, in the Road Association database the current balance on the general fund should always be equal to the sum of the three individual current balances on the three individual road funds. However, maintaining this constraint is the responsibility of the user (or, more likely, of some canned procedure)—there is no way to get the system to do it automatically. Further details of such additional constraints are beyond the scope of this book.

16   *Locking*

In a multiuser system there is always the danger that the actions of one user can interfere with those of another, unless suitable controls are in force. The classic example of such interference (not the only one possible, but the easiest to understand) is the so-called *lost update problem.* As an illustration of this problem, suppose we have a database that contains seat availability and ticketing information for a certain theater, and consider the following sequence of events:

1. Customer A walks into the office of ticket agent A and asks for a ticket for tonight's performance. Ticket agent A (henceforth referred to as *user* A) calls up the seat availability information on terminal A.

2. A few moments later customer B walks into the office of ticket agent B with the same request. Ticket agent B (henceforth referred to as user B) calls up the same seat availability information on terminal B.

3. Customer A purchases a ticket for seat K9. User A updates the seat availability information appropriately and sends it back to the database.

4. Customer B, unaware of customer A's concurrent transaction, purchases a ticket for the same seat K9. User B updates the seat availability information accordingly and sends it back to the database, overwriting the update already made by user A.

Net effect: Seat K9 has been sold twice. User B's update has caused user A's update to be lost; or, more accurately, user B has been allowed to update the database on the basis of information that is no longer current, instead of being forced to see that most current version.

Let us abstract the problem a little. In terms of SQL (or, rather, in a kind of pidgin SQL), we might represent it as shown in Fig. 16.1. The figure is intended to be read as follows: User A SELECTs some record R at time t1; user B SELECTs that same

DATABASE: A PRIMER

Figure 16.1

User A	Time	User B
—		—
SELECT R	t1	—
—		—
—	t2	SELECT R
—		—
UPDATE R	t3	—
—		—
—		—
—	t4	UPDATE R
—		—

record R at time t2; user A UPDATEs the record (on the basis of the values seen at t1) at time t3; and user B UPDATEs the same record (on the basis of the values seen at t2, which are the same as those seen at t1) at time t4. User A's update is lost at time t4.

The state of affairs illustrated in Fig. 16.1 is clearly unacceptable and so must be guarded against somehow. Hence the system should provide some kind of *concurrency control mechanism* to protect concurrent users from one another and to prevent situations like the one just illustrated from occurring. Now there are literally thousands of ways of approaching this problem in theory. In practice, however, every one of those approaches is based on one or another of a very small number of fundamental techniques, and as a practical matter almost every system currently uses an approach that is based on a technique called *locking*. We therefore concentrate on locking in this book.

Caveat: Concurrency control in general, and locking in particular, are complex subjects when treated in full generality. Moreover (and partly as a consequence of this first point), the concurrency controls provided in implemented systems are quite frequently inadequate in one way or another. In some cases the controls are simply incomplete; that is, it is possible to find situations in which the system will simply produce the wrong result (without the user being in any way aware of that fact, moreover).

In other cases systems "solve" the problem by effectively passing it back to the user; that is, the user is required to know that the database is shared and has to behave accordingly. This approach is, of course, counter to the objective of making the system look to each individual user as if it were *not* shared, and it has the added drawback that if the user does something wrong, then the results may be wrong too. As we will see, the objective of concealing the shared nature of the system cannot be totally achieved in practice; but this fact does not mean that concurrency control should be entirely the user's responsibility.

In what follows, therefore:

• We content ourselves with an introductory discussion of the topic only. We do not attempt to describe all possible problems that can arise, nor all possible solutions. However, the solution we do discuss is complete, in the sense that it does handle all possible problems correctly. It also has the virtue of being quite simple.

• We do not describe the solutions adopted by specific systems, since most of them involve additional complexities that we do not need to get into here. (However, we remark that the specific approach used in SQL amounts to an improved version of the simplified solution that we do discuss in this chapter.)

LOCKS

We now discuss that simple solution, which, as we have already indicated, is based on locking. One further disclaimer: For concreteness we frame our discussions in terms of "pidgin SQL" (using statements such as "SELECT R," "UPDATE R," etc.). You should not infer that real SQL actually behaves exactly as we describe.

The basic idea of locking is very straightforward: When a user SELECTs a record, the system automatically *locks* that record so that no other user is able to SELECT it at the same time. Thus the operation of "SELECT R" is not really just "Retrieve record R" but *"Lock record R in the database* (and then retrieve it)." If user B tries to SELECT a record that is currently locked by user A, then user B will simply have to wait until user A's lock is released.

Note: We remind you that "retrieve record R" really means "retrieve a *copy* of record R." The original record R remains in the database.

So when are locks released? In principle, the answer to this question is, "When the user has finished with them." Since only the user knows when that point is reached, it must be the responsibility of the user to inform the system of the fact at the appropriate time. We therefore need another pidgin SQL command, which we might as well call RELEASE LOCKS, the effect of which is to tell the system that the user has finished his or her transaction and therefore all locks can be released. Now another user who is waiting for one or more of the previously locked records will be able to proceed.

Let us now reexamine the lost update example (abstract version) from the previous section. With the locking scheme just outlined, events proceed as shown in Fig. 16.2.

Figure 16.2

User A	Time	User B
—		—
SELECT R (R now locked by A)	t1	—
—		—
—	t2	SELECT R (R not available, so B has to wait)
—		wait
—		wait
UPDATE R (R changed in DB)	t3	wait
—		wait
—		wait
RELEASE LOCKS (lock on R released; A's transaction is finished)	t4	wait
		wait
		wait
	t5	(B's SELECT R now takes effect; B sees R *as updated by A;* R now locked by B)
		—
	t6	UPDATE R (R changed in DB)
		—
	t7	RELEASE LOCKS (lock on R released; B's transaction is finished)

You can see that the effect of the locking scheme is to force user B to see record R *as updated by user* A. Thus user B will no longer be updating the database on the basis of out-of-date information. In the theater ticket example user B will no longer be able to sell seat K9 to customer B because user B will no longer see that seat as being available.

Aside: You may be wondering exactly what a lock is. What does it mean to say, for example, that "Record R is now locked by user A?" One way to think about these questions is as follows: Assume that the system maintains a special table, the LOCKS table, with columns HOLDER, RECORD, and WAITER. When user A successfully executes the statement "SELECT R," the system makes an entry in that table as follows:

LOCKS table:

HOLDER	RECORD	WAITER
A	R	--

If user B now tries to execute "SELECT R" in turn, the system will see from the LOCKS table that R is not available at this time and will make B wait. It will also update the entry in the LOCKS table to

LOCKS table:

HOLDER	RECORD	WAITER
A	R	B

(We are assuming for simplicity that no more than one user at a time can be waiting for any given record.) When user A executes "RELEASE LOCKS," the system will update the entry in the LOCKS table to

LOCKS table:

HOLDER	RECORD	WAITER
B	R	--

User B can now proceed.

Incidentally, do not be misled by the foregoing explanation into thinking that the LOCKS table is a table in the catalog or that you might be able to query it with SQL statements. The LOCKS table is much too ephemeral a thing to be kept in the database. It is just a *temporary* table that the system keeps in main storage while the database is actually in use.

RELEASING LOCKS

We said in the previous section that a new command (RELEASE LOCKS) was required and that it was the user's responsibility to issue that command at the appropriate time. In principle, this statement is accurate. In practice, however, matters can be simplified somewhat in a variety of ways. One simple technique is just to arrange matters so that *each database statement automatically releases any locks acquired by the immediately preceding database statement.* The explicit RELEASE LOCKS statement would no longer be necessary with this convention. However, the user would then have to understand that the values displayed for any SELECT instantly become suspect as soon as any other statement is executed—suspect in the sense that there is no guarantee that if the SELECT is repeated, it will produce the same result. (Why not?)

Another (hybrid) technique, frequently encountered in practice, is as follows:

• For an *interactive user* at a terminal, release locks at the end of the statement that acquires them. This technique has the advantage that locks are not held very long and hence that not too much time is spent waiting for them to be released. But it has the disadvantage that transactions requiring more than one user/system interaction can no longer be handled reliably from the terminal (the lost update problem becomes possible again). Instead, such transactions should be handled by a canned procedure (invoked from the terminal by a *single* user/system interaction); see below.

• For a *canned procedure*, release locks at the end of the procedure. Since the canned procedure is a program—running at machine speed and (typically) without any interaction with the human user except at the beginning when it is invoked and at the end when it displays its results (if any)—locks are still not held too long.

Note that whatever technique is selected, users still have to have some awareness of the fact that they are working with a shared system. *There is no way to conceal this fact one hundred percent.* For clarity, therefore, we continue to assume for the rest of this chapter that locks are released only when the user dictates, that is, that explicit RELEASE LOCKS statements are still required.

DEADLOCK

The locking scheme sketched in the previous two sections, while it solves the lost update problem and certain other problems not discussed in this book, unfortunately introduces problems of its own. Chief among them is the problem of *deadlock*. Deadlock occurs when two users are each waiting for the other to release a lock. For example, consider the situation shown in Fig. 16.3. In this example deadlock occurs at time t4: User B cannot proceed until user A releases the lock on R1, and user A cannot release that lock because he or she is waiting for R2, which is not available because it is locked by user B, who cannot release the lock because he or she cannot proceed, and so on, and so on.

Deadlock is unfortunately a real problem, not merely a theoretical possibility that never happens in practice. One study claims that as many as *ten percent* of all database transactions end

Figure 16.3

User A	Time	User B
—		—
SELECT R1	t1	—
—		—
—	t2	SELECT R2
—		—
SELECT R2	t3	—
wait		—
wait	t4	SELECT R1
wait		wait
wait		wait
wait		wait

in deadlock, though it is tempting to suggest that there must be something seriously wrong with the system design in that particular case. Probably a figure of about one percent or less is more typical. Nevertheless, whatever the percentage is, the fact is that deadlock definitely does occur from time to time. What can be done about it?

The answer is, again unfortunately, that drastic action is required. The system must choose one of the deadlocked programs to be a *victim* and must *cancel* that victim. ("Program" here refers either to a canned procedure or to the machine instructions the DBMS has to execute in response to end-user query language statements issued from a terminal.) Cancellation means *making it as if the program had never started in the first place.* All changes the program has made to the database so far are undone, all its locks are released, and the program starts execution again from the beginning.

Ideally, the cancellation process just described should be invisible to the user at the terminal. However, if (as we assumed) end-users hold all locks up to the point where a RELEASE LOCKS statement is explicitly issued, then *those end-users* can deadlock with each other. If an end-user deadlock occurs, then there is no choice but for the system to come back to one of those users—the victim—and say, "Sorry, you will have to start over—all the changes you have made to the database (since your last RELEASE LOCKS) have just been undone."

A consequence of the foregoing is that in a shared system it is not a good idea for end-users to carry out on-line transactions that require multiple user/system interactions. All such transactions are better done via canned procedures. This is why, as stated earlier, systems usually release locks (in the interactive case) on a statement-by-statement basis.

SUMMARY

We have discussed the question of concurrency control in a shared database system. In such a system concurrent users can interfere with each other in a variety of ways; one of the simplest examples of such interference is provided by the lost update problem, in which one user overwrites another's update without even looking at it. We described a simple locking scheme that can be used to solve that problem (and other concurrency problems), the basic idea of which is that users cannot retrieve a record unless they can acquire a lock on it, and they cannot acquire a lock on it if someone else already has such a lock. We also discussed the problem of deadlock and concluded that transactions requiring multiple user/system interactions should preferably always be handled via canned procedures in a shared system. (Locks acquired by a canned procedure will normally be held until the procedure completes, whereas locks acquired interactively are normally released "immediately.")

Finally, we remind you that we have really only scratched the surface of the concurrency control problem in this chapter. We have described one simple workable scheme, one that is, however, probably simpler than any scheme you are likely to encounter in practice. While it is true that, in principle, the complications in more realistic schemes should affect the system and not the user, the fact is that concurrency control is an area in which (a) it is impossible to conceal *all* the complexity from the user, and (b) many systems do a less than perfect job anyway.

17   *Database Design*

INTRODUCTION   The topic of this chapter (and the next)—namely, database design—is rather different in kind from those of the last few chapters. In each of those last few chapters we discussed some component of the system (e.g., the authorization mechanism), described what it looked like and in outline how it worked, and explained what it was for (security enforcement, in the case of the authorization mechanism). However, we gave little guidance on how to use that component; we had few suggestions concerning when and how to use it and when and how not to. In large part, of course, any such guidance would be superfluous: In any particular application it will be quite obvious how the various mechanisms should be used (if indeed the user has any choice in the matter; in many cases—e.g., with respect to locking—the user simply has to accept what the system does). But when we turn to the question of database design—that is, to the question of what tables there should be in the database and what fields they should contain—then matters are by no means always so obvious, as we will see. The purpose of this chapter and the next is to provide some explicit guidance in this area.

Before we proceed any further, we remark that database design is very much a human problem, not a system problem. The system does not care whether a given design is good or bad. It is the users who are affected by such considerations, not the DBMS.

Who then does the database design? In a single-user system, of course, that single user does. But in a shared system no single end-user will have sufficient information to design the overall database in its entirety; instead, there will be some specially designated person—probably the database administrator—who has that responsibility. That person will have to work with users to understand their individual requirements and will have to merge all those requirements together to produce an appropriate integrated design for the total database. Note, however, that individual users or user groups will be responsible for describing their own requirements to the DBA, and a good way of doing that is by producing a preliminary design for their own piece of the database. Thus even in a shared environment it is a good idea for users to have at least a nodding acquaintance with some of the principles of good design, even though they will probably not be responsible for the final overall design itself.

Database design is a big subject. Whole books have been written about it. Traditionally, it has always been regarded as a very difficult task, one involving highly specialized skills and consuming a great deal of time and effort. Now it is true that the design of large shared databases can indeed be quite difficult; but it is also true that the design of small and/or nonshared databases can be fairly easy (this *must* be true, or databases on minis and micros would not be a feasible proposition). The design of large databases is not *always* difficult, either, especially in the newer systems (older systems tend to introduce too many unnecessary complications into the task). What is more, the design principles that apply to small databases are still applicable when the database is large; it is just that the design of large databases has to take into account a number of additional considerations that are not relevant to the small case. In this book we content ourselves with identifying and illustrating some of the basic principles that apply to both cases.

Caveat: As stated above, database design can be simple. *Talking* about it is frequently not! It is a fact that, in simple cases at least, it is often easier just to do the design than it is to try and explain exactly what it was you did. The reason for this state of affairs is that in order to talk about design in the abstract, it is necessary to introduce a certain amount of abstract terminology; and it is that terminology that is at the root of the problem. Papers on this topic typically involve a *lot* of abstract terms and tend therefore to be very difficult to read. I will do my best in what follows to be as concrete as possible. (Of course, I am saved from having to use a great deal of special terminology by the fact that I am not delving very deeply into the subject anyway. I am not denying the need for abstract terms in a more far-reaching discussion.)

To pursue the point of the previous paragraph one moment longer: Talking about database design at all is a slippery slope. However far you go, it is possible to find some case that the guidelines discussed thus far do not adequately handle, which makes it tempting to go just a little bit further—and before you know it, you are wallowing in a great morass of abstraction and complexity. Such temptations will be firmly resisted in these two chapters.

Our discussion is divided into two pieces (corresponding to the two chapters). In each, we consider a simple example—one sufficiently simple that the "right" design is intuitively obvious—and then examine the question of exactly why that design is right. From these considerations we will extract some fundamental principles of good design, principles that (to repeat) apply to large databases as well as small ones.

DEPARTMENTS AND EMPLOYEES: A GOOD DESIGN

As stated in the "Introduction" section, database design is the process of deciding what tables you should have in the database and what fields those tables should contain. Our first example (a very hackneyed one, but none the worse for that) concerns departments and employees. To be more specific, we wish to design a simple personnel database, in which we need to represent (or *model*) the following situation:

• The company has some number of departments. As time progresses, new departments can be created and existing ones eliminated.

• Each department has a department number (unique), a name, a manager, a budget, and a set (possibly empty) of employees. No manager can manage more than one department at a time.

• Each employee has an employee number (unique), a name, a job, and a salary. Employees can leave and join the company at any time. Every employee is in a department; no employee can be in more than one department at a time. Managers are considered to be in the department that they manage. (We are assuming a "flat" structure, for simplicity. That is, all departments are assumed to be at the same level; there is no notion of one department containing other, lower-level departments, or of one manager being senior to another.)

What tables and fields do we need to model this situation? The obvious (and right) answer is as follows (using a simplified form of the SQL CREATE TABLE statement):

```
CREATE TABLE DEPT      [Departments]
        DEPTNO         [Department number]
        NAME           [Department name]
        MGR_EMPNO      [Employee number of manager]
        BUDGET         [Department budget]


CREATE TABLE EMP       [Employees]
        EMPNO          [Employee number]
        NAME           [Employee name]
        JOB            [Employee job]
        SALARY         [Employee salary]
        DEPTNO         [Employee's department number]
```

For the purposes of this chapter, however, the following representation of the design will turn out to be more useful:

DEPT	DEPTNO	NAME	MGR_EMPNO	BUDGET

EMP	EMPNO	NAME	JOB	SALARY	DEPTNO

DEPARTMENTS AND EMPLOYEES: A BAD DESIGN

Now, why exactly is the design shown above the right one? Well, let us consider some alternatives. There are basically two possible alternatives, both involving a single table instead of two. The first involves moving employee information into the department table, yielding (say) a design of the form shown in Fig. 17.1 (a table of 40 fields). The advantage of this design is that it is no longer necessary to specify the department number for each employee separately. But the disadvantages are obvious. Among them are the following:

1. The table is very wide. It will not fit conveniently on the screen or (more important) on a printed page. Reports from this database will be clumsy and difficult to read—a very practical consideration!

2. We have had to set an upper limit (nine in the example) on the number of employees in a department. The first department to

Figure 17.1

```
DEPT │ DEPTNO │ NAME │ MGR_EMPNO │ BUDGET │ · · ·

              ◄─────  1st EMP in this DEPT  ─────►
        · · · │ EMPNO1 │ NAME1 │ JOB1 │ SALARY1 │ · · ·

                       ◄─────  2nd EMP in this DEPT  ─────►
                 · · · │ EMPNO2 │ NAME2 │ JOB2 │ SALARY2 │ · · ·
                                              ·
                                              ·
                                              ·
                              ◄─────  last EMP in this DEPT  ─────►
                        · · · │ EMPNO9 │ NAME9 │ JOB9 │ SALARY9 │
```

acquire a tenth employee will cause major disruption to the data-base and to programs that use the database.

3. Departments having fewer than nine employees will have records containing a lot of null values. For example, the record for a department with only three employees will contain 24 null values, which is not very elegant and may waste storage space on the disk. (As a matter of fact, each DEPT record in this design would probably include an additional field, NEMPS say, indicating the number of employees it does have. That field could appear immediately following the BUDGET field.)

4. It is likely that employee data for each department would be kept in some specific order within the department record—for example, by alphabetical order of employee names, as in Fig. 17.2. (All fields following SALARY3 in that figure will be null, since NEMPS is 3 for this department.) Now consider the processing involved if a new employee (Clark) joins the department, or if Adams leaves, or if the instructor (Smith) gets married and changes her name to Anderson. Each of these changes will lead to an awkward shuffling of data within the record.

Figure 17.2

DEPT	DEPTNO	NAME	MGR_EMPNO	BUDGET	NEMPS	
	M27	Education	42713	200K	3	...

	EMPNO1	NAME1	JOB1	SALARY1	
...	61126	Adams	Secretary	25K	...

	EMPNO2	NAME2	JOB2	SALARY2	
...	42713	Cook	Manager	50K	...

	EMPNO3	NAME3	JOB3	SALARY3	
...	50708	Smith	Instructor	30K	...

	EMPNO9	NAME9	JOB9	SALARY9
...	?	?	?	?

5. Comparatively simple queries can require very clumsy formulations. For example: "Which department is employee 61126 in?" In SQL:

```
SELECT DEPTNO
FROM   DEPT
WHERE  EMPNO1 = '61126'
OR     EMPNO2 = '61126'
OR     EMPNO3 = '61126'
OR     EMPNO4 = '61126'
OR     EMPNO5 = '61126'
OR     EMPNO6 = '61126'
OR     EMPNO7 = '61126'
OR     EMPNO8 = '61126'
OR     EMPNO9 = '61126'
```

6. Another example: "What is the average salary for department K82?" First, we need to find out how many employees there are in that department:

```
SELECT  NEMPS
FROM    DEPT
WHERE   DEPTNO = 'K82'
```

Suppose the result is 8. Then we compute the average salary as follows:

```
SELECT  (SALARY1 + SALARY2 + SALARY3 + SALARY4 +
           SALARY5 + SALARY6 + SALARY7 + SALARY8) / 8
FROM    DEPT
WHERE   DEPTNO = 'K82'
```

Now we consider briefly how the "right" design overcomes each of these problems:

1. Instead of having one very wide record for each department, the "right" design has (n + 1) narrow records for each department (one DEPT record and n EMP records, where n is the number of employees in the department under consideration).

2. There is no upper limit on n.

3. A department with n employees will have exactly n EMP records. There is no question of an (n + 1)st record in which field values are null.

4. Ordering is not maintained within the database but is imposed on data as it is retrieved. For example:

```
SELECT  EMPNO, NAME, JOB, SALARY
FROM    EMP
WHERE   DEPTNO = 'M27'
ORDER   BY NAME
```

Inserting, deleting, and updating records is straightforward and does not involve any awkward shuffling of data:

```
INSERT INTO EMP ( . . . , NAME, . . . , DEPTNO )
        VALUES ( . . . , 'CLARK', . . . , 'M27' )

DELETE
FROM    EMP
WHERE   DEPTNO = 'M27'
AND     NAME = 'Adams'
```

```
UPDATE  EMP
SET     NAME = 'Anderson'
WHERE   DEPTNO = 'M27'
AND     NAME = 'Smith'
```

5. Which department is employee 61126 in?

```
SELECT  DEPTNO
FROM    EMP
WHERE   EMPNO = '61126'
```

6. What is the average salary in department K82?

```
SELECT  AVG (SALARY)
FROM    EMP
WHERE   DEPTNO = 'K82'
```

DEPARTMENTS AND EMPLOYEES: ANOTHER BAD DESIGN

The second alternative design for departments and employees is, in effect, the converse of the previous one. Instead of moving employee information into the department table, it moves department information into the employee table, as follows:

EMP

EMPNO	ENAME	JOB	SALARY	DEPTNO	DNAME	MGR_EMPNO	BUDGET

Note that we have to distinguish between employee names and department names, so we have renamed the fields concerned ENAME and DNAME, respectively. Let us look at some sample data for this design:

EMP

EMPNO	ENAME	JOB	SALARY	DEPTNO	DNAME	MGR_EMPNO	BUDGET
61126	Adams	Secretary	25K	M27	Education	42713	200K
42713	Cook	Manager	50K	M27	Education	42713	200K
50708	Smith	Instructor	30K	M27	Education	42713	200K

The advantage of this design is that all the department information for a given employee is right there in that employee's record (retrieval of that information will otherwise require a join operation, as explained in Part I). The principal disadvantage is *redundancy*, as the sample data above clearly illustrates. Some consequences of that redundancy are as follows:

1. It is wasteful of storage space on the disk.

2. It is possible to update the database in such a way that it becomes inconsistent. For example, the statement

```
UPDATE EMP
SET    MGR_EMPNO = '12345'
WHERE  EMPNO = '61126'
```

will leave the database in an inconsistent state (the manager for department M27 will be shown as 12345 in one record but as 42713 in others).

3. Suppose the department has just one employee in it. For example, suppose 61126 is the only employee in department M27. If we delete that employee:

```
DELETE
FROM   EMP
WHERE  EMPNO = '61126'
```

then we lose all information about the department, too. (The department has become a department with no employees in it, and the design is incapable of representing such a department.)

4. (This point is really the converse of the previous one.) Suppose a new department H45 (department name Publishing, budget 400K, no manager yet assigned) has been established, but it contains no employees as yet. Then we cannot conveniently insert that information into the database, because we are not allowed to create a record such as

EMPNO	ENAME	JOB	SALARY	DEPTNO	DNAME	MGR_EMPNO	BUDGET
?	?	?	?	H45	Publishing	?	400K

The reason for this restriction is that EMPNO is the primary key of the EMP table, and (as mentioned in Chapter 15) primary keys are usually not allowed to take on null values. (The precise reason for this latter rule will be explained in the next section.)

Once again let us consider briefly how the "right" design solves these problems.

1. There is no redundancy, so there is no waste.

2. There is no redundancy, so there cannot be any inconsistency. (Department M27's manager is given in exactly one place—namely, in M27's DEPT record—so it cannot be shown as 12345 in one place and 42713 in another.)

3. If we delete the only employee (61126) in M27:

```
DELETE
FROM    EMP
WHERE   EMPNO = '61126'
```

then no department information is lost. The record for M27 still exists in the DEPT table.

4. We can insert a department that has no employees:

```
INSERT INTO DEPT ( DEPTNO, NAME, BUDGET )
        VALUES ( 'H45', 'Publishing', 400K )
```

DISCUSSION

Let us now try and analyze what is going on in this example and see if we can extract some broad and useful principles from it. The situation to be modeled in the database involves two types of "entity" (i.e., two basic kinds of object), namely, departments and employees, and in the "right" design each of these *entity types* maps into a table of its own. Hence we have the following:

- **Principle 1:**

  Represent each entity type as a separate table.

  Second, each individual entity (each individual department or employee in the real world) has its own *identifier*, unique with respect to all entities of the type in question, that is used to distinguish that particular entity from all others of that type. The unique identifier for departments is of course *department number*, that for employees is *employee number*. These unique identifiers become *primary keys* in the database design (see Chapter 15).

- **Principle 2:**

  Decide the primary key for each table.

  Values of the primary key of a table must be unique *and must not be null*. (We can now see the reason for this "no nulls" restriction, incidentally. A record with a null primary key value would have to correspond to an entity with a null identifier; and an entity with a null identifier is an entity with *no* identifier, which is a contradiction in terms. If there is no identifier, then there is no entity.)

Each entity has certain *properties:* Departments have names, budgets, and so on; employees have jobs, salaries, and so on. These properties are represented by fields within the entity tables.

- **Principle 3:**

    Assign each property of an entity type to a field within the table representing that entity type.

By following these three principles, we will always finish up with a design that conforms to the following simple pattern:

Each table consists of:
1. a primary key, representing the unique identifier for some particular entity type;

together with
2. Together with zero or more additional fields, representing properties of the entity type identified by the primary key *and not of some other entity type.*

Both of the bad designs shown earlier fail to conform to this simple pattern. In the first case DEPT records included fields (such as SALARY1, SALARY2, etc.) that represented properties of employees rather than departments. In the second case EMP records included fields (such as BUDGET, DNAME, etc.) that represented properties of departments rather than employees. As a result, the (single) table in each case was *overloaded* with information. The three principles stated above, by contrast, will lead to a clean design in which each table contains information about one entity type only. That clean design will be easier to understand, easier to use, and (most important) easier to extend if new information is to be added to the database later on. In a nutshell, the design will be *stable* and will be a good foundation for future growth.

Another way of expressing the clean design objective is: *One fact in one place.* Each "fact" (e.g., the fact that a given department has a given budget) appears at exactly one place in the design. Yet another way of characterizing it (very informally) is: *Each field represents a fact about the key, the whole key, and nothing but the key* (where "key" is shorthand for "entity identified by the primary key of the table that contains the field in question").

DATABASE: A PRIMER

So far we have said nothing about the *relationship* that connects the two entity types in the example (i.e., the relationship between departments and employees). In fact, departments and employees provide the standard example of a *one-to-many relationship:* For each department there are many corresponding employees (where "many" includes the possibilities of one and zero, of course). This relationship must be understood to be *directed* (from departments to employees); the converse relationship, from employees to departments, is *many-to-one* (many employees have the same department). The example illustrates how such relationships are represented in the database: The "many" table (EMP in the example) includes a *foreign key* (field EMP.DEPTNO), whose values match values of the *primary key* (field DEPT.DEPTNO) of the "one" table (table DEPT). Diagrammatically, we have the situation shown in Fig. 17.3. (See Chapter 15 if you need to refresh your memory on the topic of foreign keys.)

As a matter of fact, there is another relationship that holds between DEPTs and EMPs: Each department has a manager, and that manager is of course an employee. (That relationship is *one-to-one:* Each department has exactly one manager. "One-to-one" is just a special case of "one-to-many," however.) So we have another foreign-key/primary-key match: Field DEPT.MGR_ EMPNO is a foreign key in the DEPT table that matches the primary key (EMP.EMPNO) of the EMP table. Figure 17.4 shows both matches.

Figure 17.3

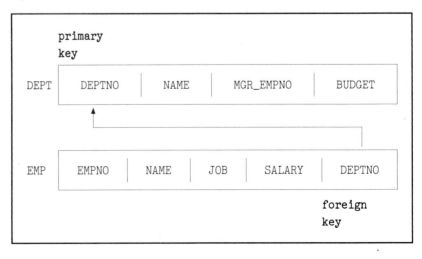

Figure 17.4

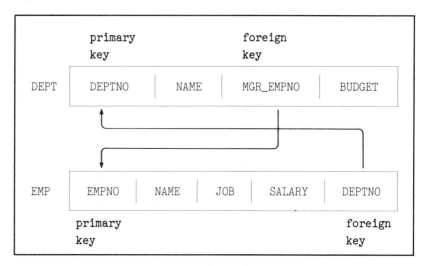

An alternative design would drop the foreign key MGR__EMPNO from the DEPT table and would add a foreign key MGD__DEPTNO (say) to the EMP table, representing the department managed by the employee in question. See Fig. 17.5. However, this design is less satisfactory because it involves a lot of null values (MGD__DEPTNO will be null for every employee who is not a manager). But it does illustrate a point that we have not explicitly mentioned before—namely, that the *general* rule for foreign keys is not that each value of the foreign key must be equal to some existing primary key value, but rather that each value of the foreign key *either* must be equal to some existing primary key value *or must be null*. Sometimes, of course, null values will not be allowed; for example, the foreign key EMP.DEPTNO is not allowed to take on null values, since every employee must be in a department.

Aside: To describe departments-to-managers as one-to-one is in fact an oversimplification. A more accurate statement is as follows: For one department there is either one manager or none (allowing for the case in which no manager is yet assigned); for one employee there is either one department or none that is managed by that employee. The relationship is thus really "(zero-or-one)-to-(zero-or-one)." But it is usual to ignore such refinements in informal discussion.

Figure 17.5

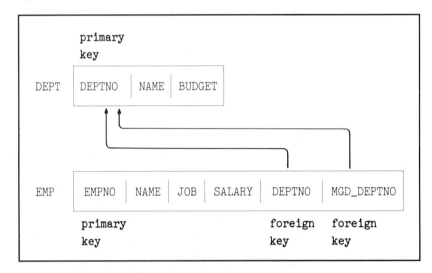

To return to the main topic: Foreign-key/primary-key matches are the glue that holds the database together. Identifying those matches is a crucial part of the database design process. So we have the following:

- **Principle 4:**

  Represent each one-to-many relationship between entity types by a foreign key in the "many" table that matches the primary key of the "one" table.

This concludes the first of our two chapters on database design. You might try the following exercise before moving on to the next chapter (which deals with more complex kinds of relationship).

Exercise: Take a look at the sample databases in Chapter 2 (the wine cellar database, the flight information database, etc.). For each one, identify the primary keys. Verify that the designs satisfy the "one fact in one place" objective. Identify foreign keys, where applicable. Do those examples give rise in your mind to any further design questions? Can you deduce any further generally applicable principles from them?

18   *Database Design (Continued)*

INTRODUCTION

In the previous chapter we considered the departments-and-employees database and used it to introduce a number of important principles of database design. In particular, we showed how to deal with one-to-many relationships. In this chapter we treat a more complicated kind of relationship, namely, the many-to-many relationship. Again we approach the problem by way of a well-known but useful example, this time the suppliers-and-parts example.

SUPPLIERS
AND PARTS:
A GOOD DESIGN

The suppliers-and-parts database is intended to model the following situation:

- A company uses a number of different kinds of parts and obtains them in the form of shipments from a number of different suppliers.

- Each supplier supplies many different kinds of parts; each kind of part is supplied by many different suppliers. However, at any given time there will be at most one shipment outstanding for a given kind of part from a given supplier. Different shipments may involve different quantities of the part being shipped.

- Each supplier has a supplier number (unique), a name, a status (i.e., a rating value), and a city (supplier location).

- Each part (or, rather, each *kind* of part) has a part number (unique), a name, a color, a weight, and a city (location at which parts of that kind are stored).

Figure 18.1 shows a design that is intuitively (and actually) a good one for this database. Figure 18.2 shows some sample values to illustrate that design.

Figure 18.1

SUPPLIER	SUPPNO	SNAME	STATUS	CITY

PART	PARTNO	PNAME	COLOR	WEIGHT	CITY

SHIPMENT	SUPPNO	PARTNO	QUANTITY

Figure 18.2

Table SUPPLIER:

SUPPNO	SNAME	STATUS	CITY
S1	Smith	20	London
S2	Jones	10	Paris
S3	Blake	30	Paris
S4	Clark	20	London
S5	Adams	30	Athens

Table PART:

PARTNO	PNAME	COLOR	WEIGHT	CITY
P1	Nut	Red	12	London
P2	Bolt	Green	17	Paris
P3	Screw	Blue	17	Rome
P4	Screw	Red	14	London
P5	Cam	Blue	12	Paris
P6	Cog	Red	19	London

Table SHIPMENT:

SUPPNO	PARTNO	QUANTITY
S1	P1	300
S1	P2	200
S1	P3	400
S1	P4	200
S1	P5	100
S1	P6	100
S2	P1	300
S2	P2	400
S3	P2	200
S4	P2	200
S4	P4	300
S4	P5	400

DISCUSSION

Note first of all that the suppliers-and-parts example does involve a many-to-many relationship, because (a) for each supplier there will typically be any number of outstanding shipments and hence many corresponding parts, and (b) for each part, likewise, there will typically be many outstanding shipments, from many distinct suppliers. More succinctly: For each supplier there are many parts; for each part there are many suppliers.

How did we arrive at our "good" database design? Well, note first of all that tables SUPPLIER and PART are obtained by application of the principles established in the previous chapter:

- Table SUPPLIER consists of a primary key (SUPPNO) identifying some entity type (suppliers), together with three additional fields (SNAME, STATUS, and CITY) representing properties of that entity type.

- Table PART consists of a primary key (PARTNO) identifying some entity type (parts), together with four additional fields (PNAME, COLOR, WEIGHT, and CITY) representing properties of that entity type.

Turning now to shipments, we observe first that we cannot put shipment information into the SUPPLIER table. If we did, we would get a design of the form shown in Fig. 18.3, say. That design obviously violates the principles already established in the previous chapter. We cannot put shipment information into the PART table either, for exactly the same reason. So we must introduce another table, the SHIPMENT table. Each record in that table represents a single shipment and specifies (a) the supplier involved, (b) the part involved, and (c) the shipment quantity. Note the following points:

Figure 18.3

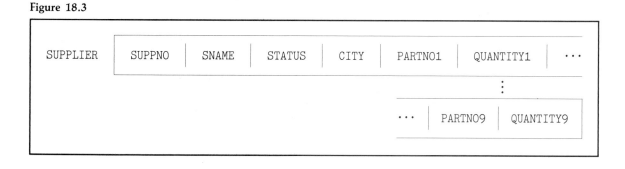

• Fields SHIPMENT.SUPPNO and SHIPMENT.PARTNO are *foreign keys*, matching primary keys SUPPLIER.SUPPNO and PART.PARTNO, respectively. See Fig. 18.4.

• Field SHIPMENT.QUANTITY does not represent a property of a supplier, nor of a part, but of a shipment. *Shipments are entities in their own right, just like suppliers and parts.* As entities, they can have properties of their own. (Note, however, that shipments are not *independent* entities, in the same way that suppliers and parts are independent entities; they depend on suppliers and parts, in the sense that a given shipment can exist only if the corresponding supplier and part both exist also.)

• As entities, shipments must have unique identifiers and hence *primary keys*. The primary key of the SHIPMENT table is the combination (SHIPMENT.SUPPNO,SHIPMENT.PARTNO): It requires both a supplier number and a part number together to

Figure 18.4

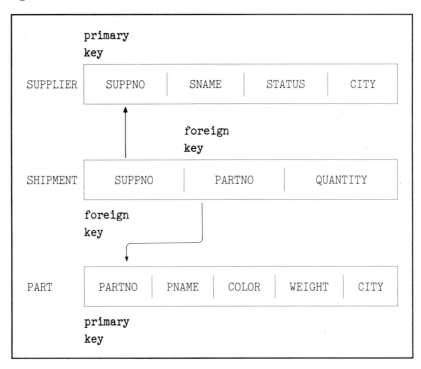

identify a shipment uniquely, as the sample data shown in Fig. 18.2 illustrates. (Recall from the definition in Chapter 15 that primary keys can consist of *combinations* of fields as well as of single fields.)

Abstracting the foregoing discussion, we are led to the following:

• **Principle 5**

Represent each many-to-many relationship between entity types as a separate table. Use foreign keys within that table to identify the entity types involved in the relationship. Use the combination of those foreign keys as the primary key for the table. Represent properties of the relationship by fields in the relationship table.

FURTHER REMARKS The suppliers-and-parts example gives rise to a number of further observations.

• It is common to talk of many-to-many relationships as if they were the most complicated kind of relationship to arise in practice. But many-to-many-to-many (etc.) relationships are by no means unknown. By way of illustration, we might extend the suppliers-and-parts example to involve *projects* also: Each shipment is a shipment of a certain part by a certain supplier to a certain project. A suitable design for this case would be as shown in Fig. 18.5. The SHIPMENT table now represents a many-to-many-to-many relationship and involves three foreign keys and a primary key with three components. Thus the technique for dealing with many-to-many-to-many (etc.) relationships is no more than a generalization of that for dealing with many-to-many relationships (Principle 5), and does not really require any special consideration.

Exercise: Invent some sample data for this extended design.

• Returning now to the simple suppliers-and-parts example (i.e., forgetting projects): Note that the relationship of suppliers to shipments is one-to-many, and the relationship of parts to shipments is also one-to-many. Principle 4 (for dealing with one-to-many relationships) should therefore apply; and so indeed it does, if we look

Figure 18.5

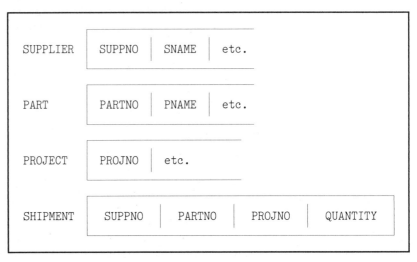

at suppliers-to-shipments and parts-to-shipments separately. The fact is, a many-to-many relationship can *always* be regarded as a combination of two one-to-many relationships. (Similarly, a many-to-many-to-many relationship can always be regarded as a combination of three one-to-many relationships, etc.)

• We said earlier that foreign-key/primary-key matches are the glue that holds the database together. Broadly speaking, this statement is true. However, there may be other intertable relationships that are not represented by keys at all. An example is provided in the suppliers-and-parts database by the fields SUPPLIER.CITY and PART.CITY. Suppliers located in London, for example, do have some kind of relationship with parts that are stored in London, namely, "colocation"; but that relationship is represented by matching values in two fields that are not primary or foreign keys. (Those fields could *become* foreign keys if a "city" table were to be added to the database later on.)

**INDIVIDUAL
USER VIEWS**

It is important to understand the distinction between database design and data definition. Database design, as already explained, is the process of deciding what tables and fields you need. *Data definition* is the process of specifying the results of that design process to the database management system—that is, the process of mapping your design into appropriate CREATE TABLE statements and so forth (or whatever data definition statements your particular system provides). Then, having issued those data definition statements, and so built an empty database, it is still necessary to go on and load data into that database before you can really start doing some useful work.

Now, many systems provide another data definition statement, namely, CREATE VIEW (discussed in Chapter 13). The design process we have been describing in this chapter and its predecessor tells you how to go about designing the database *independently of how that database is going to be used.* In essence, we have simply been saying, "Decide what entities you are interested in; decide what their properties are; decide what relationships (one-to-many or many-to-many) exist among them"; and we have totally ignored the question of how that information will be used in any particular application. But (especially in a shared environment) it is quite likely that each individual application will require its own individual view of the database: Each application may wish to see—or indeed may only be *allowed* to see—some subset of the total database (it may be interested only in a subset of the entities, properties, and relationships that are represented in that total database). Moreover, it may require that subset to be restructured and/or renamed in a variety of ways. All of these requirements—subsetting, restructuring, renaming—are accommodated by the view mechanism. Thus in a shared environment, at least, database design and data definition will typically be followed by a stage in which individual user views are defined for individual applications. It may even be desirable during that stage to provide user views that violate some of the design principles we have been establishing. For example, in the departments-and-employees database we might define a view as follows:

```
CREATE VIEW EMPDEPT ( EMPNO, ENAME, JOB, SALARY,
                      DEPTNO, DNAME, MGR_EMPNO, BUDGET )
     AS SELECT EMPNO, EMP.NAME, JOB, SALARY,
               DEPT.DEPTNO, DEPT.NAME, MGR_EMPNO, BUDGET
        FROM   EMP, DEPT
        WHERE  EMP.DEPTNO = DEPT.DEPTNO
```

This view corresponds precisely to the second of the bad designs from Chapter 17 (it involves a lot of redundancy, inasmuch as department information for any given department is repeated for every employee in that department). However, for a user who is interested in department information for given employees *and is performing retrieval operations only,* this view may be exactly what is required. It makes the formulation of a query such as "Who is employee 61126's manager?" considerably simpler than would otherwise be the case. It is not a "bad design" *for that user.*

So let us retrench a little. In the previous chapter we stressed the importance of *design stability.* It is important to arrive at a design that is fundamentally stable, to serve as a good base for the extensions that will inevitably be needed in practice as the database grows to incorporate more information (i.e., more *kinds* of information). But that stable design is, as explained earlier, *application-independent.* It is possible (to some extent) subsequently to tailor, restructure, and slant that design to meet the needs of individual applications by means of the view mechanism. However, this tailoring (etc.) is very much a secondary consideration. The primary objective is to get the application-independent design right in the first place.

SUMMARY

We have now come to the end of our discussion of database design. As indicated in the introduction to the previous chapter, it is possible to go very much further with this topic than we have done in these two chapters. However, we have covered enough to enable you to approach database design problems with some confidence, particularly in a small or single-user environment. By way of conclusion, we repeat from Chapter 15 the definitions of primary and foreign key (since those concepts are so crucial to the design process), and we then repeat the five design principles identified in this chapter and its predecessor.

- *Definition:* The *primary key* of a table is a field of that table, or perhaps a combination of several fields of that table, that can be used as a unique identifier for the records in that table.

- *Definition:* A *foreign key* is a field or field combination in one table whose values are required to match those of the primary key in some other table.

- *Design principle 1:* Represent each entity type as a separate table.

- *Design principle 2:* Decide the primary key for each table.

- *Design principle 3:* Assign each property of an entity type to a field within the table representing that entity type.

- *Design principle 4:* Represent each one-to-many relationship between entity types by a foreign key in the "many" table that matches the primary key of the "one" table.

- *Design principle 5:* Represent each many-to-many relationship between entity types as a separate table. Use foreign keys within that table to identify the entity types involved in the relationship. Use the combination of those foreign keys as the primary key for the table. Represent properties of the relationship by fields in the relationship table.

EXERCISES

Some of the following exercises deliberately go a little beyond the design principles discussed so far in order to make you realize the never-ending nature of the database design problem. Further discussion is given in the "Answers" section, where appropriate.

1. Refer to the Road Association database in Chapter 4. Identify all primary and foreign keys in that design. Are there any many-to-many relationships? Can you see any way to improve the design?

2. We stated in the body of this chapter that an important objective for good design is to provide a stable base for growth. What modifications are required to the design of the Road Association database if it becomes necessary to incorporate the following additional information?

   (a) The area of each parcel;

   (b) The number of parcels owned by each owner;

   (c) The distance of each parcel from the entrance to the road system (i.e., the distance from the start of Redwood Road);

   (d) The length of each of the three roads;

   (e) The name of the person (the "road manager") in charge of maintenance on each of the three roads;

   (f) The number of parcels on each road.

   What effect, if any, do these changes have on the queries and updates shown in Chapters 4 and 5?

3. Modify the Road Association database design to allow for the possibility that one parcel can have multiple owners.

4. Design a database for the following application (the courses-and-students database):

   • A certain company maintains an internal education department whose responsibility is to run training courses for the company's employees. It currently offers a variety of such courses, each one having a course number (unique) and a subject. New courses can be added and old ones eliminated at any time.

   • Each course is taught many times (i.e., has many *offerings*), in general. Each offering has a date, a location, one or more teachers, and a number of students.

   • Each course also has a number of immediate prerequisite courses (e.g., an employee will not be allowed to enroll in an offering of course C22 without having first attended offerings of courses C17 and C20).

   • Each teacher of an offering is identified by employee number (unique among employees).

   • Each student on an offering is identified by employee number (unique among employees). A student's enrollment record also shows the grade that person obtained on that offering.

   You may find it helpful to invent some sample data for this problem before embarking on your design.

5. Consider the suppliers-and-parts database. Suppose parts come in multiple colors and are stored in multiple cities (e.g., part P1 is available in red, white, or blue and is stored in both London and Nice). Modify the design accordingly.

6. Again consider the suppliers-and-parts database. Suppose that it is possible for multiple shipments for a given part from a given supplier to be outstanding at any given time, but that no two such shipments can be due for delivery on the same day. Modify the design accordingly. Does this situation violate any of our established design principles? If so, how?

ANSWERS

2. Change the design as follows:

(a) Add an AREA field to the PARCELS table.

(b) Add a NO_OF_PARCELS_OWNED field to the OWNERS table.

(c) Add a DISTANCE field to the PARCELS table.

(d) Add a new table called ROADS containing exactly three records (one for each of the three roads). That table contains two fields: ROAD and LENGTH. Note that ROAD is the primary key for ROADS and that the ROAD field in tables PARCELS and SPECIAL_ASSESSMENTS will now be a foreign key in each of those two tables matching the primary key of ROADS.

(e) Add a MANAGER field to the ROADS table.

(f) Add a NO_OF_PARCELS field to the ROADS table.

SELECT operations will continue to work essentially as before (except that the meaning of "SELECT *" will be extended in some cases). UPDATE and DELETE operations will be unaffected. IN-SERT operations will generate null values for new fields; for example, an INSERT INTO PARCELS that does not mention the new AREA field will set AREA to null in the new record. A subsequent UPDATE operation can be used to change the AREA to some non-null value.

3. Drop the OWNER field from the PARCELS table. Add a new table called PARCEL_OWNERS, with fields APN and OWNER. That table represents a many-to-many relationship between parcels and owners; APN is a foreign key matching the primary key of PARCELS, and OWNER is a foreign key matching the primary key of OWNERS. The primary key of PARCEL_OWNERS is the combination (APN,OWNER).

Note that this change will definitely affect certain existing queries (basically, any query that involved the assumption that each parcel had a single owner).

4. The obvious entity types are courses, offerings, prerequisites, teachers, and students. However, there is another entity type, namely, employees, the existence of which is somewhat hidden by

the manner in which the problem is stated. (Teachers and students are both employees.) The following relationships exist:

Courses-to-offerings	One-to-many
Courses-to-prerequisites	Many-to-many
Offerings-to-teachers (i.e., -to-employees)	Many-to-many
Offerings-to-students (i.e., -to-employees)	Many-to-many

A possible design is as follows (we use a simplified form of SQL once again):

```
CREATE TABLE COURSE
     COURSENO
     SUBJECT
     PRIMARY KEY ( COURSENO )

CREATE TABLE OFFERING
     COURSENO
     OFFNO     [Offering number within course: 1, 2, 3, . . .]
     DATE
     LOCATION
     PRIMARY KEY ( COURSENO, OFFNO )
     FOREIGN KEY ( COURSENO MATCHES COURSE.COURSENO )

CREATE TABLE PREREQS
     COURSENO
     PRENO     [Course number of prerequisite course]
     PRIMARY KEY ( COURSENO, PRENO )
     FOREIGN KEY ( COURSENO MATCHES COURSE.COURSENO )
     FOREIGN KEY ( PRENO    MATCHES COURSE.COURSENO )

CREATE TABLE TEACHES
     COURSENO
     OFFNO
     EMPNO
     PRIMARY KEY ( COURSENO, OFFNO, EMPNO )
     FOREIGN KEY ( EMPNO MATCHES EMP )
     FOREIGN KEY ( ( COURSENO, OFFNO ) MATCHES
                                OFFERING.( COURSENO, OFFNO ) )
```

```
CREATE TABLE ATTENDS
      COURSENO
      OFFNO
      EMPNO
      GRADE
      PRIMARY KEY ( COURSENO, OFFNO, EMPNO )
      FOREIGN KEY ( EMPNO MATCHES EMP )
      FOREIGN KEY ( ( COURSENO, OFFNO ) MATCHES
                                  OFFERING.( COURSENO, OFFNO ) )


CREATE TABLE EMP
      EMPNO
            .
            .
            .
      PRIMARY KEY ( EMPNO )
```

The PREREQS, TEACHES, and ATTENDS tables all represent many-to-many relationships.

5. Replace table PART by the following three tables:

```
PART   ( PARTNO, PNAME, WEIGHT )

PCOLOR ( PARTNO, COLOR )

PCITY  ( PARTNO, CITY )
```

Sample values:

PART table:

PARTNO	PNAME	WEIGHT
P1	Nut	12

PCOLOR table:

PARTNO	COLOR
P1	Red
P1	White
P1	Blue

PCITY table:

PARTNO	CITY
P1	London
P1	Nice

In effect, we are treating "part color" and "part city" as *separate entities in their own right.* However, those entities are not independent—they do not have "independent existence"—but are instead existence-dependent on the corresponding PART entity. If, for example, the record for P1 is deleted from the PART table, then the records for P1 must be deleted from the PCOLOR and PCITY tables also. Note that fields PCOLOR.PARTNO and PCITY.PARTNO are foreign keys matching the primary key of PART. (What are the primary keys for PCOLOR and PCITY?)

6. Add a DUE_DATE field to the SHIPMENT table. The primary key for that table will now be the combination (SUPPNO,PARTNO, DUE_DATE). This design does violate one of our design principles, namely Principle 5, because DUE_DATE is not a foreign key, and the primary key is therefore more than just "the combination of foreign keys identifying entity types involved in the relationship." In other words, although it commonly will be the case that the combination of foreign keys will have the uniqueness property (required if that combination is to serve as the primary key), it is not *necessarily* the case.

This example touches on yet another principle, namely: Whenever a primary key is composite (i.e., involves more than one field)—and especially if it involves more than two fields—you should consider the possibility of introducing another (noncomposite) field to act as the primary key instead. For example, introduce a unique *shipment number* for each shipment:

```
SHIPMENT ( SHIPNO, SUPPNO, PARTNO, DUE_DATE, QUANTITY )
```

Composite primary keys can be rather clumsy to deal with.

Afterword

Database technology is here to stay. More than that, applications for that technology are likely to expand dramatically over the next few years, with the rapid spread of personal computers and the fast-growing availability of database systems for those personal machines. At the same time the more traditional applications on larger machines will also increase in both numbers and scope. In this book we have tried to indicate the potential of database technology by describing, in user-oriented terms, what database systems are capable of. Most of our discussions have been in terms of four specific systems:

- SQL, which is already available on a number of larger machines and looks set to become a de facto standard for machines of all sizes (in fact, moves are already afoot within the American National Standards Institute to develop SQL into an official standard, not just a de facto one);

- QBE, which exhibits a quite different, and arguably more user-friendly (forms-oriented), mode of operation;

- NOMAD, which combines in a single self-contained system a very wide range of sophisticated facilities, including powerful report-writing capabilities, graphical output functions, and a reasonably comprehensive integrity enforcement mechanism;

- dBASE, which is the only one of these four systems to be commercially available on microcomputers at the time of writing (although this statement may no longer be true by the time this book is published).

As indicated earlier, we concentrated on these systems not because we wish to disparage any of the many others on the market, but rather because between them they provide a good illustration of the range of capabilities to be found in modern database management systems.

The major topics we discussed were as follows:

- Basic database concepts
- Retrieval operations
- Maintenance operations
- Canned procedures
- Database definition
- Report writing
- The catalog
- Indexes
- Views
- Security
- Integrity
- Locking
- Database design

How can we expect database technology to evolve in the future? Although much has already been achieved, much still remains to be done. Improvements can be expected in all of the areas listed above; for example, systems are likely to provide better support for integrity control (as mentioned in the text, this area is one in which most systems are somewhat weak today). In addition, research is being actively pursued in a number of broader areas, and some of that research will doubtless emerge eventually in the form of products or product enhancements. Here are some of those broader areas:

1. Higher-level interfaces

"Interface" is a term used to refer to the manner in which user/system interactions are expressed. It covers both the manner in which users formulate commands to the system and the manner in which the system communicates results to the user. Current systems typically provide "stylized English" interfaces (as in SQL) or, less commonly, forms-oriented interfaces (as in QBE), though a few systems are beginning to provide "natural language" interfaces in which user commands can be expressed in something closely resembling written English. Research into other kinds of interface—involving, say, spoken English as opposed to written English, pictures (not just forms, but, for example, photographs, both still and moving), sound recordings, and so on—is currently being undertaken in a number of universities and similar institutions.

2. Distributed data

Currently most databases are *centralized*: All of the data is stored at one central location. A number of prototype systems are under construction, however, in which the data can be stored at any number of geographically dispersed sites—say, New York, London, and Rio de Janeiro—and users at any site can access *all* of the data without having to know where any piece of it is. The various sites are all linked together in some kind of *communications network*. The advantage of such an arrangement is that more data is available to more people; at the same time it is possible to store each piece of data close to where it is most frequently used (in the interests of efficiency). For example, each branch of a bank could keep its own local database of account records for the customers of that branch, but at the same time could access the remote databases at other branches; thus, for example, a customer of the New York branch who happened to be in London could easily obtain funds at the London branch on the presentation of some suitable identification.

3. Other kinds of data

Existing systems are quite good at handling data that exhibits a simple, regular structure, of the kind that is commonly found in the business world. However, not all data is like that. Some counterexamples are (a) telemetry data (e.g., signals from a probe or satellite), which typically consists of enormously long sequences of bits; (b) miscellaneous facts (e.g., footnotes or margin notes on regular data, such as a note on the EMP table to the effect that employee Jones is president of the Camera Club); (c) ordinary text, such as the text of a letter or article, which can be thought of as a very long character string with a certain internal structure of its own (paragraphs, sentences, words, etc.). We need to enhance our existing systems to handle these additional kinds of data.

4. Semantic modeling

The term "semantic modeling" refers to the activity of *representing knowledge* (or meaning) in the database. Existing systems do not really understand very much about the data they are storing. If they did understand a little more, then they could behave in a more intelligent fashion with respect to that data. As a simple example, if SQL understood about foreign keys, it could make sure that the Road Association database never contained a PARCEL_ACCOUNTS record that referred to a nonexistent parcel. Thus making the system aware of foreign keys is (in small part) putting more meaning into the database and making the system more intelligent. We can expect to see many improvements of this nature over the next several years.

Appendix A
The Relational Model

As mentioned in the Foreword, all of the systems described in this book are *relational* systems. The purpose of this appendix is to explain in a little more detail (but still somewhat informally) what is meant by such a statement. Basically, a relational system is a system that is constructed in accordance with a set of principles that together form what is called *the relational model*. The relational model is *a way of looking at data*—that is, a prescription for how to represent data and how to manipulate that representation. To be more specific, the relational model is concerned with three aspects of data: data *structure*, data *manipulation*, and data *integrity*. We examine each of these in turn.

- **Data structure**

    The structural part of the model specifies how data should be represented—namely, as tables, just like all the tables you have seen in examples in this book. (Note clearly that the data representation we are talking about here is the data representation that is *seen by the user*. The representation on the disk will not be so simple, involving, as it necessarily must, all kinds of implementation-specific details. See the discussion of data independence at various points in this book.)

    Here is a more formal definition of the tables of the relational model:

    Definition: A *table* consists of a row of *column headings* together with zero or more rows of *data values*. For a given table, (a) the column heading row specifies one or more columns; (b) each data row contains exactly one value for each of the columns specified in the column heading row.

    Notice the phrase "exactly one" in this definition. The significance of this phrase is that a table such as the one labeled ILLEGAL in Fig. A.1 is not a valid table within a relational database (the

Figure A.1

ILLEGAL		LEGAL	
SUPPNO	PARTNO	SUPPNO	PARTNO
S1	P1, P2, P3	S1	P1
S2	P2, P4	S1	P2
		S1	P3
		S2	P2
		S2	P4

rows of ILLEGAL do not contain "exactly one" value in the PARTNO column). Instead, the same information must be represented in the simpler form illustrated by the table labeled LEGAL.

Tables such as LEGAL are said to be *normalized,* and the process of converting an illegal table into an equivalent normalized form is called *normalization.* The relational model does not allow unnormalized tables. (All data can be represented in normalized form, so this rule does not impose any real restriction on the user. Moreover, the resulting simplification in data structure leads to corresponding simplifications in numerous other areas—in particular, in the data manipulation operators, as you will see below.) Exercise 5 in Chapter 18 was concerned with this question of normalization, although we did not use the term at that point in the text.

We can now explain why the model is called "relational." The reason is that tables such as those just described are actually a special case of the construct known in mathematics as a *relation.* (As far as this book is concerned, in fact, "relation" and "table" mean exactly the same thing.) The whole relational model is founded on elementary mathematical relation theory.

• **Data manipulation**

The manipulative part of the model provides a set of operators for manipulating data that is represented in the form of tables. "Join" is an example of such an operator. We will examine such operators in more detail in a few moments.

- **Data integrity**

    The integrity part of the model consists of two general integrity rules that are applicable to all databases. We have touched on both of those rules in this book already, but we repeat (and summarize) them here for completeness:

1. Every table should have a primary key—that is, a field, or field combination, that serves as a unique identifier for the records in that table. Primary keys should not accept null values.

2. If table T2 includes a foreign key FK matching the primary key PK of table T1, then every value of FK in T2 must either (a) be equal to the value of PK in some record of T1, or (b) be null.

    In addition to these two general rules, a given database will normally be required to satisfy a set of specific integrity rules that apply only to that particular database. But such specific rules are outside the scope of the relational model per se.

    Let us now, as promised, take a more detailed look at the manipulative part of the model. First, let us make explicit something that we have been tacitly assuming throughout this book:

    The result of any retrieval operation is another table.

In other words, whatever query—whatever SELECT statement, in SQL terms—we execute, the result of that query is a new table, constructed in some way from the tables in the database. Thus the process of retrieval is, precisely, *a process of constructing tables.* Intuitively, you can think of retrieval as a kind of cut-and-paste operation, by which the required result is built up out of the tables you start with in the database. The cut-and-paste operation involves extracting rows, extracting columns, joining on the basis of matching values, and so on; and these fundamental operations (extracting rows, extracting columns, joining, etc.) are exactly the operations provided by the manipulative part of the model.

    Let us now make the foregoing discussion a little more precise. The manipulative part of the relational model consists of a set of operators known collectively as the *relational algebra.* Each operator of the relational algebra takes either one or two relations (tables) as its operand(s) and produces a new relation (table) as its result. Many such operators can be defined; in this appendix we consider only three of the most important, namely, SELECT, PROJECT, and JOIN.

- **SELECT (sometimes called RESTRICT)**

The SELECT operator (not to be confused with the SELECT of SQL, NOMAD, or dBASE!) extracts a *row subset* of a given table—that is, that subset of rows from the given table for which a given condition is satisfied. The condition can be as complex as desired, provided only that it can be evaluated for a given row by looking at that row in isolation (i.e., without having to look at any other rows in the database at the same time). Examples:

```
SELECT PARCEL_ACCOUNTS WHERE APN = '93-282-55'

SELECT PARCELS WHERE ROAD = 'CREEK' OR ROAD = 'MILL'

SELECT PART WHERE WEIGHT > 15
```

- **PROJECT**

The PROJECT operator extracts a *column subset* of a given table—that is, that subset obtained by selecting specified columns (and then eliminating redundant duplicate rows within the columns selected, if necessary; see the second example below). Examples:

```
PROJECT GENERAL_LEDGER OVER ENTRY, DATE, AMOUNT, BALANCE

PROJECT PARCELS OVER ROAD
```

Suppose in the second of these examples that the PARCELS table contains 32 rows. Then the ROAD column in that table will, of course, contain 32 values. However, it will contain only three *distinct* values, namely, 'REDWOOD', 'CREEK', and 'MILL'. Hence the result of the PROJECT is a table containing three rows, not 32 (because redundant duplicates are eliminated).

- **JOIN**

The JOIN operator takes two tables T1 and T2 and joins them together to yield a new, wider table T. More precisely, the join of table T1 on column C1 with table T2 on column C2 consists of all possible rows r such that r is the concatenation of a row r1 of T1 and a row r2 of T2, and the value of C1 in r1 is equal to the value of C2 in r2. Figure A.2 presents a simple example.

The join just defined is sometimes known as the *equijoin*. Notice that the result of an equijoin necessarily contains two identical columns (namely, C1 and C2, in the example). If we eliminate one

Figure A.2

T1					T2			

A	B	C1	D
a1	b1	x	d1
a2	b2	x	d2
a3	b3	y	d3

E	C2	F	G
e1	x	f1	g1
e2	y	f2	g2
e3	y	f3	g3

JOIN T1 ON C1 WITH T2 ON C2

A	B	C1	D	E	C2	F	G
a1	b1	x	d1	e1	x	f1	g1
a2	b2	x	d2	e1	x	f1	g1
a3	b3	y	d3	e2	y	f2	g2
a3	b3	y	d3	e3	y	f3	g3

of these columns (which we can do via PROJECT), the result is called the *natural* join. The natural join corresponding to the equijoin of Fig. A.2 is shown in Fig. A.3. For symmetry we have named the join column in that figure as simply "C."

With just these three relational algebra operations (SELECT, PROJECT, and NATURAL JOIN), it is possible to formulate quite complicated retrieval requests. We give a single example:

Figure A.3

NATURAL JOIN T1 ON C1 WITH T2 ON C2

A	B	C	D	E	F	G
a1	b1	x	d1	e1	f1	g1
a2	b2	x	d2	e1	f1	g1
a3	b3	y	d3	e2	f2	g2
a3	b3	y	d3	e3	f3	g3

List all improved parcels, with owners' names, addresses, and phone numbers. (Example 11 in the section "Sample Queries" in Chapter 4.)

Step 1: `SELECT PARCELS WHERE IMPROVED = 'Y'`

Let the result be P, say.

Step 2: `NATURAL JOIN P ON OWNER WITH OWNERS ON OWNER`

Let the result be Q, say.

Step 3: `PROJECT Q OVER APN, OWNER, ADDRESS, PHONE`

This step produces the desired final result.

It is also possible to write the entire query as a single (nested) expression:

```
PROJECT
  ( NATURAL JOIN
          ( SELECT PARCELS WHERE IMPROVED = 'Y' ) ON OWNER
            WITH OWNERS ON OWNER )
                OVER APN, OWNER, ADDRESS, PHONE
```

We are now (at last) in a position to define what we mean by a *relational database management system* (relational DBMS). A system is *relational* if and only if it supports at least the following subset of the total relational model:

- Relational databases (i.e., databases that are perceived by the user as tables and nothing but tables);

- At least the operations SELECT, PROJECT, and JOIN of the relational algebra (without any restrictions on those operations having to do with the way the data is physically stored on the disk).

Note carefully that a system does not necessarily have to support SELECT, PROJECT, and JOIN *explicitly*. It is only the functionality of those operators that we are talking about here. For example, SQL provides the functionality of all three of those operators (and more besides) within its own SELECT operator.

Note also that a system that supports relational databases (i.e., tables) but not these three operators does not qualify as a relational system under our definition. Likewise, a system that allows (say) the user to SELECT rows from a table according to values of some field F only if that field F is *indexed* also does not qualify (because it is placing physical restrictions on the operations).

Appendix B
A Guide To Further Reading

The field of database literature is so vast that any list of suggestions for further reading must necessarily be highly selective. In this appendix we give only a few references that are particularly relevant to the theme and topics of this book.

Warning: Most of these references are considerably more technical and/or theoretical in nature than this book.

GENERAL

• C. J. Date. *An Introduction to Database Systems.* Reading, Mass.: Addison-Wesley, Volume I, 3rd edition, 1981; Volume II, 1st edition, 1983.

These two volumes provide a much more detailed and technically complete treatment of the subject than this book does. They also include many annotated references on specific topics and so could act as a good starting point for a more systematic or detailed study of the subject. However, they are definitely oriented toward the data processing professional reader. Some knowledge of programming is required.

Note: In the rest of this appendix we refer to these two books as simply Volume I and Volume II, respectively.

• James Martin. *An End-User's Guide to Data Base.* Englewood Cliffs, N.J.: Prentice-Hall, 1981.

Martin's book addresses some of the same topics as this book. However, it seems to be oriented more toward end-user *management* rather than end-users per se. It contains the following chapters:

1. What is data base?

2. Productivity and flexibility

3. Who does what?

4. What are data?

5. Data modeling

6. Design tools for end-users

7. How to succeed with data modeling

8. Data-base languages for end-users

9. Ownership of data, and privacy

10. Considerations which affect performance

11. Separate end-user systems

• David Kruglinski. *Data Base Management Systems: A Guide to Microcomputer Software.* New York: Osborne/McGraw-Hill, 1983.

Kruglinski discusses a number of microcomputer systems, including in particular the dBASE II system discussed in Chapter 10 and elsewhere in the present book.

CHAPTER 2: AN OVERVIEW OF DATABASE MANAGEMENT

• E. H. Sibley. "The Development of Data Base Technology." Guest Editor's Introduction, *ACM Computing Surveys* 8, No. 1 (March 1976); special issue on data base management systems.

• J. P. Fry and E. H. Sibley. "Evolution of Data Base Management Systems." *ACM Computing Surveys* 8, No. 1 (March 1976); special issue on data base management systems.

• See also Volume I, Chapters 1 and 3.

CHAPTER 3: WHAT THE MACHINE IS DOING

• I. D. Hill. "Wouldn't It Be Nice If We Could Write Computer Programs in Ordinary English—Or Would It?" *British Computer Society Computer Bulletin*, June 1972.

This article illustrates very clearly (and in a nontechnical manner) some of the problems involved in attempting to communicate with a computer in natural language.

CHAPTERS 4 AND 5: A CASE STUDY

• IBM Corporation. *SQL/Data System for VSE: A Relational Data System for Application Development.* IBM Form No. G320–6590 (1981).

This volume is an introductory manual on SQL/DS, an implementation of SQL for medium-size IBM machines. Other, more advanced manuals on this system are also available from IBM. Most of our discussions of SQL in this book are based on this implementation.

- ORACLE Corporation. *ORACLE Version 3.0 Introduction Manual.* Menlo Park, Calif.: 1982.

   This manual describes ORACLE, an implementation of SQL for DEC VAX–11 and PDP–11 machines. A version for IBM machines has also been announced.

- D. D. Chamberlin *et al.* "SEQUEL 2: A Unified Approach to Data Definition, Manipulation, and Control." *IBM Journal of Research and Development* 20, No. 6 (November 1976).

   SEQUEL 2 was the forerunner of SQL. This paper provides a complete definition of that language.

- M. M. Astrahan *et al.* "System R: Relational Approach to Database Management." *ACM Transactions on Database Systems* 1, No. 2 (June 1976).

   System R was the prototype forerunner of the SQL/DS product. This paper describes the structure and design of that prototype.

- See also Volume I, Chapters 5–8.

**CHAPTER 8:
QUERY BY
EXAMPLE**

- IBM Corporation. *Query By Example Terminal User's Guide.* IBM Form No. SH20–2078 (1978).

   This book describes the IBM implementation of QBE. Other manuals on this system are also available from IBM.

- See also Volume I, Chapter 11.

**CHAPTER 9:
NOMAD**

- National CSS, Inc. *NOMAD2 Reference Manual.* Wilton, Conn.: 1982.

- Daniel D. McCracken. *A Guide to NOMAD for Applications Development.* Reading, Mass.: Addison-Wesley, 1980.

   This book is a very readable tutorial on some of the major features of the NOMAD system.

**CHAPTER 10:
dBASE II**

- Ashton-Tate. *dBASE II Assembly-Language Relational Database Management System.* 1982. Available from Ashton-Tate, 9929 W. Jefferson Boulevard, Culver City, Calif. 90230.

CHAPTER 12:
INDEXES

• D. Comer. "The Ubiquitous B-tree." *ACM Computing Surveys* 11, No. 2 (June 1979).

Most modern database systems support a particular kind of multilevel index called a *B-tree*. This paper provides a good tutorial on B-trees.

• R. Morris. "Scatter Storage Techniques." *Communications of the ACM* 11, No. 1 (January 1968).

Another commonly found technique (not discussed in this book) for organizing data on the disk for good performance is called *hashing*. This paper surveys a variety of hashing methods.

• R. Fagin *et al.* "Extendible Hashing—A Fast Access Method for Dynamic Files." *ACM Transactions on Database Systems* 4, No. 3 (September 1979).

This paper describes a particularly elegant form of hashing.

• See Volume I, Chapter 2, for an overview of methods for organizing data in storage. Volume I, Chapter 10, describes the techniques used in System R.

CHAPTER 13:
VIEWS

• See Volume I, Chapter 9, and Volume II, Chapter 4.

CHAPTER 14:
SECURITY

• D. E. Denning and P. J. Denning. "Data Security." *ACM Computing Surveys* 11, No. 3 (September 1979).

• M. Gardner. "A New Kind of Cipher That Would Take Millions of Years to Break." *Scientific American* 237, No. 2 (August 1977).

• See Volume II, Chapter 4.

CHAPTER 15:
INTEGRITY

• C. J. Date. "Referential Integrity." *Proceedings of 7th International Conference on Very Large Data Bases* (September 1981). Available from IEEE Computer Society and ACTI, Cannes, France.

This paper gives a detailed discussion of foreign keys.

• See also Volume II, Chapter 2.

**CHAPTER 16:
LOCKING**

• K. P. Eswaran, J. N. Gray, R. A. Lorie, and I. L. Traiger. "The Notions of Consistency and Predicate Locks in a Data Base System." *Communications of the ACM* 19, No. 11 (November 1976).

This is the paper that first put the theory of concurrency control (specifically, locking) on a firm footing.

• J. N. Gray. "Notes on Data Base Operating Systems." In *Operating Systems: An Advanced Course*, edited by R. Bayer, New York: Springer-Verlag, 1978.

This paper contains a discussion of locking (and many other topics) from the point of view of a system implementer with a strong theoretical bent (or a theoretician with a strong pragmatic streak). It is rather specialized, but essential reading for the serious student.

• See also Volume II, Chapter 3.

**CHAPTERS 17
AND 18:
DATABASE DESIGN**

• C. J. Date. *A Practical Guide to Database Design*. IBM Technical Report TR 03.220 (December 1982).

This report consists of a greatly expanded treatment of the material found in these two chapters.

• R. Fagin. "Normal Forms and Relational Database Operators." *Proceedings ACM SIGMOD International Conference on Management of Data* (May 1979). Available from ACM, Boston, Mass.

The principle "every fact should be a fact about the key, the whole key, and nothing but the key" (see Chapter 17) is an informal statement of what is frequently expressed in a more formal (or at least more abstract) manner: "Each relation should be in *third* (or sometimes *fourth*) *normal form*." The fact is, any given relation (table) might be in any one of five "normal forms"—first, second, . . ., or fifth (abbreviated 1NF, 2NF, . . ., 5NF). "First normal form" just means the same as "normalized" (see Appendix A). "Second normal form" means that the table is normalized but that it also satisfies some additional conditions; "third normal form" means that it is in second normal form but satisfies still further conditions; and so on. Generally speaking, each normal form is more desirable from a database design standpoint than the one before;

that is, 3NF is more desirable than 2NF, and so on. Fagin's paper is the definitive statement on the theory of the five normal forms.

• W. Kent. "A Simple Guide to Five Normal Forms in Relational Database Theory." *Communications of the ACM* 26, No. 2 (February 1983).

• See also Volume I, Chapter 14.

APPENDIX A: THE RELATIONAL MODEL

• E. F. Codd. "A Relational Model of Data For Large Shared Data Banks." *Communications of the ACM* 13, No. 6 (June 1976). Republished in *Communications of the ACM* 26, No. 1 (January 1983).

Codd was the inventor and original proponent of the relational model. This classic paper is the one in which the ideas of that model were first published (except for some internal IBM documents).

• E. F. Codd. "Relational Completeness of Data Base Sublanguages." In *Data Base Systems*, Courant Computer Science Symposia Series, Volume 6. Englewood Cliffs, N.J.: Prentice-Hall, 1972.

This paper contains a formal treatment of the relational algebra.

• E. F. Codd. "Extending the Database Relational Model to Capture More Meaning." *ACM Transactions on Database Systems* 4, No. 4 (December 1979).

This paper presents some ideas for an enhanced version of the relational model called RM/T.

• See Volume I, Chapters 4, 12, and 13 (basic relational model, including the relational algebra), and Volume II, Chapters 5 and 6 (more formal treatment and discussion of RM/T).

INDEX

advantages of a database system, 12, 15, 38
advantages of COBOL, 37
advantages of views, 184–185
ALTER TABLE (SQL), 97
ampersand variable (NOMAD), 128
APPEND (dBASE), 142, 150
application backlog, 38
application generator, 80
ASCII, 40
audit trail, 193
authorization constraint, 191

B-tree, 260
builtin functions
   QBE, 104
   SQL, 56ff
byte, 155, 166

canned procedure, 77ff
   dBASE, 143ff
catalog, 91ff, 190
   dBASE, 154
   NOMAD, 131
   QBE, 110ff
central processing unit, 26
CHANGE (NOMAD), 129
CHANGE KEY (NOMAD), 199
CHANGE WITHIN DB (NOMAD), 130
character string data, 19
   dBASE, 137
   NOMAD, 117
   QBE, 110
   SQL, 19
Codd, E. F., 262
column, 18
COLUMNS table, 92
command, 16
computer system structure, 25ff
constant element (QBE), 102
COPY (dBASE), 150

CPU, 26
CPU instructions, 26, 32
creation of indexes
   dBASE, 174
   NOMAD, 175
   QBE, 175
   SQL, 174, 200
creation of tables
   dBASE, 136
   NOMAD, 117
   QBE, 109
   SQL, 19, 46ff
creation of views
   SQL, 178ff

D. (QBE), 108
data definition, 18
data independence, 40ff, 165, 169, 170, 185
data manipulation, 11, 16
data sharing, 41
database, 24
database administrator, 162
database language, 16
database management, 20, 25, 42
database management system, 30
database system, 9
DATE data
   NOMAD, 117
   QBE, 110
DBA, 162
DBA authority (SQL), 189
DBMS, 30
deadlock, 213
decimal data
   dBASE, 137
   NOMAD, 117
   QBE, 110
   SQL, 19, 48
DEFINE EXTRACT (NOMAD), 118, 183
DELETE (dBASE), 142

DELETE (NOMAD), 130
DELETE WITHIN DB (NOMAD), 130
DELETE (SQL), 11, 69
dictionary, 97
direct access, 167, 169
directory, 91
disk, 28
DISPLAY (dBASE), 137ff
distributed data, 247
DO (dBASE), 147
DO WHILE (dBASE), 148
DROP INDEX (SQL), 174
DROP TABLE (SQL), 97

EDIT (dBASE), 140
equijoin, 252
encryption, 194
entity, 226, 234
    dependent, 234, 243
    independent, 234, 243
errors, 70
example element (QBE), 102
exceptions, 70
EXISTS (SQL), 62ff
EXTRACT (NOMAD), 124

fact (database design), 227
field, 18
foreign key, 200, 228, 229, 251
FORMAT (SQL), 86ff
format constraints, 202
formatting, 18

GRANT (SQL), 189
GROUP BY (SQL), 64

HEADING (NOMAD), 117
hidden data, 185, 190

I. (QBE), 107
I/O, 29
I/O device, 29
I/O operation, 29
IF (dBASE), 147
index, 165ff
index lookup, 165
indexed field, 167
input/output, 29

INSERT (NOMAD), 127
INSERT (SQL), 11, 52
integrity, 197
    relational model, 251
INTELLECT, 38
interface, 246
interrelationship, 13, 91, 92
item (NOMAD), 117

join
    dBASE, 139
    NOMAD, 119, 123ff
    QBE, 106
    relational model, 252
    SQL, 60ff

keyboard, 28

LIST (NOMAD), 120ff
loading the database, 51ff
LOCATE (NOMAD), 129
lock, 209ff
lost updates, 207

machine code, 32
machine instruction, 26, 32
machine language, 32
main memory, 27
main storage, 27
master (NOMAD), 117
MERGE (NOMAD), 125
modeling (database design), 219
multilevel index, 171
multistatement updates, 72ff

NAME data (NOMAD), 117
natural join, 253
natural languages, 38ff
nested queries (SQL), 14, 58
normalization, 250, 261, 262
null, 52, 58, 204

ORDER BY (SQL), 15, 62
overloading (database design), 227

P. (QBE), 101ff
PACK (dBASE), 143
page, 165, 167

password, 188, 192, 193
pointer, 167
primary key, 198, 226, 228, 234, 244,
    251
    not null, 226
primary USE table (dBASE), 139
PRINT (SQL), 18
printer, 29
program, 29
programming language, 33
PROJECT (relational model), 252
PROMPT (NOMAD), 129
property (database design), 227

query language, 16

range constraint, 203
read instruction, 27
RECALL (dBASE), 142
record, 18
REJECT (NOMAD), 125
relation, 250
relational algebra, 251ff
relational database, 254
relational model, 249ff
relational system, 254
relationship, 228
    many-to-many, 233, 235
    many-to-one, 228, 230
    one-to-many, 228
    one-to-one, 229, 230
RELEASE LOCKS, 210ff
REPLACE (dBASE), 142, 143
report writing, 85ff
    dBASE, 149ff
    NOMAD, 121ff
    SQL, 85ff
response time, 170
REVOKE (SQL), 191

schema (NOMAD), 131
screen, 29
scrolling, 18, 83
secondary storage, 28

secondary USE table (dBASE), 139
security, 188, 197
segment (NOMAD), 120
SELECT (NOMAD), 183
SELECT (relational model), 252
SELECT (SQL), 9ff, 54ff
SELECT * (SQL), 10
SELECT PRIMARY (dBASE), 139
SELECT SECONDARY (dBASE), 139
semantic modeling, 248
sequential access, 168, 170
sequential scan, 165
SLIST (NOMAD), 131
SORT (dBASE), 140, 151
stability (database design), 238
standardization, 245
statement, 16
SUBSET (NOMAD), 125
subtotal, 87
SUM (dBASE), 139

table, 249
table description, 97
table in USE (dBASE), 137
TABLES table, 91
terminal, 29
third normal form, 261
TOP (NOMAD), 129
total (reports), 87ff

U. (QBE), 108
update, 17
UPDATE (SQL), 10, 70
USE (dBASE), 137
user, 3
user identification, 192

view, 177ff
virtual data, 118, 119, 182, 183
virtual table, 177
visual display, 29

WHERE, 10
write instruction, 27

Other books in the Microcomputer Books Series, available from your local computer store or bookstore. For more information write:

General Books Division
Addison-Wesley Publishing Company, Inc.
Reading, Massachusetts 01867
(617) 944-3700

(10341) **Pascal: A Problem Solving Approach**
Elliot B. Koffman

(03115) **A Bit of BASIC**
Thomas A. Dwyer and Margot Critchfield

(01589) **BASIC and the Personal Computer**
Thomas A. Dwyer and Margot Critchfield

(05247) **The Little Book of BASIC Style**
John M. Nevison

(05248) **Executive Computing**
John M. Nevison

(10187) **How to Choose Your Small Business Computer**
Mark Birnbaum and John Sickman

(05735) **Low-Cost Word Processing**
Laurence Press

(10242) **Executive VisiCalc for the Apple Computer**
Roger E. Clark

(10158) **Pascal From BASIC**
Peter Brown

(10355) **CP/M and the Personal Computer**
Thomas A. Dwyer and Margot Critchfield

(10243) **Executive VisiCalc for the IBM Personal Computer**
Roger E. Clark

(05092) **Microcomputer Graphics**
Roy E. Myers

(06577) **Pascal for BASIC Programmers**
Charles Seiter and Robert Weiss

(09666) **The Urgently Needed Parent's Guide to Computers**
Brian K. Williams and Richard J. Tingey

(16455) **The Addison-Wesley Book of IBM Software 1984**
Robert Wells, Sandra Rochowansky, and Michael Mellin

(10285) **The Addison-Wesley Book of Apple Software 1984**
Jeffrey Stanton, Robert Wells, Sandra Rochowansky, and Michael Mellin

(10286) **The Addison-Wesley Book of Atari Software 1984**
Jeffrey Stanton, Robert Wells, Sandra Rochowansky, and Michael Mellin

(11208) **The Beginner's Guide to Computers**
Robin Bradbeer, Peter DeBono, and Peter Laurie

(10256) **A Guide to the Best Business Software for the IBM PC**
Richard C. Dorf

(07769) **Discovering Apple Logo**
David D. Thornburg

(05464) **Pascal for the IBM Personal Computer**
Ted G. Lewis

(14775) **Applesoft BASIC Toolbox**
Larry G. Wintermeyer

(05663) **BASIC Business Subroutines for the Apple II and IIe**
Alan Porter and Martin Rezmer

(10241) **Executive SuperCalc for the Osborne 1**
Roger E. Clark